Forward Exchange, Speculation, and the International Flow of Capital

Forward Exchange, Speculation, and the International Flow of Capital

Herbert G. Grubel

Best wishes to Mr. Dubberly,

Herbert Grubel

Stanford University Press, Stanford, California 1966

Stanford University Press
Stanford, California
© 1966 by the Board of Trustees of the
Leland Stanford Junior University
Printed in the United States of America
L. C. 65-21490

To My Parents

Preface

My interest in the subject of forward exchange was aroused by the international short-term capital movements of 1961 and the speculative pressures on the dollar in that year, most particularly because it had been argued that the disturbing effects of these capital flows could be prevented by the appropriate exercise of forward-exchange policy.

My search of the literature in quest of an understanding of the issues surrounding the use of such a policy revealed the theory of forward exchange to be in a peculiar state. On the one hand, a body of unco-ordinated theory could be found in a number of articles in professional economic journals. On the other hand, the complete theories of forward exchange published by Einzig in 1937 and 1961 failed to employ the rigorous, modern tools of economic analysis developed by other authors in their contributions to the journals. These two works thus stand outside the mainstream of professional developments, but do serve as a valuable source on institutional aspects of the forward-exchange markets. Empirical work in the postwar period has been limited to Reading's analysis of the sterling–dollar relationship during the 'fifties.

This book, then, represents the outcome of my effort to integrate and synthesize the existing theoretical work, and to collect and analyze empirical evidence relating to current experience. Parts of the book have already been published: in the *Yale Economic Essays* ("A Multi-country Model of Forward Exchange: Theory, Policy and Empirical Evidence 1955–61"); in *The Journal of Finance* ("A Neglected Aspect of Forward Exchange Theory and Policy"); and in the *Quarterly Journal of Economics* ("Profits from Forward Exchange Speculation"). I thank the publishers of these journals for their permission to reprint passages from these articles.

In the process of building a systematic model of forward-exchange determination, I have drawn heavily on the work of Einzig, Spraos, Jasay, and Reading. The integration of forward-exchange theory with the theory of portfolio selection under uncertainty was stimulated by work in this field by my teacher, James Tobin. While working on the theoretical model, I found that the literature had failed to recognize triangular arbitrage in forward exchange as an important influence on the theory and on its use for policy decisions in a world consisting of more than two countries. I therefore modified the basic model to incorporate this phenomenon and enlarged my empirical work to cover multicountry relationships of a type not previously investigated.

The model was useful in shedding light on some other important questions of theory that had received inadequate attention in the literature, such as the influence of official spot intervention points, the maturity structure of forward rates, and the choice of interest-rate differentials. The last two of these were also subjected to empirical testing. The application of the model to forward-exchange policy provided insights into the cost and benefits of intervention, differences in methods of market entry, and the influence of triangular arbitrage in forward exchange.

The most important data used in this study are found in the two Statistical Appendixes to the book. These statistics, plus some daily exchange-rate observations, are stored on a magnetic tape which can be duplicated and will be made available at cost to anyone interested in using the information for further research.

In the process of completing this study I have incurred many obligations. Above all ranks that to Robert Triffin, of Yale University, whose ideas and encouragement were very important to me. Other members of the Yale faculty, Michael Lovell, Gustav Ranis, and Raymond Powell, aided my work with many suggestions. Egon Sohmen's lectures had aroused my curiosity in the topic at an early stage of my studies at Yale.

The empirical work was made possible through the generosity of the Dresdener Bank, Frankfurt, The Morgan Guaranty Trust Company, New York, and the Bank of France, Paris. These institutions have allowed me to use statistical data drawn from their internal books. My friends Hans-Rudolf Ebel, in Frankfurt, and Claude Hubert, in Paris, have been instrumental in getting these data to me. For this, I am deeply indebted to them.

Robert Aliber, of the Committee for Economic Development, very generously arranged for me to meet and discuss problems of forward exchange with several persons in government, industry, and banking. My colleagues at Yale, Gerald Helleiner and Larry Lynn, read an earlier version of Part I, and I have made good use of their valuable comments. Chapter 12 has benefited from comments by Jacques Dreze, Milton Friedman, and Harry G. Johnson on an earlier draft.

Financial assistance from the Cowles Foundation for Research in Economics, at Yale University, and from the Ford Foundation have made possible the statistical computations and the microfilming of the data. A substantial part of the work on this book was done while I was supported in part by funds made available by the Rockefeller Foundation for a larger research project directed by Harry G. Johnson at the University of Chicago.

I wish to thank also Mrs. Muriel Porter, who efficiently and patiently typed the manuscript, and William W. Carver, of Stanford University Press, who patiently edited the manuscript and removed innumerable blemishes of style and presentation.

Finally, I acknowledge deep indebtedness to my wife, Toni. Her untiring and patient assistance in the preparation of the data and graphs, and in improving style, has been invaluable.

None of these people, of course, should be held responsible for any errors remaining in the book.

H. G. G.

Chicago, June 1, 1964

Contents

Part I

The Theoretical Model

The first part of this book presents the pure theory of forward exchange, in the form of a systematic analysis of the forces guiding the actions of participants in the forward-exchange markets. The resulting model is tested against available empirical evidence in Part II, and serves as the basis for Part III, in which the theory of international short-term capital movements and forward-exchange policy is presented. The two statistical appendixes following the text contain weekly exchange-rate and interest-rate data that serve as the basis for most of the empirical work discussed in Part II.

Part I is divided into eight chapters. The first is a glossary of basic terms and symbols used in the discussion and analysis of forward-exchange markets. The second and third deal with interest arbitragers and triangular arbitragers, respectively. The fourth and fifth chapters analyze the behavior of other groups of market participants—speculators and traders. The sixth explores the interaction of the speculator–trader group and the arbitragers, in order to explain how forward rates are determined in static equilibrium and as a process through time. In the seventh chapter, the model is modified to account for the existence of official spot-intervention points. The last chapter is an analysis of two problems concerning the structure of forward rates and interest rates.

1. Fundamental Terms and Symbols

The analysis of forward-exchange markets is not difficult in the sense that Einstein's theory of relativity, or capital theory, are difficult. Whereas relativity and capital theory demand highly abstract reasoning, most difficulties with the theory of forward-exchange markets arise out of a necessity to manipulate price and quantity relationships much in the manner of what has been called mental gymnastics. So that mental entanglement may be minimized during the development of the theory, this chapter presents a number of definitions and concepts that serve to introduce the subject and may be useful for reference during the reading of the book.*

Spot rate. The cost of one unit of foreign currency, in terms of domestic currency, for delivery on the following day. In theoretical discussions the spot rate is represented by the symbol X_0. Where necessary, and for empirical purposes, the symbols of the two currencies involved are used; thus $(\$ \cdot £)_0$ is the spot rate for dollars and pounds sterling in the New York–London market. Other monetary units mentioned frequently in the book are C$ (Canadian dollars), DM (Deutsche marks), and F (French francs). The prices used in the empirical study may be either day-opening or noon rates, or may be some average of the rates at which transactions took place during the day. In theoretical discussions the price is assumed to be the weighted mean of all transactions.

Forward rate. The cost of one unit of foreign currency, in terms of domestic currency, for delivery at a stipulated future date. The symbol

---

* The terms defined are widely used in the literature, especially by Paul Einzig, in *The Theory of Forward Exchange*, London, Macmillan 1937, and in *A Dynamic Theory of Forward Exchange*, London, Macmillan 1961; by B. Reading, "The Forward Pound 1951–59, "*Economic Journal*, June, 1960; and by S. C. Tsiang, "The Theory of the Forward Exchange Market" *International Monetary Fund Staff Papers*, April 1959.

used is X_t, or $(\$ \cdot \pounds)_t$, where the subscript t is the interval between the day the contract is made and the day the forward currency is to be delivered. Although t may be one day or several years, market rates are usually quoted for 30 and 90 days.

Future spot rates. Certain useful distinctions may be made in analytical contexts by specifying two variants to the spot rate; I have added *expected future spot rate* $E(X_0^t)$, i.e., the expected cost of the foreign currency at time t, and *actual future spot rate* X_0^t, i.e., the actual cost of the currency at time t.

Discount and premium. From the New York viewpoint, sterling (i.e., the foreign currency) is said to sell at a *forward discount* when it will cost less in dollars at some future date than it does currently, i.e., $X_t < X_0$. This implies that the domestic forward currency is at a premium.* When $X_t > X_0$, the sterling is said to sell at a *forward premium*, and the domestic forward currency is implied to be at a discount.

Implicit interest rate. Premiums and discounts are often expressed as percentage earnings per year. This earning rate, called the *implicit interest rate* IR, is defined as

$$IR = [(X_t - X_0)/X_0](360/T)$$

where T is time to maturity, in days. This means that the implicit interest rate is the difference between the spot rate and the forward date, expressed as a percentage of the spot rate, multiplied by the number of times the length of the contract would allow the repetition of the transaction within one year.

Interest-rate differential. The difference between domestic and foreign interest or discount rates in percentage per year on "equivalent" securities. In symbols, $ID = R_d - R_f$, where $R_d - R_f > 0$ represents an *interest-rate differential* in favor of the domestic market, $R_d - R_f < 0$

---

* To illustrate the mental gymnastics involved in this subject, and to prepare the reader for the confusion that may arise from usage in British writings, the following difference between practices in London and in all other exchange markets is presented. London quotes exchange rates in terms of the number of foreign units of exchange required to purchase one pound sterling. The forward discount rule stated above must therefore be reversed. As an illustration, consider the following sterling–dollar rates quoted in London: spot, 2.80; forward, 2.82. If we were to compare $X_t > X_0$ to the above condition, we would conclude that the foreign currency sells in London at a premium. But, given these exchange rates, the foreign currency is at a discount. That this is so can be seen by "normalizing" the rates, i.e., expressing them in terms of the number of domestic units it takes to purchase one dollar. This is done by making spot equal to 1/2.80 and forward equal to 1/2.82, with the result that $X_t < X_0$. The foreign currency is at a discount. The usage employed *elsewhere* than in London is implicit in all subsequent use of the terms *premium* and *discount*.

represents a differential in favor of the foreign market, and $R_d - R_f = 0$ expresses equality of interest rates.

Covered interest arbitrage. The purchase of foreign spot currency, investment of the proceeds in the foreign market, and the simultaneous elimination of the exchange risk by the sale of an essentially equal amount of the foreign forward currency.

Covered-interest-arbitrage margin. The difference ID − IR. Whenever the advantage possessed by a foreign money market in terms of a simple interest-rate differential is not completely wiped out by the cost represented by the implicit interest rate, a positive intrinsic interest-rate differential, or *positive covered-interest-arbitrage margin*, exists.

Parity forward rate. When X_t is such as to make ID − IR = 0, X_t is called X_t^*, the *parity forward rate*. A more precise definition is

$$X_t^* = \left(\frac{R_d - R_f}{1 + R_f}\right)\left(\frac{T}{360}\right)X_0 + X_0 \qquad (1.1)$$

Triangular arbitrage. Taking riskless advantage of an inequality in the equation $(\$ \cdot \pounds) = (\$ \cdot DM)(DM \cdot \pounds)$ by buying and selling the currencies involved. The equation tends toward equality regardless of whether the three rates are spot rates or forward rates.

Speculation. Deliberately exposing oneself to additional risk of exchange uncertainty. A speculative "long position" is taken by *purchasing* foreign currency forward without incurring an obligation to make a spot payment at the time of delivery, in the expectation that the spot sale of the foreign currency at that time will produce a profit. A "short position" is taken by *selling* foreign currency forward without currently owning an equivalent amount of this currency, again in the expectation that the spot rate obtaining at the specified future date will make the transaction profitable.

Hedging. Buying or selling forward currency so as to eliminate an exchange risk due to (a) normal international commercial transactions or (b) foreign investment of short-term capital funds, where (b) is undertaken as part of the covered interest arbitrage described above.

Swapping. Buying (or selling) a foreign currency at spot while at the same time selling (or buying) an equal amount of the same currency forward. Both transactions are at stated prices and to the same customer.

2. Interest Arbitragers

The theory of forward exchange presented in this chapter, the *parity theory*, was first formulated by Keynes[*] and later elaborated by Einzig.[†] I shall use it as a point of departure for the analysis, and incorporate it as an essential element of my own, more extensive model of forward exchange rate determination. The extended model will be seen to be necessary when the parity theory is shown to be logically incomplete and incapable of explaining many of the empirical phenomena presented in Part II.

Algebraic Formulation of the Parity Theory

This chapter analyzes the market behavior of a group of forward exchange market participants known as *interest arbitragers*. These participants have the common characteristic of using forward exchange as a means of eliminating the exchange risk caused by their basic activity.

The analysis requires some important assumptions. First, it is assumed that government regulations interfere neither with the arbitragers' basic activity that gives rise to the exchange risk nor with the act of eliminating the risk, and moreover that the tax treatment of profits does not differ in the countries involved. Second, for purposes of exposition, it is convenient to assume the existence of only two countries, the United States and the United Kingdom, and to demonstrate basic relationships in this framework. In Chapter 3, the analysis is expanded to include more than two countries. Finally, it is assumed that exchange rates are flexible without limit; the removal of this assumption is undertaken in Chapter 7.

---

[*] John Maynard Keynes, *A Tract on Monetary Reform*, London: Macmillan, 1923, Part IV of Chap. iii.
[†] Paul Einzig, *The Theory of Forward Exchange*, London: Macmillan, 1937; and *A Dynamic Theory of Forward Exchange*, London: Macmillan, 1961.

Interest arbitragers can be considered as forming two analytically distinct groups: owners of funds, and borrowers. I shall discuss these in turn.

Owner Arbitragers

Individuals, industrial organizations, banks, and institutional investors often accumulate liquid funds that are earmarked for expenditure at some point in the near future or that serve as regular transactions balances or as a liquidity buffer for unforeseen expenditures. For example, dividend or interest payments on capital or tax liabilities are due on specific dates in large sums and must be accumulated over time. And capital raised through new issues often accumulates in lump sums but is deployed only gradually on real expenditures. Investments in the relatively capital-certain money-market instruments, such as Treasury bills, bankers' acceptances, and trade or finance paper, permit these investors to retain ready access to their funds while at the same time earning some interest. Competing for the funds of investors with these domestic instruments are foreign money-market papers. The basic considerations determining the investors' choice of domestic or foreign assets are as follows.

If foreign-exchange transactions were not required in the acquisition of foreign assets, investors would purchase these assets whenever their yield exceeded that on equivalent domestic assets. The complication, important for forward-exchange theory, arises from the fact that foreign investment requires two exchange transactions, at separate points in time. The first transaction is the purchase of the foreign currency (in our case, sterling) with which to buy the foreign asset. The second becomes necessary when the capital plus interest are to be repatriated and exchanged into dollars, upon maturity of the investment. If the foreign exchange rate has not in the meantime changed—so that the sterling can be sold at exactly the rate it was bought for—the investment will have produced a rate of return exactly equal to the interest-rate yield. But at the time of the initial investment and purchase of sterling, there can of course be no certain knowledge of the exchange rate likely to exist at maturity. If the rate at maturity is higher than the original rate, the investment yields a capital gain in addition to the interest yield; if on the other hand it is lower, a capital loss is the result.

Capital gains and losses expressed in terms of an annual rate of return on the invested sum are very sensitive to even small changes in the exchange rate. Consider the case where sterling is bought at 2.79 but can be sold for only 2.78 just one month later, when the short-term investment matures. The loss would appear to be small—only one cent on the pound sterling, or 0.35 per cent of the sum invested. However, the loss has occurred within one month, which on an annual basis is equivalent to a loss of 4.2 per cent on the invested capital. It is clear that the capital loss on the same annual-return basis would be only 1.4 per cent on a three-month investment. But the longer the time between the initial purchase and the resale of the foreign currency, the greater the risk of a change in its price. At the same time that the risks of capital gain or loss are great, the interest differentials between centers of international finance are often quite small, and capital losses can quite easily wipe out any gains made from investing in foreign, rather than domestic, securities.

Thus it can be seen that the foreign placement of funds in the fashion described is quite risky and bears a strong element of speculation. Investors, however, are often conservative, and in order for them to be encouraged to lend, there must be a means of removing the investment from the realm of speculation. The market for forward exchange provides such a means: it allows the investor to determine, at the time he initially purchases the sterling, the price at which he can resell it. He simply enters a contract to deliver the sterling at a certain, fixed price so many days hence, normally on the day his investment matures. If the price of forward sterling is above the initial spot price, the investor makes a capital gain; if it is below the spot price, he takes a capital loss. But since this terminal loss or gain is known at the time he considers his investment alternatives, he can include it with the interest rate as factors determining the overall yield on the foreign investment, which is now as free from exchange risk as a domestic investment.

The decision rules and the relevant variables guiding an investor's choice have been formulated carefully: an owner of short-term funds in New York will be willing to move them to London if the return he can earn in New York (R_d for 90 days) is smaller than that in London (R_f for 90 days) after deduction of the transactions costs; these costs arise during the process of, on the one hand, buying sterling (at X_0 plus C per cent commission) with which to purchase the London securities, and, on the other hand, eliminating the exchange risk by selling the sterling forward (at X_t, T for 90 days, again with a commission of C per cent). An equation makes this condition precise.* Funds will flow from New York to London when

$$(1 + R_d) < (1/X_0)(1 - C)(1 + R_f)X_t(1 - C) \qquad (2.1)$$

Disregarding transactions costs, which may in fact be quite negligible, and simplifying the expression, we may rewrite the equation as

$$1 + R_d < (X_t/X_0)(1 + R_f) \qquad (2.2)$$

When the inequality is reversed, i.e., when

$$1 + R_d > (X_t/X_0)(1 + R_f) \qquad (2.3)$$

funds will flow from London to New York. Finally, no funds will flow when

$$1 + R_d = (X_t/X_0)(1 + R_f) \qquad (2.4)$$

Traditionally, the equilibrium condition (2.4) has been said to be equivalent to the statement $R_d - R_f = (X_t - X_0)/X_0$; i.e., the interest-rate differential is equal to the implicit interest rate. The difference between the two sides of this equation has been called the *crude arbitrage margin*. Algebraic transformation of the more basic equilibrium statement, however, produces the *precise arbitrage margin* PM:

$$PM = (R_d - R_f)/(1 + R_f) - (X_t - X_0)/X_0 \qquad (2.5)$$

If R_f is large, the difference between the crude and precise margins may be significant.†

Borrower Arbitragers

Another group of market participants—the *borrower arbitragers*—is motivated by the same considerations as the owners of investible funds. This group is made up of people who borrow spot funds in a foreign country and purchase forward currency in order to cover the exchange

---

* The algebraic presentation was adapted from John Spraos, "The Theory of Forward Exchange and Recent Practice," *Manchester School of Economic and Social Studies*, May 1953, p. 88. The continuous case is presented by Egon Sohmen, *Flexible Exchange Rates*, Chicago: University of Chicago Press, 1961, pp. 66–69.

† In empirical work, two different approaches are possible. In the first, the R_d and R_f, usually quoted in rates per year, can each be divided by 4 so as to correspond to the 90-day implicit interest rate $(X_t - X_0)/X_0$, which is left uncorrected. In the second approach, the R_d and R_f are left unchanged, and $(X_t - X_0)/X_0$ is multiplied by 4. The difference between crude and precise arbitrage margins is smaller in the first case than in the second. Published empirical work that has come to my attention relies exclusively on the second method, and uses the crude margin. See S. C. Tsiang, "The Theory of the Forward Exchange Market," *International Monetary Fund Staff Papers*, April 1959, p. 80, n. 2, on the theoretical size of error between the crude and precise margins. The use of an electronic computer made it practical to compute precise margins for the empirical work presented in Part II of this book.

risk. This activity is to be separated analytically from the simple purchase of forward currency to guarantee an exact revenue in domestic currency from a commercial transaction (see Chapter 5). The distinction between the two operations—not always made clear and often not observed in the literature—is important because one operation involves spot funds directly, and therefore a country's reserves, whereas the other does not.

Usually these borrowers are businessmen in need of financing their trade. What is involved can be demonstrated most easily by using an example. A New York importer purchases a stock of British goods; if his supplier wants immediate payment of the value in sterling, the importer may have to borrow the money to meet this demand. Let us assume he intends to repay the sum after the goods' arrival and sale in New York three months later. He can take out a loan either in London, in which case he owes sterling three months later, or in New York, where by buying spot sterling he settles his merchandise debt and ends up owing dollars. If interest cost were the only consideration, he would borrow where the rate is the lowest, but choosing the first alternative carries a concomitant exchange risk, because the trader cannot know how many dollars it may take to repay his sterling loan three months hence. Purchasing forward sterling, on the other hand, permits him to eliminate this risk. Which of the two available alternatives he chooses depends on which is cheaper—paying the New York interest rate and buying sterling at the current spot rate, or paying the London interest rate and purchasing sterling at the current forward rate.

The following reasoning, presented in terms of the symbols, shows the equivalence between borrower-arbitrager behavior and fund-owing-arbitrager behavior.

The borrower arbitrager in New York is indifferent to the choice between London and New York if the sterling obligation N, times the spot rate X_0, borrowed at the New York interest rate R_d, is equal to the cost of interest at R_f on N pounds sterling converted to a certain dollar obligation by purchase of forward sterling at X_t; i.e., $N(X_0)(1 + R_d) = N(1 + R_f)X_t$, which can be written $1 + R_d = (1 + R_f)(X_t/X_0)$, and is the familiar equilibrium condition for owner arbitrage. By simple manipulation it can be shown that in the case of the inequality $1 + R_d > (1 + R_f)(X_t/X_0)$, the fund-owning arbitragers would move their funds to New York, and the borrower arbitragers would borrow in London. The two actions have equivalent effects on the exchange rates, interest rates, and reserves of the two countries. Borrowing delays the remittance of value for exports and is one way in which the well-known "lags" in the balance of payments are brought about.

The Euro-Currency Market

Since about 1958 the new institutional arrangement of the Euro-currencies, involving both borrowers and owners of funds, has brought the money markets of the world closer together.* It is based on the following considerations. A foreign businessman, let us say an Italian exporter, earns dollars that are on deposit in a New York bank. If he wants to make a temporary money-market investment he can do so by purchasing foreign assets in New York, using his dollar balances there, and covering himself against the exchange risk by the forward sale of dollars. Alternatively, he can sell the dollars at spot and invest in the domestic market. The Euro-dollar market opens a third possibility to him. He can lend the dollars to a domestic intermediary who may pay him a higher interest rate than he can get in New York. Repayment of the loan by the intermediary can be in dollars or in local currency. If the repayment is in dollars, the owner covers himself in the forward market. A favorable constellation of spot, forward, and interest rates can thus produce, for this third alternative, a return superior to that accruing from domestic or direct foreign investment.

The intermediary who has gained command of these dollars can use them for his own business as means for direct settlement, or he can lend them to a customer. If he decides on the latter course, he will more likely than not exchange the dollars against local currency and cover the exchange risk through forward purchase of dollars. He can, of course, also use them to finance imports from the United States. For the final user of the dollars, as well as for the original lender and the intermediary, the exchange is advantageous, or it would not have been entered into. The net advantage is in large part due to the fact that the final user in the example can obtain dollars (or domestic funds) cheaper in this way, simply because his credit rating is likely to be better with the intermediary, with whom he may be doing regular business, than it would be in New York, where he might otherwise be forced to borrow. He therefore pays the intermediary a lower rate of interest than would be required in New York. Yet, the rate may be—and most often is—

---

* *Bank for International Settlements, Annual Report*, Basel, 1964, pp. 127–41.

high enough to allow the intermediary to pay a higher interest to the original supplier of the dollars than the direct New York market investment might have brought. This is so because the intermediary requires a smaller-risk premium on the loan, or his overhead may be smaller than that of his New York counterpart (i.e., the difference between lending and borrowing rates may be greater in the United States than in Europe). Because dollars can always be exchanged against domestic currency, some firms are able to obtain, through the Euro-dollar market, credit in domestic currency that otherwise would have been unavailable to them at any price because of central bank credit-rationing, as in Japan, for example.

Markets for other currencies have developed, and function in a way similar to that for the Euro-dollar. Activities in all of these currencies have tied world money markets closer together and tend to push spot and forward rates in the direction of the parity relationships outlined above. Whether the comparison is with London, Paris, or Frankfurt, the funds will be placed outside New York only if the yields from New York investments are lower than the return earned by lending out dollars directly, properly hedged against the exchange risk. This tends to raise interest rates in New York and lower them outside, and to exert pressure on the forward rate until the advantage of one market over the other is wiped out.

Thus, through the development of these secondary markets for currencies, forward-exchange uses have increased and the markets for forward exchange have consequently been deepened and made more perfect.

Modern Portfolio Theory and Foreign Assets

The Model

One of the puzzling phenomena to be explained by economic theory is that people who are maximizing the return on their net worth tend to hold diversified portfolios rather than to concentrate wealth in one type of asset with the highest yield. We may ask, for example, why people do not switch entirely to foreign assets as soon as the covered yield exceeds that on domestic assets. The modern portfolio theory developed by Markowitz* and Tobin† can be used to explain how greater

---

* Harry M. Markowitz, *Portfolio Selection: Efficient Diversification of Investments*, New York: Wiley, 1959.
† James Tobin, "Liquidity Preference as Behavior Towards Risk," *Review of Economic Studies*, February 1958.

arbitrage margins cause increased holdings of foreign assets and an expansion of forward exchange in a smooth and continuous way. In the following, the basic Tobin model is presented, and applied to foreign assets covered against the exchange risk.

When traders decide on the proportions they wish to allot for holdings of various types of monetary assets* in their portfolios, they are usually not certain what the return from any given asset will be. Rather, they have in mind a number of possible outcomes, each carrying a certain probability of occurring. These outcomes rest essentially on capital gains or losses due to changes in the market value of the assets. In the case of covered foreign assets, there are also uncertainties concerning gains or losses that result when forward contracts and spot-currency sales must be undone because spot funds must be repatriated before their maturity. Investors also see in foreign investments certain other risks not typically associated with domestic assets, such as potential unavailability due to payments moratoria or exchange controls.

We assume that all of these differences between domestic- and foreign-asset advantages are reflected in the investor's estimates of probable future outcomes. The mean of a probability function of possible outcomes associated with each asset is called the *expected rate of return* E(R) (or μ_R; see the Appendix to Chapter 2). The *standard deviation σ* of the function is a convenient measure for the riskiness of the asset. The investor maximizes his expected utility by assembling from a menu of assets those assets combining return and risk in a manner best suited to his personal preference. Figure 2.1 illustrates such a choice. The vertical axis measures E(R), and the horizontal axis, σ. The investor is assumed to face a choice of only two assets, cash with E(R) = 0 and σ = 0, and a foreign asset with E(R) = a and σ = α. The line OA is the *opportunity locus* of combinations of E(R) and σ open to the investor. He can place his portfolio anywhere along OA by varying its proportions of cash and foreign assets. The proportion is unity at point A, and 0.75 and 0.5 at the other points shown. The *indifference curve* I—i.e., the combinations of rates of return and risk at which the investor considers himself equally well off—is tangent at the point where the proportion of foreign assets to cash in the portfolio is 0.5. The shape of the indifference curve is an essential part of the argument. The derivation of the curve, and the manner of justifying

---

* Although in the current context we are concerned only with alternative assets all having a fixed rate of return, the theory can also be used to explain choices between bonds and equity capital.

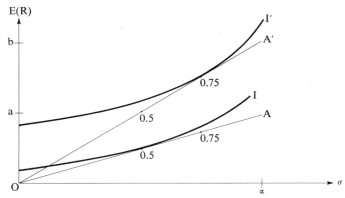

FIG. 2.1. Model of portfolio choice; OA and OA′ are opportunity loci; I and I′ are indifference curves.

its use, are beyond the scope of this book, but can be found in Tobin's work.*

The E(R) on foreign assets is an increasing function of the arbitrage margin. If we assume that the risk associated with the assets is independent of the size of the arbitrage margin, then a higher E(R) on foreign assets b, caused by a widening of the differential between parity and the actual forward rate, results in a new opportunity locus OA′. The point at which the higher indifference curve I′ is tangent to the new opportunity locus OA′ indicates that the higher return on the foreign asset has caused a substitution of the foreign assets for cash, so that the proportion is now 0.75. Thus, the higher return on the foreign asset causes its demand to be increased. The principle applies equally to owner arbitragers and borrower arbitragers.

An analysis involving two assets each with nonzero risk is more complicated, but its conclusions remain essentially the same. Worth mentioning, however, is the following. If foreign assets are considered to have the same expected rate of return but higher risk than their domestic counterparts, and are considered essentially equivalent in all other respects, diversification will still occur, because as long as the risks on the two types of asset are independent, diversification reduces overall risk without changing the rate of return. On the other hand, a foreign asset with a lower expected rate of return and higher risk than

---

* *Op. cit.*, pp. 73–77. See also the appendix to this chapter.

its equivalent domestic counterpart is clearly inferior, and will not be included in the portfolio.

As demonstrated mathematically in the appendix to this chapter, substitution of cash for foreign assets requires an increasingly larger arbitrage margin as the proportion of cash in the portfolio approaches zero. The demonstration in the appendix is limited to the case of a two-asset portfolio where one asset yields no return. For the more complicated and more realistic situation where both assets carry a positive expected rate of return and risk, the following intuitive explanation is offered. An investor with an initial portfolio consisting of $500 asset W, yield w, and $500 asset X, yield x, may require a yield y on asset X to induce him to hold another $100 of X, where $y > x$. Before he can be encouraged to add still another $100 of X he is likely to require an even higher yield z, where $z > y$.

The possibility of borrowing, which can lead to the attainment of higher levels of satisfaction, has been incorporated systematically into portfolio theory by Tobin* and will only be sketched here. Borrowing leads to an extension of the existing opportunity locus at its upper end by a line less steep in slope than the line OA in Fig. 2.1, given the same $E(R)$ and σ for asset A as the basis for the diagram. The outermost point represents the combination of $E(R)'$ and σ' that can be had by assembling a portfolio consisting only of asset A. The new $E(R)'$ is greater than the old $E(R)$ because the interest rate on the loan is presumably lower than the expected rate of return on asset A, thus allowing a greater rate of return on the equity. On the other hand, the risk increases proportionately more than the expected rate of return, since the interest on the loan must be paid regardless of the realized rate of return on the portfolio. Since all losses on that part of the portfolio must be absorbed by the earnings on the equity, the risk in the return on the equity is increased accordingly. The point of tangency of an indifference curve and the extended opportunity locus again determines the proportions of the assets held in the portfolio and whether borrowing actually takes place or not.

The modern inventory theory of the demand for cash can serve as an additional explanation of the interest elasticity of funds moving into foreign assets. The theory states that the proportion of an investor's equity allocated to cash balances for transactions purposes, rather than

---

* In lectures and in an unpublished manuscript.

to the purchase of income-yielding assets that are subject to the rules of portfolio management just described, depends on the institutional patterns of receipts and expenditures, the absolute size of transactions, the cost of switching into and out of revenue-yielding securities, and the level of return on such a portfolio. As Tobin has shown,[*] the level of working balances is a decreasing function of the yield on securities.

Since many of the demand deposits held domestically and in foreign countries are used essentially for transactions purposes, they are likely to be reduced as the yield on covered foreign assets increases. Including the concept of transactions balances therefore reinforces the previous conclusion that demand for foreign assets is an increasing function of forward margin because it increases the yield on alternative uses for funds in portfolios containing foreign securities free from exchange risk.

Implications for Forward-Exchange Theory

Modern portfolio theory carries two important implications for the formulation of a theory of forward exchange. One is that foreign assets covered against exchange risk tend to be added to domestic portfolios in a continuous, smooth fashion, and that there exist no critical interest-rate differentials at which large amounts are suddenly shifted from one group of assets to another. Arguments for the evidence of such critical values have appeared in the literature, and are implicit in the graphic analyses of both Jasay and Reading.[†]

The second implication is that substantial covered-earnings advantages of foreign assets over domestic equivalents can persist for prolonged periods. This can happen when the *other* determiners of the forward rate—i.e., the sellers of the forward exchange that arbitragers are buying when making their transactions—are willing to sell forward exchange at a nonparity rate in amounts exceeding the quantity of the arbitrage funds that portfolio managers, acting within the given preferences and risk estimates, are willing to move.[‡] Without the portfolio theory, explanations of statistically observed persistent arbitrage margins had to rely on such arguments as the existence of market imperfections and institutional limitations on the quantity of shiftable funds. Such explanations were made necessary by the fact

---

[*] James Tobin, "The Transaction Demand for Money," *Review of Economics and Statistics*, August 1956.

[†] Anthony Egan Jasay, "Bank Rate or Forward Exchange Policy," *Banca Nazionale del Lavoro Quarterly Review*, March 1958, pp. 72–73; B. Reading, "The Forward Pound 1951–59," *Economic Journal*, June 1960, pp. 304–19.

[‡] A fuller explanation of these conditions is found in Chapter 6, where market equilibrium is analyzed.

that, although higher foreign rates of return could be earned, people nevertheless would not or could not borrow at the lower market rate in the one country and earn the certain higher return in the other country. Modern portfolio theory tells us that even if an investor could borrow infinite amounts at going interest rates he might not want to do so, because his utility is a function not simply of the expected rate of return but also of the risk entailed by his actions.

The Arbitrage Schedule

Economic relationships can often be expressed in greater detail and clarity by diagrams. In the following sections the relationship between quantity of arbitrage funds moved and implicit interest-rate differentials is represented by the *arbitrage schedule*. This schedule is a kind of demand curve, and its intersection with the supply curve determines the forward rate in the market. The supply curve is derived in Chapters 4 and 5, and equilibrium is analyzed in Chapter 6.

A Simplifying Assumption

Before turning to a presentation of the arbitrage schedule proper, I shall introduce another diagram, one that allows a clear statement of the simplifying assumption required for graphic expression of the arbitrage schedule.

Figure 2.2 shows graphically* the combinations of forward-rate discount or premium (in percentage per annum) and interest-rate differential (in percentage per annum) that cause arbitrage inflows and outflows, following directly from the algebraic conditions derived in Section A of this chapter. Thus in the northeast quadrant, below the *interest parity line*, the forward-exchange premium is so large as to offset the domestic market's interest-rate advantage and to cause an outflow of funds. More precisely, consider the combination of forward-exchange premium and interest-rate differential represented by point A. Arbitrage outflow will tend to move point A toward the interest parity line. But where, and how near the parity line, the new point A' will be depends on two forces represented by vectors in the graph. The horizontal force is a narrowing of the forward-exchange premium resulting from the arbitragers' demand for spot and their sale of forward exchange; the vertical force results from an upward pressure on domestic interest rates and a downward pressure on foreign interest

---

* The graph is adapted from Alan R. Holmes, *The New York Foreign Exchange Market*, Federal Reserve Bank of New York, 1959.

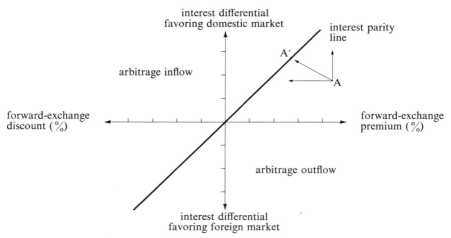

Fig. 2.2. Direction of adjustments.

rates, both of which tend to increase the interest-rate differential. The interesting question is how the sizes of the two vectors are determined: we find them to depend on the supply elasticities of spot funds with respect to interest rates in the two countries, and on the price elasticity of supply for spot and forward exchange.

In the remainder of this part of the book we shall assume that all quantities except forward exchange are in perfectly elastic supply. The effect of this assumption is that, when an equilibrium condition is disturbed by an autonomous change in the interest-rate differential or in the level of the spot rate, interest-arbitrage flows will affect only the forward rate; neither the spot rate nor the two interest rates will change. Thus we assume in effect that spot and interest rates are exogenously determined—as they could be in the real world—by government pegging operations, so that we may concentrate on the determination of the forward rate. This assumption does not alter the substance of the model, but simplifies the exposition considerably.

The AA Schedule

We turn now to a geometrical exposition of the arbitrage schedule. In Fig. 2.3 the vertical axis measures spot and forward rates.* The

---

* The diagrammatic exposition owes much to its originator, A. E. Jasay, and to B. Reading, who improved on it. See also the note on p. 16.

stock of forward sterling bought is along the horizontal axis to the right of zero, and the stock of forward sterling sold is along this axis to the left of zero. According to the theory presented thus far, with the spot rate X_0 and the interest-rate differential given exogenously, the parity forward rate X_t^* is known. To illustrate this point, consider the following, which is based on Eq. (2.5):

$$X_t^* = \left(\frac{R_d - R_f}{1 + R_f}\right)X_0 + X_0 \qquad (2.6)$$

If we assume $[(R_d - R_f)/(1 + R_f)]$ to have a value of $+0.01$ (representing a domestic interest-rate advantage of approximately 1 per cent), and assume X_0 to be 3.00, then X_t^* is 3.03.

The arbitrage schedule AA shows the quantity of forward commitments at which interest arbitragers are in portfolio balance with alternative values of the forward rate X_t, given the interest-rate differential and spot rate. When X_t is equal to X_t^*, no arbitrage takes place and forward commitments are zero. At values of X_t greater than X_t^*, forward sales are an increasing function of the absolute difference between X_t and X_t^*. When X_t is less than X_t^*, capital flows in, leading to forward-sterling purchases measured to the right of zero. Thus, at a forward rate X_t^a, interest arbitragers are willing to commit themselves to a purchase of ON pounds forward sterling. The horizontal line PP, the interest parity line, passing through X_t^* serves as a reference for the visual interpretation of the magnitude by which the exchange rate for

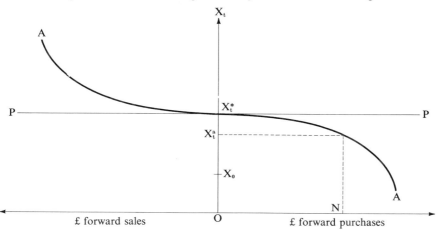

FIG. 2.3. Arbitrage schedule AA.

arbitrage equilibrium differs from the parity rate at varying quantities of forward commitments.

The shape of the AA schedule shown follows directly from portfolio theory. When there are zero foreign assets in investors' portfolios, small earnings advantages will at first lead to large purchases, making the schedule elastic around zero. However, when some stocks of these assets are held already, increasingly larger earnings differentials are required to induce further additions, a phenomenon that explains the inelastic part of the schedule. At some quantity of forward commitments, it is conceivable even that the schedule would become perfectly inelastic, and no higher rates of return would induce further arbitrage movements.

One implication of this analysis is that the simple interest-parity equation introduced above must be modified as follows: equilibrium for interest arbitragers does not require that the equation

$$1 + R_d = \frac{X_t}{X_0}(1 + R_f)' \tag{2.7}$$

hold, nor is it necessary that the equilibrium point A′ in Fig. 2.2 be on the interest parity line.

Mathematical Appendix to Chapter 2

This appendix* demonstrates that, given the quadratic utility function and assumptions concerning the investment-opportunity locus, the holding of a foreign asset is an increasing function of the return on that asset, but that the function increases at a decreasing rate. Consider:

A_1 = proportion of portfolio held in cash

A_2 = proportion of portfolio held in foreign asset
    Condition: $A_1 + A_2 = 1$; neither A_1 nor A_2 can be negative

$R = A_2(r + g)$, where

R = return on portfolio

g = random variable with expected value equal to zero

r = rate of return on foreign asset, an increasing function of the difference between spot and forward exchange rates

$E(R) = \mu_R = A_2 r$

$\sigma_R = A_2 \sigma_g$, where

σ_g = standard deviation of g

* This presentation was adapted from James Tobin, "Liquidity Preference as Behavior Towards Risk," *Review of Economic Studies*, February 1958.

Thus the proportion of foreign assets held by investors determines σ_R and E(R).

$\mu_R = r\sigma_R/\sigma_g$, the equation for the opportunity locus of Fig. 2.1; the slope of that line is r/σ_g.

The indifference curve is based on a quadratic utility function

$$U(R) = (1 + b)R + bR^2$$

where $-1 < b < 0$ for the risk-averter. Thus,

$$E[(U)R] = \int U(R)\, f(R)\, dR = (1 + b)\mu_R + b(\sigma_R^2 + \mu_R^2)$$

The slope of this indifference curve is derived by holding $E[U(R)]$ constant and differentiating with respect to σ_R, so that

$$\frac{d\mu_R}{d\sigma_R} = \frac{\sigma_R}{-\left(\dfrac{1 + b}{2b}\right) - \mu_R}$$

The optimum position is at the point of tangency between the opportunity locus and the indifference curve, i.e., where the two slopes are equal:

$$\frac{r}{\sigma_R} = \frac{\sigma_R}{-\left(\dfrac{1 + b}{2b}\right) - \mu_R} = \frac{A_2\sigma_g}{-\left(\dfrac{1 + b}{2b}\right) - A_2 r}$$

$$A_2 = \frac{r}{r^2 + \sigma_g}\left(-\frac{1 + b}{2b}\right)$$

Differentiating with respect to r, we have, for $r < \sigma_g$,

$$\frac{dA_2}{dr} = \frac{\sigma_g^2 - r^2}{(\sigma_g^2 + r^2)^2}\left(-\frac{1 + b}{2b}\right)$$

since

$$\left(-\frac{1 + b}{2b}\right) > 0$$

for risk-averters, the proportion of foreign assets held increases with a rise in the interest rate r. The second derivative, however,

$$\frac{d^2A_2}{dr^2} = \left\{-\frac{2r}{(\sigma_g^2 + r^2)^2} - 2\left[\frac{(\sigma_g^2 + r^2)(2r)}{(\sigma_g^2 + r^2)^3}\right]\right\}\left(-\frac{1 + b}{2b}\right)$$

is positive, which means that the rate of increase in the proportion of foreign assets in a portfolio decreases, for a given change in the interest rate, with an increase in the level of the interest rate itself.

3. Triangular Arbitragers in Forward Exchange

In this chapter an aspect of forward-exchange trading that has generally been neglected in the literature on the subject* is systematically integrated into the general theory of forward exchange. The aspect to be considered is *triangular arbitrage*.

Einzig, in a book published as recently as 1962, stated: "It is characteristic of the neglected state of the study of forward exchange that this important aspect of the subject [i.e., London's role as an intermediary for triangular operations] has hitherto been neglected by everybody who has written about it—including myself."† This statement may be somewhat inaccurate, however, because Spraos had earlier worked triangular arbitrage in forward exchange into his theoretical model of the forward-exchange market.‡ Einzig's analysis of London's role as an intermediary is implicit in Spraos' more general model. With the exception of my own paper on the subject, only these two authors have mentioned the subject in the literature, and both have failed to point out the implications of triangular arbitrage for the general theory of forward exchange.

The relative neglect of this aspect of forward-exchange theory may be due to the fact that past analysis and empirical research were commonly focused on the world's most significant market relationship, that between New York and London. But now that other currencies have gained in importance, the analysis must be expanded to include more than simply the two centers of finance.

---

* This chapter is based in part on my "A Neglected Aspect of Forward Exchange Theory and Policy," *Journal of Finance*, September 1963.
† Paul Einzig, *A Dynamic Theory of Forward Exchange*, London: Macmillan, 1961, p. 259.
‡ John Spraos, "The Theory of Forward Exchange and Recent Practice," *Manchester School of Economic and Social Studies*, May 1953.

Equilibrium Conditions

Triangular arbitrage is known to keep cross-spot exchange rates consistent. The equilibrium condition, disregarding transactions costs, is the condition wherein the price of sterling in terms of dollars $(\$ \cdot £)_0$ is equal to the price of sterling obtained by exchanging the dollars against Deutsche marks $(\$ \cdot DM)_0$ and using the marks to obtain sterling $(DM \cdot £)_0$; i.e.,

$$(\$ \cdot £)_0 = (\$ \cdot DM)_0 (DM \cdot £)_0 \tag{3.1}$$

It is important to point out how easy it is to profit from any inequality in this equation. If, for example $(£ \cdot \$) = 2.50$, and $(£ \cdot F) = 10.00$ (where F is francs), then $(\$ \cdot F)$ must be $(£ \cdot F)/(£ \cdot \$) = 4.00$. If $(\$ \cdot F) = 5.00$, \$ will be bought via the £ for 4.00 F and resold for 5.00 F. Moreover, the individual engaging in triangular arbitrage does not need to own any spot funds, since the operation can be carried out in a very short time. The marginal cost of the transaction to banks and foreign-exchange dealers, who often maintain direct teletype or telephone communications with foreign financial centers for commercial purposes, is likely to be very small.

Triangular-arbitrage operations are of course feasible in spot exchange as well as forward exchange. The question then arises whether any opportunities for profitable triangular arbitrage on forward rates remain when the cross-spot rates are consistent and the three relevant pairs of markets are also in interest-arbitrage equilibrium, in the sense of Eq. (2.1). The following proof that the resultant cross-forward rates are consistent is taken from Spraos.* The symbols R_F, R_L, and R_{NY} represent the interest rates in Frankfurt, London, and New York, respectively. The equilibrium conditions in the three markets with respect to interest arbitrage are

$$(\$ \cdot £)_0 = (\$ \cdot £)_t \left(\frac{1 + R_L}{1 + R_{NY}} \right) \tag{3.2}$$

$$(\$ \cdot DM)_0 = (\$ \cdot DM)_t \left(\frac{1 + R_F}{1 + R_{NY}} \right) \tag{3.3}$$

$$(DM \cdot £)_0 = (DM \cdot £)_t \left(\frac{1 + R_F}{1 + R_L} \right) \tag{3.4}$$

---

* *Op. cit.*, p. 88.

Substituting in Eq. (3.1), we get

$$(\$ \cdot \pounds)_t\left(\frac{1 + R_L}{1 + R_{NY}}\right) = \left[(\$ \cdot DM)_t\left(\frac{1 + R_F}{1 + R_{NY}}\right)\right]$$
$$\times \left[(DM \cdot \pounds)_t\left(\frac{1 + R_L}{1 + R_F}\right)\right] \quad (3.5)$$

which reduces to

$$(\$ \cdot \pounds)_t = (\$ \cdot DM)_t(DM \cdot L)_t \quad (3.6)$$

and is the equilibrium condition for consistent cross-forward rates, making triangular arbitrage unprofitable.

Modification of the AA Schedule

What influence triangular arbitrage has on the AA schedule can best be seen by assuming that equilibrium exists in the three markets represented by Eqs. (3.1), (3.3), and (3.4) above, while condition (3.2), the dollar–sterling market, is in disequilibrium. Under these circumstances, triangular arbitrage in forward exchange becomes profitable, and at any given dollar–sterling forward rate at which interest arbitragers are willing to offer a certain amount of forward exchange, triangular arbitragers will come forward with a similar amount. The result is that a given AA curve initially representing interest arbitragers alone will be made more elastic over its entire range when triangular arbitragers are included. These relationships are expressed in Fig. 3.1 by the curves AA and A'A'. In subsequent sections of this

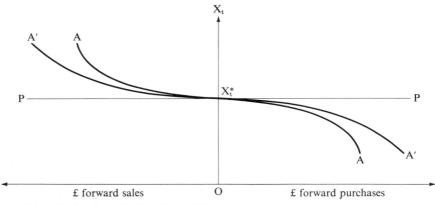

FIG. 3.1. AA schedule and triangular arbitrage.

book, graphic representations of the AA schedule include triangular arbitragers, unless otherwise indicated.

The new schedule has an important additional characteristic that further differentiates it from the old one. Under the original assumptions, the quantity of forward commitments was equal to the sterling spot funds actually moved between two countries. The model that includes triangular arbitrage breaks this one-to-one relationship, because here the operators in forward exchange do not deal in spot currency at all. However, this does not mean that the activities of triangular arbitragers will necessarily fail to lead to spot fund movements. In their efforts to return to dollars from marks (or sterling, as the case may be), they disturb the interest-arbitrage equilibrium condition in these markets and can induce capital inflows. But whether they actually do so depends on whether they enter their forward mark (or sterling) contracts with interest arbitragers or with speculators. If they deal with the latter, no spot flows take place because speculators do not deal in spot funds, as will be seen below. The important point is that the quantity of forward-sterling contracts does not correspond to the amount of short-term capital flow between New York and London.

4. Speculators in Forward Exchange

Speculators are a potent force in the forward-exchange market. They are an important source of the exchange required by interest arbitragers in carrying out their operations.

The Mechanism of Speculation

As defined in Chapter 1, a speculator is an investor who exposes himself deliberately to the risk of uncertainty in future exchange prices. By taking definite views on what these prices will be, he expects to make a profit.

For example, the forward-exchange speculator's profit P per unit of speculative commitment arises from the difference between the price at which he contracts to deliver (or accept delivery of) a unit of forward exchange (say sterling) some time (say 90 days) hence (X_t) and the actual price of sterling on the day his contract matures (X_0^t); i.e., $P = (X_t - X_0^t)$. Thus, if he guesses correctly, sells forward sterling, and finds that X_0^t at maturity is actually below the value of X_t at which he committed himself, he makes a profit.

More precisely, if he *sells* sterling forward and $(X_t - X_0^t) > 0$, then $P > 0$; if $(X_t - X_0^t) < 0$, then $P < 0$. On the other hand, if he *buys* sterling forward, the relationships are reversed; i.e., if $(X_t - X_0^t) > 0$, then $P < 0$; if $(X_t - X_0^t) < 0$, then $P > 0$.

The speculator's total profits P_T depend, of course, on the number of pounds sterling N to which he commits himself; i.e., $P_T = PN$. Foreign-exchange dealers charge no commissions; rather, they obtain payment for their services by buying and selling at different rates. Since competition among foreign-exchange dealers is very keen, the difference between buying and selling rates is very small, typically $2.7980 buy and $2.7983 sell.

Since on the day of contract maturity the speculator has offsetting obligations, he theoretically needs no capital. In practice, however, banks require a margin deposit, which in August 1961, was 10 per cent in the case of a large New York bank. Furthermore, a speculator may want to protect himself against unexpected increases in margin deposits resulting from exchange-rate changes by keeping some additional funds in liquid form. The opportunity cost of speculation thus consists of the loss of earnings on the 10-per-cent margin deposit and the loss due to keeping some funds in liquid form. It is quite obvious that in spite of these costs speculators obtain considerable leverage from their equity.

A speculator has two decisions to make, and can be thought of as having two parameters to consider in doing so. The first decision, whether to buy or to sell forward exchange, depends on what he expects the future spot rate $E(X_0^t)$ will be, given the current forward rate. Having decided whether to buy or to sell, he must make up his mind on how much to commit. This decision depends on his confidence in his own prediction of the actual future spot rate. This notion of confidence can be formalized by saying that speculators usually hold expectations about a whole set of possible outcomes. Each of these possible outcomes carries a certain subjective probability of becoming reality, and $E(X_0^t)$ can be considered to be the mean of that probability distribution. In general, the greater the dispersion of possible outcomes around this mean—i.e., the greater the standard deviation σ—the greater the possibility of large losses or gains. The deviation σ can therefore be regarded as an expression for risk. It is clear that the amount of forward contracts a speculator is willing to enter depends not only on the relation between $E(X_0^t)$ and X_t but also on σ. If the speculator is not a risk-lover, his willingness to hold speculative forward commitments is an increasing function of the expected rate of return $E(R)$—i.e., $E(R) = E(X_0^t) - X_t$—and a decreasing function of σ.

The parameters of this probability distribution are purely subjective. But if individual demand and supply are netted out, the resulting net-market speculative condition reflects the central tendency among the family of speculators. There is every reason to believe that the net tendency is much like that of individual speculators, and that it changes in response to the same stimuli.

The Speculators' Schedule

The speculators' schedule SS in Fig. 4.1 shows the relationships just discussed, and represents another step in the direction of deriving

a set of demand and supply curves whose intersection determines the
forward rate. The horizontal axis again (as in Fig. 2.3) measures the
quantity of forward commitments, and the vertical axis measures
exchange rates. The SS schedule is associated with an expected future
spot rate $E(X_0^t)$ and a risk estimate σ_0; it passes through the point of
zero forward commitments, where the present forward rate X_t is equal

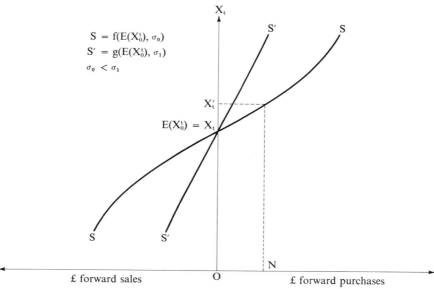

FIG. 4.1. Speculators' schedule.

to $E(X_0^t)$. The locus of points on the schedule indicates the relationship
between actual values of X_t and the quantity of forward commitments
resulting from the given $E(X_0^t)$ and σ_0.

Thus, for example, the forward rate X_0^t results in forward sales of
ON pounds sterling by speculators, in the expectation that the pounds
can be purchased spot at the lower $E(X_0^t)$ when the forward contract
matures. At the extreme end, the SS curve becomes inelastic under the
assumption of diminishing returns to risk-taking. The schedule $S'S'$
is associated with $E(X_0^t)$ and σ_1, where $\sigma_0 < \sigma_1$. The same risk estimate
σ_0 but a different $E(X_0^t)$ would shift the SS schedule up or down, parallel
to its position with the previous $E(X_0^t)$.

5. Demand for Forward Exchange from Importers and Exporters

One potentially very large source of forward-exchange demand and supply originates with importers and exporters whose transactions enter the current-accounts section of the balance of payments. This chapter systematically integrates these market participants into the formal model of forward exchange rate determination.

Origins of Demand for Forward Exchange

Importers' and exporters' demand for forward exchange arises out of the following business practice. Contracts for the payment of goods or services are normally drawn up months before payment is due, and are expressed in terms of the currency that is the domestic unit for one of the two partners in the transaction. The other partner, therefore, faces the uncertainty of not knowing exactly what the size of his receipts (or payments) will be in terms of his own domestic currency. This uncertainty involves a risk that is alien to his basic business activity; to eliminate it, a rational trader should cover himself in the forward market, and if he is fully rational the price at which he signs his contract ought to depend on the level of the forward rate at the time.

Among traders in the real world,* however, there appears to be a willingness to assume exchange risks, and in fact to become speculators to the extent of their involvement as traders. Some traders may be unwitting speculators, out of ignorance of the existence of a forward cover. So long as these traders are neither primarily importers nor exporters, their failure to cover themselves has no impact on the demand for forward exchange, since they deal only in spot currency. It is important to emphasize that the direct demand for spot currency remains

---

* See William H. White, "Interest Rate Differences, Forward Exchange Mechanism, and Scope for Short-term Capital Movements," *International Monetary Fund Staff Papers*, November 1963.

unchanged between the time the commercial contract is signed and the time it matures, regardless of whether forward cover is bought or not.

But let us return now to the case where exporters and importers are not ignorant of the existence of forward-exchange markets. In order to analyze how the needs of these traders add to the demand for and supply of forward currency, it is convenient to assume that all foreign trade between the United States and the United Kingdom is covered in the forward market, regardless of whether it is billed in sterling or in dollars. This means that either an American or a British businessman will be purchasing the forward cover. Because of bilateral arbitrage, the London and New York markets can be considered as one, and we can continue to concentrate on the demand for and supply of forward sterling for dollars.

For analytical purposes, we distinguish between three cases:

Case 1. All transactions are covered in the forward market, and the levels of exports and imports are completely independent of the current forward rate; i.e., they are exogenously determined. Since imports give rise to forward purchases, and exports to forward sales, the two can be "married." Depending on whether the exogenously determined exports, or the imports, are the greater, traders will cause at any given moment in time either excess demand for or supply of forward exchange in the market.

Case 2. The demand for imports and exports is assumed to be a function of the forward rates, as indicated by the rather inelastic demand and supply schedules shown in Fig. 5.1. The quantity of

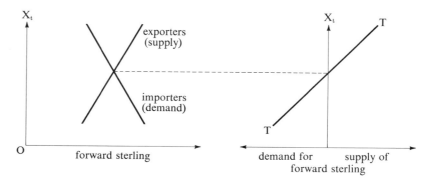

Fig. 5.1. Demand and supply of forward exchange from traders.

unmarried excess forward sterling thus differs in size and sign at the various values of the forward rate X_t, as the traders' schedule (TT) in the figure indicates. The value of X_t at which the demand and supply curves intersect depends on domestic levels of income, demand and supply, and elasticities of goods and services with respect to prices, etc., the analysis of which goes beyond the scope of this study. The demand and supply curves in the figure can be assumed to result from the covering of sales and purchases by all exporters and importers. Alternatively, these curves can be considered the consequence of the actions of a certain proportion of both exporters and importers in the economy. The latter assumption is probably the most realistic, since some of the businessmen engaged in foreign trade are aware of the existence of forward-exchange markets and use them regularly. The important difference between the two assumptions is that the TT schedule in the figure is less elastic under the second assumption than under the first.

Case 3. Exports and imports are again assumed to be exogenously determined, as in case 1. However, whether traders cover themselves or not depends on their expectations about actual future spot rates, which implies that they are in essence willing to speculate. Let us assume that each trader has in mind a probability distribution of what the spot rate will actually be at the time when he must make the transaction. A situation that typically confronts an importer is the following. The currently quoted forward rate is 2.82. If the importer is confident that the actual spot rate at the time of his payment will not be above 2.82, and will perhaps be lower, he is likely to gain an advantage by not purchasing the forward currency. The most unfavorable result would be that he would have to pay 2.82 for the pound sterling when he settles his bill. But there may also be the chance that he would pay less than 2.82. Analogous reasoning applies to exporters,* and, given a probability distribution for expected future spot rates, for other values of the forward rate.

These considerations respecting the behavior of exporters and importers in case 3 are given precision in Fig. 5.2. The demand for forward sterling by importers is shown (on the left-hand side of the figure) to be smaller the further the forward rate X_t exceeds some rate

---

* In a conversation with the author, the head of the Foreign Exchange Department of the Chase Manhattan Bank of New York described this type of behavior by businessmen as typical. In a large number of cases, the decision to cover or not to cover is made on the basis of the Bank's recommendations.

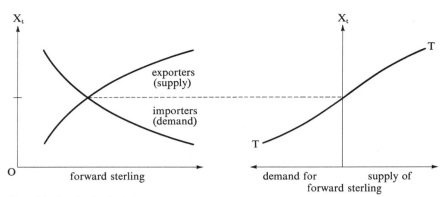

Fig. 5.2. Traders' schedule.

considered "normal," and to increase with values of X_t below that. Exporters behave in corresponding fashion, and the market schedule for forward exchange demanded and supplied is the rather elastic TT curve.

The Speculator–Trader Schedule

The demand for forward exchange from traders—as from speculators—does not involve spot currency. In the following, the three cases of trader schedules just analyzed are integrated into the speculator diagram.

Under the assumptions of case 1, the SS schedule will be shifted up (or down) by an equal distance over its entire range to an extent corresponding to the excess of imports over exports (or exports over imports).

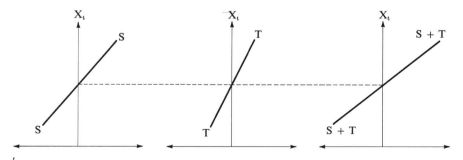

Fig. 5.3. Trader and speculator schedules combined.

In both case 2 and case 3, the TT schedule must be added horizontally to the SS schedule to form the combined S + T schedule shown in Fig. 5.3. As a result, the S + T schedule is more elastic than either the SS schedule (Fig. 4.1) or the TT schedule (Fig. 5.2). If speculators and traders share the same expectation about the actual future spot rate, the SS, TT, and S + T schedules will all intersect zero at the same point on the X_t axis, as shown by the dotted line in the figure; otherwise, the intersections will be at different forward rates. The difference between the S + T schedule under case 2 and that under case 3 is essentially a quantitative one upon which it is difficult to generalize. The most important point is that the inclusion of traders tends to make the schedule more elastic than if speculators alone are considered.

6. Market Equilibrium and Adjustments through Time

Market Equilibrium

The arbitrager and speculator–trader schedules are now used to show how forward rates and quantities of forward-exchange contracts are determined.

In Fig. 6.1, X_0 is the spot rate, X_t is the forward rate, and X_t^* is the parity forward rate. Since X_0 is less than X_t^*, it follows that the interest-rate differential favors New York. The speculator–trader schedule $(S + T)'$ crosses the zero axis near the current spot rate, demonstrating that, in general, speculative sentiment expects a stable spot rate. The intersection of the $(S + T)'$ schedule with the AA schedule produces a forward rate of X_t' and a forward commitment of OM.

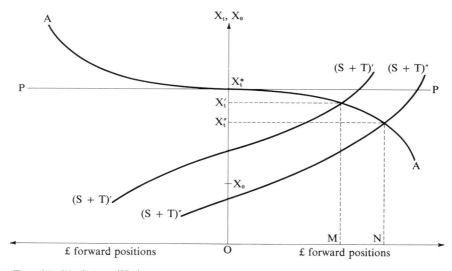

FIG. 6.1. Market equilibrium.

According to the assumptions underlying the (S + T) schedule, the expectations and the balance of trade are such that, at this equilibrium forward rate, speculators and traders are willing to hold commitments for the delivery of no more than OM pounds of forward sterling. Interest arbitragers and triangular arbitragers—given the spot rate, the interest-rate differential, and the other forward rates at their interest parity—hold at the forward rate X_t' commitments to accept delivery of OM pounds. Since the interest rate favors New York, these pounds are needed to repatriate the funds originally invested in New York.

A new market equilibrium, typified by a "speculative situation," is shown in Fig. 6.2. The spot rate is now greater than X_t^*, which means that the interest-rate differential favors London. The position of the (S + T)′ schedule indicates that speculators expect a devaluation of sterling. As a result of these expectations, the intersection of the AA and (S + T)′ schedules is to the right of the zero line, signifying a capital flow to New York of OM pounds sterling at the forward rate X_t'. We have here the case where forward-exchange speculation attracts the flow of spot funds away from the high-interest country toward the low-interest country. Forward-exchange speculation is thus seen to be capable of putting pressure on the spot-exchange rate and international reserves, by causing flows of spot funds away from the country with the high interest rate, raised perhaps just for the purpose of attracting such spot funds. This analysis of the case described by Fig. 6.2 is

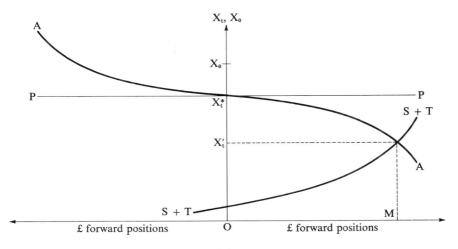

Fig. 6.2. Market equilibrium under speculation.

important for forward-exchange policy, which will be discussed in Part III.

Returning to Fig. 6.1, we consider a shift in the $(S + T)'$ schedule from its original position to $(S + T)''$. Such a shift can be brought about by a change in expectations about the future spot rate $E(X_0^t)$ or in the certainty with which these expectations are held σ (the standard deviation). Alternatively, the shift can be due to an increase in covered-trade surplus, or to a combination of changes in these three parameters. The shift shown is sufficient, given the AA schedule, to produce an X_t significantly different from X_t^*, although at that forward rate the market is again in equilibrium. The forward contracts outstanding increase from OM to ON.

A change in X_t' and OM can also occur as the result of a narrowing or widening of the interest-rate differential. In the diagram, this would be reflected in a shift of the PP and AA schedules. Unless such a change in the interest-rate differential causes a very specific shift of the speculative schedule, the new equilibrium, as well as the quantity of forward commitments outstanding, is likely to be different.

As was shown in Chapter 3, the relationship between changes in the quantity of forward-exchange commitments and changes in short-term capital movements in this two-country model is *not* one-to-one, because of the presence of triangular arbitrage. What proportion of a given increase in forward commitments is due to triangular arbitrage and what to interest arbitrage is a question that cannot be settled on theoretical grounds. In both cases, institutional factors determine the elasticities of demand and supply, and therefore the size of the covered-interest-arbitrage operations. The critical question of the elasticities of these schedules is thus a problem for empirical research.

Adjustments through Time

In the analysis thus far, several important problems have been ignored. Some of these will be taken up now. The first concerns the impact of investments of different length on the theory of forward exchange as so far presented. To illustrate what is involved, consider that in equilibrium a stock of $1 billion in short-term funds is invested in London, having moved there in response to a covered margin of 0.6 per cent. Looking at the figures at any given point in time during a year when the margin remains unchanged, we note that $1 billion in forward contracts is outstanding. This is obvious in the case where the forward contract is for a year. But if the initial investment has been in one-month bills, covered by one-month forward sales, the case is not so obvious. What has happened is that at the end of each month the investor has had to go through the same considerations that underlay his initial shift, so as to decide where to keep his funds. Where the covered-earnings differential has persisted, he has kept the funds in London. Logically, he has then gone through the following steps: receipt of funds from maturing investment, exchange of the funds for home currency on the basis of the old forward contract, purchase of spot currency, reinvestment, and cover through a new forward contract. This process is short-circuited, in practice, in that deliveries of funds in the exchange dealings are not made, but rather the forward contract is renewed and the difference between spot and forward is settled in cash.

Another important problem is the behavior of interest arbitragers and speculators when interest or exchange rates change before contracts mature. The diagrams and the underlying analysis have until now been exercises in comparative statics; they say nothing about the actions of arbitragers or speculators between equilibrium positions—i.e., about how they pursue portfolio adjustments when the arbitrage margin changes. For this, dynamic analysis is required, and its use raises formidable problems.

It is convenient to concentrate first on interest arbitragers, and to introduce the following assumptions in order to make the problem manageable:

1. All foreign investments occur in 90-day bills, and are covered in the 90-day forward market.

2. There exist no facilities for odd-day forward contracts, and all investments are held to maturity.

3. Arbitrage margins are caused by change in the forward rate and the implicit rate of return, i.e., $(X_t - X_0)/X_0$; interest rates and spot rates in the two countries do not change.

4. The investor is not concerned with the maturity structure of his portfolio.

Under these assumptions, when changes in forward rate cause the arbitrage schedule to call for an increase in forward-exchange holdings, investors effect the adjustment by purchases of additional forward-covered foreign investments. A reduction of forward commitments by arbitragers, when required by a change in the forward rate, can be achieved only by letting old contracts mature and neglecting to renew them, which implies a domestic reinvestment of the equivalent sum.

If the assumptions are dropped, the investor must consider so many variables in deciding by what method to adjust his foreign-asset and forward-exchange holdings that generalizations are not possible. All that can be done here is to enumerate some of the factors an investor must consider in deciding how and with what speed to adjust his foreign-asset holdings.

When the expected return on foreign assets is raised, the consequent increase in holdings is accomplished simply by the purchase of assets with the desired maturity. The matter is more complicated when the change in the expected return calls for reduced holding of foreign assets. There may or may not be a capital gain or loss from the sale of the security itself. Similarly, the undoing of the forward contract may result in a capital gain or loss which can either mitigate or accentuate the results of the security disposal. And of course the investor has always the choice of letting his asset mature, so as to earn the rate originally sought. Entering into this choice may be expectations of the rates on the day of maturity. All these considerations are influenced by an examination of the way in which the reduction in the arbitrage margin has been brought about: whether by changes in forward rate, spot rate, or domestic or foreign interest rates; or by changes of these parameters in some combination. No simple statements are possible concerning adjustments through time by interest arbitragers responding to arbitrage-margin changes, but once all parameters relevant to the decision are specified, it is possible to determine what actions a rational and profit-maximizing arbitrager is likely to undertake.

The speculator faces similar problems in establishing speculative commitments in accord with his preferences, when the parameters determining his choice have changed. For illustration, assume that a speculator sells forward a certain amount of sterling for delivery 90 days hence. Given the forward rate and his expectation about the future spot rate, he is in equilibrium. Ten days later, as the result of new information, he raises his estimate of what the spot rate is likely to be on the day his contract matures, and is as convinced of his new estimate as he had been of the old. This means that he has shifted his schedule in a parallel fashion and must lower his outstanding forward commitments to return to equilibrium. If a market for 80-day forward exchange exists, he buys sterling forward for delivery on the date of his original commitment. This act effectively reduces his net speculative position. It may be that this can be achieved only by incurring a definite cost; i.e., the selling price under the 90-day contract may be lower than the buying price under the 80-day contract. But the cost thus incurred may nevertheless be smaller than the expected cost of maintaining an open position after the events that changed the speculator's expectations.

If the speculator finds that he can make his forward commitments only in 90-day contracts, he cannot repair his open position quite so readily. But since his being bound by 90-day contracts enters his estimate of risk it thus bears upon the size of his speculative engagements at any time. On the other hand, if the speculator's expectation of the spot rate on the day he owes sterling has changed such that he feels he must lower this debt, there is a roundabout way he can do it. He can simply buy sterling forward for delivery 90 days after his change of expectations; if the two contract-maturity dates are not far apart, and the estimate changes for both days are closely correlated, the speculator's open position has been closed effectively. In today's markets, forward contracts for odd days are readily available and the 30-day market is highly developed, so that he should be able to close positions directly without much difficulty and should only rarely have to resort to the indirect method.

Traders wishing to undo their forward commitments when changes occur in the basic variables that initially determined their actions have essentially become speculators. As such, they are influenced by the same principles as the speculators. Triangular arbitragers in forward exchange, on the other hand, are never tempted to undo their commitments as a result of future price developments, since their profits are made by taking advantage of a certain configuration of prices at one instant in time.

One problem facing the arbitrager of short-term funds covering his exchange risk by the purchase of forward cover is that this investment is not really as liquid as a domestic investment. If the arbitrager suddenly needs cash, in local currency, to settle an unexpected obligation, he may find that his foreign investment is not easily liquidated. The difficulties he faces are those that arise with other adjustment-through-time problems. There may have been an interest-rate change in the foreign country, causing a capital loss or gain to result from the sale of the security. The forward contract may be of an odd-day length for which no ready market is available. If a market does exist, the sale of the forward contract may yield a capital loss or gain which may or may not offset the gain or loss from the sale of the security. For instance, if the spot rate and the interest rate in the investor's domestic market has remained unchanged while the foreign interest rate has fallen, then under normal circumstances the foreign security can be sold and the capital repatriated at a capital gain. If the forward rate has moved to parity after the change in the interest-rate differential, then the sale of the forward contract that arose from the original covering operation is likely to occur at a capital loss, since the parity forward rate on the relevant maturity is now lower than that of the contract originally entered. As in the analysis before, too many variables enter the gain-loss computations here to permit us to draw simple conclusions or to make reliable estimates of likely events.

Logically, however, all these problems can be short-circuited by considering the development of a new market—a market that does not yet seem to have been developed but that sooner or later should come into existence, simply because the case for one is so strong. This market is one in which packages for forward-covered short-term foreign investments can be discounted. For the New York investor the combination of the foreign-security, forward-exchange ownership represents a known and certain dollar cash value at a specified date, with risk arising only from the possibility of default of the forward-exchange contract and from the overall chance of a national payments moratorium.

Were such a discount market to develop, covered interest arbitrage would become even more widespread than it is under the present circumstances. Not only would the foreign investment be more liquid in the relevant sense, but also, in turn, odd-day contracts would be more easily obtained than before, thus further increasing the demand. Any group of brokers willing to create a market for odd-day, foreign-security, forward-exchange, contract packages is bound to find many customers.

7. Intervention Points and Forward-Exchange Theory

The theory of forward exchange presented so far rests on the assumption that spot rates are flexible without limits. Clearly, this assumption is not realistic. Under the IMF agreements, countries have obliged themselves to maintain spot rates within 1 per cent on either side of par.* During the 'fifties, par rates changed only rarely, as countries showed new awareness of their obligation to prevent domestic instabilities and speculative runs through responsible economic management. The longer these par values remain unchanged, the more confident the public will be that the accompanying intervention points will be maintained. This development has important implications for the theory of forward exchange, implications based on the fact that if an investor is certain the rate for sterling will not fall below 2.78 (the lower intervention point) within the time period concerning him, he can be confident that when the rate *is* 2.78, it can only go up. In this chapter the model of forward-rate determination is modified to accommodate this fact, and the behavior of the individual groups of market participants is suitably reexamined. Finally, market equilibrium is analyzed.

Arbitragers

The following analysis is carried out for the case where the spot rate for the pound sterling is 2.78, i.e., at its lower intervention point. By analogous reasoning the conclusions reached can easily be applied to the case where the spot rate is 2.82, its upper intervention point. When the spot rate is 2.78, the parity forward rate can be above or below the spot rate. We shall examine first the situation where the interest-rate differential favors London, so that the parity forward rate is therefore

---

* International Monetary Fund, *Articles of Agreement*, Article IV, Section 3.

below the spot rate and also below the lower intervention point. The assumption of great confidence in the 2.78 floor encourages a movement of funds from New York to London *without cover*. For by the time a London investment matures, the worst that can happen to an investor is that the spot rate has remained unchanged. Any appreciation of the rate represents a capital gain that accrues in addition to the higher interest earnings. Owner and borrower arbitragers stand to benefit in the same way. The important question is whether these considerations mean that as the spot rate approaches 2.78 the arbitrage schedule will become progressively smaller, and when the lower intervention point is finally reached the demand for forward exchange from arbitragers will be zero.

There are two reasons why we can answer No to this question. First, the triangular arbitragers remain in the market. Second, there is a significant difference between having great confidence in the maintenance of the exchange-rate floor and being certain about it. As long as there is a nonzero probability of currency devaluation and an accompanying change in invervention points, the uncovered movement of funds is essentially speculation in spot rates. In principle, the closer the spot rate approaches the lower intervention point, and the longer it remains there, the greater are the chances that a fundamental disequilibrium of the rate will require that it be reduced. The rate of 2.78 is in fact rarely reached, and then only when the currency is in danger of requiring a basic readjustment. Such devaluations are often on the order of 5 to 10 per cent, and the corresponding loss on a three-month investment would be equivalent to a negative rate of return of 20 to 40 per cent per year. Thus, even though the probability of change in the intervention point is rather small, the certainty of very heavy losses should it occur makes many conservative investors eager to obtain forward exchange and cover this risk.

Given these considerations, it seems reasonable to assume that forward-exchange supply and demand from interest arbitragers remains in spite of strong confidence in the maintenance of the exchange-rate floor. This is so especially if we are correct in presuming that substantial covered-interest arbitrage is carried out by large finanical institutions, which generally use borrowed funds and are known for their aversion to risk-taking and speculation. Furthermore, borrowing arbitrage may retain its demand for forward cover in pursuing the highly competitive, low-profit, margin trade in world staples.

However, there are likely to be some groups of investors willing to gamble on the existing odds by moving their funds without cover more readily the closer the spot rate approaches the intervention points. These actions have the effect of reducing the quantity of funds available for covered shifts. As a result, the supply of forward currency available from arbitragers is reduced from the level it would have attained in the absence of intervention points.

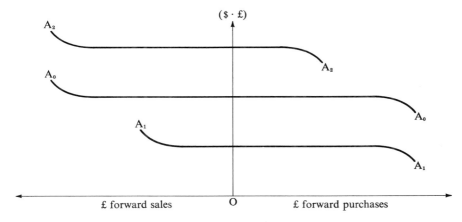

Fɪɢ. 7.1. Arbitrage schedule and intervention points.

In terms of the graphic analysis, this means that the inelastic parts of the arbitrage schedule are proximate to the zero origin as a function of spot rate, given the interest-rate differential. Figure 7.1 shows this relationship. The somewhat stylized arbitrage schedule A_0A_0 is the normal one, which by assumption we associate with the parity forward rate of 2.80. Schedule A_1A_1 prevails when the spot rate is near the lower intervention point and the interest-rate differential favors London. Schedule A_2A_2 obtains when the spot rate is close to the upper intervention point and New York interest rates exceed those in London. The interpretation of the example is as follows. With the spot rate at 2.78 and the interest-rate differential in favor of London, schedule A_1A_1 applies. At forward rates above the parity forward rate, funds flow to London and the left-hand side of the diagram becomes relevant. As can be seen, the inelastic part of the schedule on the left-hand side is reached at smaller quantities of forward sales than is normally the case. This is because the spot rate at the lower intervention point has attracted uncovered arbitrage to London, and has left fewer funds for covered arbitrage in New York. The right-hand side of the arbitrage schedule is shown with its normal length because the portfolios of London investors are not reduced by uncovered outflows; the right-hand side of the schedule also indicates the forward rates at which covered shifts to New York are profitable.

Let us turn now to the case where the spot rate is at the lower intervention point but the interest-rate differential favors New York, so that the parity forward rate is above the lower intervention point. This is empirically an unlikely case, since the low sterling spot rate indicates British balance-of-payments deficits; under such circumstances, the London interest rate is likely to be high in order to attract foreign short-term capital and thereby to deflate domestic demand.

However, the analysis of the case is of some interest. The expectation that the spot rate can only appreciate will not attract uncovered flows into New York because New York asset holders already enjoy the higher interest rate. For London investors, on the other hand, the near-certain expectation of a rise in the sterling rate means a near-certain expectation of a capital loss if funds are moved without cover. One pound sterling brings only 2.78 when the initial New York investment takes place, and very likely will have to be repurchased at more than 2.78 at maturity. Thus it follows that in the case where the spot rate is at the lower intervention point and the interest-rate differential favors the strong center, the arbitrage schedule will retain its normal shape because there are no flows of uncovered funds to distort it.

A spot rate at the upper intervention point implies a weak dollar and a strong pound sterling. The arbitrage schedule will be distorted if the interest-rate differential favors New York, but will not be distorted if the differential favors London.

The essential difference between arbitrage schedules drawn under the assumption of perfectly flexible spot rates and spot rates flexible within official limits is that under the latter conditions the arbitrage schedule sometimes takes on a distorted shape. However, under either assumptions the schedule shifts in response to changes in the spot rate or the interest-rate differential.

Speculators and Traders

The speculator who is confident of the stability of par sterling at 2.80 should be willing to sell large amounts of forward sterling when the forward rate is at the upper intervention point of 2.82. Analogously, he should be willing to buy forward sterling in large amounts when the rate is at its lower intervention point. On the strength of that confidence, the worst outcome he can expect is that the actual spot rate on the contract-maturity date will be the same as the forward rate at which the contract was made. At any actual future spot rate between 2.78 and 2.82, a positive profit is made.

For the graphic analysis, this modification means that the SS schedule becomes almost perfectly elastic as the forward rate approaches the intervention points, as shown in Fig. 7.2. On the other hand, the

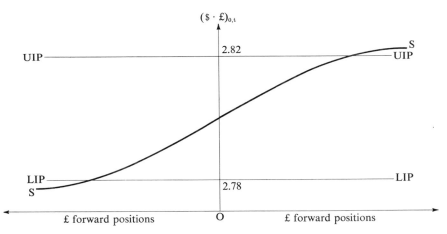

FIG. 7.2. Speculators' schedule and intervention points.

probability that a devaluation will occur is never zero. Entering an open position therefore carries a positive risk, and the size of the potential loss increases with the size of the open position. At some quantity of forward commitments, the positive utility associated with the possibility of gain from buying or selling one more unit of currency is equal to the disutility of the additional risk arising from the transaction. If the speculator is to be coaxed into entering larger forward commitments, more substantial possible gain must be offered him. Given expectations, this may occur only at a forward rate outside the intervention points. The section of the SS schedule between the ranges of perfect elasticity is also somewhat more elastic than a schedule drawn under the assumption of perfect rate flexibility. This mid-range section intersects the vertical axis where the expected future spot rate is equal to the actual forward rate.

As with arbitragers, the demand for forward exchange by individuals engaged in international trade is influenced by the existence of official intervention points and a widespread confidence in their maintenance. If an American exporter wishes to make ccrtain the dollar equivalent of his future sterling receipts, he will want to sell sterling forward. But if the forward price is 2.78, and he believes the spot rate can be no lower than 2.78 when he receives his foreign currency—with some chance that it will be higher—he will not want to cover himself. For the worst that can result from his not purchasing forward exchange is that his dollar receipts will be equal to what they would have been had he bought it.

Just as with arbitragers and pure speculators, however, there is always *some* risk that a change in par value may occur. This risk causes some risk-averting traders to cover themselves in every transaction, regardless of the odds on losses or gains from speculating on the exchanges. When compared with conservative financial arbitragers, however, the proportion of risk-avoiding traders is likely to be rather small. Thus we can assume that the supply of forward sterling originating in the transactions of exporters approaches zero when the forward rate is at the lower intervention point, and becomes larger the more the forward rate approaches the upper intervention point. This relationship produces the function SS in Fig. 7.3. For importers, the function is a mirror image of the exporters' function, as shown by the line DD. The excess of demand over supply of forward exchange at various forward rates is therefore highly elastic, as TT shows.

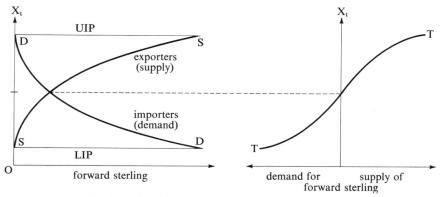

FIG. 7.3. Demand and supply of forward exchange from traders.

Underlying the functions in Fig. 7.3 could be an assumption that the level of exports or imports is completely independent of the forward rate and depends rather on the spot rate or some expected future spot rate. Or, alternatively, the assumption could be made that the level of exports and imports is always determined by the forward rate. Under this assumption, the negative or positive excess of forward sterling demanded over that supplied would be greater at all rates than under the first assumption—greater not only because of the effect of specula-tion, but also because at high rates the supply of forward currency is greater than the demand. Whichever of these two behavioral assump-tions is chosen, the TT schedule is more elastic than the one drawn in Chapter 5 under the assumptions of the basic model outlined there.

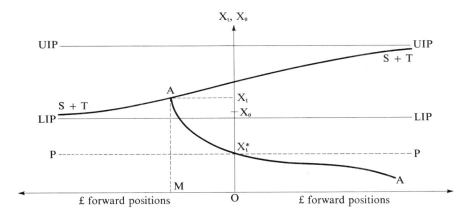

Fig. 7.4. Market equilibrium and intervention points, interest-rate differential favoring London.

The S + T schedule shown in Fig. 7.4, obtained by combining the SS and TT schedules, is distinguished from the schedule drawn under the assumption of perfectly flexible exchange rates by its greater elasticity over its entire range, including a long stretch of almost perfect elasticity near the intervention points. The S + T schedule indicates again the stock of forward sterling held by speculators and traders at any given forward rate. The schedule shifts in response to changes in either the expected future spot rate (or the confidence with which the expectations are held) or the parameters underlying the traders' demand and supply schedule.

Market Equilibrium

The model of forward exchange, modified by the assumption that intervention points and great confidence in their maintenance exist, is summarized in Figs. 7.4 and 7.5.

In the first figure, the spot rate X_0 is near the lower intervention point LIP. The position of the parity forward rate X_t^* below the spot rate indicates that the interest-rate differential favors London. Because of these circumstances, uncovered flows to London are encouraged and the arbitrage schedule AA is shorter on the left-hand side than on the right. The speculator-trader schedule crosses the zero line near X_t^*, thus indicating that speculators expect that rate to be maintained. Consequently the resultant forward rate X_t leads to OM forward commitments, which in the absence of triangular arbitrage would correspond to the amount of covered funds moved to London from New York.

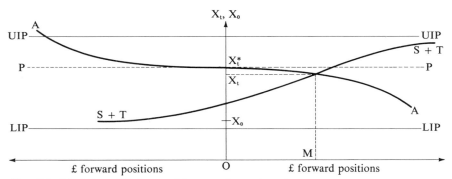

Fig. 7.5. Market equilibrium and intervention points, interest-rate differential favoring New York.

In Fig. 7.5, X_0 is again near the lower intervention point but the interest advantage lies with New York. The arbitrage schedule associated with the resultant value of X_t^* has the normal shape. The very elastic speculators' schedule intersects the arbitrage schedule in the right-hand side of the diagram, thus indicating an inflow of covered London funds into New York equal to OM except for some triangular-arbitrage contracts.

From these diagrams and the verbal analysis, the conclusion can be drawn that the introduction of intervention points into the basic model does not influence the *qualitative* conclusions, but with respect to *quantitative* estimates, the following important differences are introduced:

1. When the spot rate is not close to the intervention points, the quantity of forward positions in equilibrium is likely to be much larger because of the greater elasticity of the S + T schedule.

2. When the spot rate is very close to or at the intervention points, and the interest-rate differential favors the country whose currency is depreciated with respect to the other, the inelastic part of the AA schedule shifts toward zero. At such times, the effect of the greater elasticity of the S + T schedule may or may not be offset by this shift in the AA schedule. Because of these offsetting tendencies, a given constellation of interest rates, spot and forward rates, and expectations about the future spot rate can result in a larger or smaller forward position than in the basic model.

3. When spot and interest rates are such that the parity forward rate is outside the intervention points, a larger-than-average covered-arbitrage margin is likely to arise.

4. The relationship between forward positions and actual capital movements, which is less than one-to-one in the basic model because of the triangular arbitrage, is made more unpredictable by the uncovered movement of funds.

8. Two Theoretical Problems

The models of forward exchange rate determination presented so far have all assumed implicitly that it is possible to speak of a single interest rate in London and a single rate in New York, on the basis of which arbitragers make their decisions. But a look at the financial pages of newspapers reveals that on any one day there exists a whole collection of interest rates. Which of these rates are the relevant ones for arbitrage purposes? Closer examination of the published rates shows that the differences among them can be attributed to two analytically distinct causes: first, interest rates differ on securities with different maturities; second, interest rates on assets with equal maturities differ with the credit ratings of the borrowers.*

This chapter employs this classification in analyzing the implications of interest-rate structure for the theory of forward exchange. We shall first examine the problem of determining which pairs of equal-maturity securities have interest-rate differentials relevant for arbitrage considerations. We shall then turn to an analysis of the interaction between interest-rate maturity structure and forward-exchange-rate maturity structure.

Choice of Interest-Rate Differentials

Money markets have developed many kinds of securities with equal maturity. At the short end of the maturity structure, the New York market offers such diverse money-market papers as bankers' acceptances, trade bills, Treasury bills, finance-company paper, and savings deposits. Papers with similar names and distinguishing characteristics exist in the

---

* For a theory of the structure of interest rates, see Joseph Conard, *Introduction to the Theory of Interest*, Berkeley: University of California Press, 1959; and David Meiselman, *The Term Structure of Interest Rates*, Englewood Cliffs: Prentice-Hall, 1962.

London market and in other financial centers. For simplicity we shall assume that it is possible to identify corresponding and equivalent investment opportunities in various money markets. By "equivalent" I mean here papers with approximately equal default risks, such as Treasury bills issued by the British and American central governments.

It is analytically possible to assume that an investor's primary interest is in the maturity of his investment. Under these circumstances he might, for example, compare the yield on U.S. Treasury bills with that on all United Kingdom money-market papers of equal maturity. But such behavior in the real world is not likely to occur. If an American investor chooses U.S. Treasury bills as investment because he dislikes the risks associated with the higher-yield American finance-company paper, he would be irrational to contemplate higher-risk investments in a foreign market. It is possible that because of imperfect information the American investor might today consider only United Kingdom Treasury bills as a relevant foreign alternative to higher-risk domestic investments.* But it is surely only a matter of time before the market will supply the needed information in such cases and thus permit foreign securities to compete on equal terms with domestic securities of equal maturity and default risk.

We are led by these considerations to reexamine the problem of determining which pairs of yields are relevant as bases for planning covered-interest-arbitrage operations, and to conclude that the problem can be simplified to determining which interest-rate differential between securities of equal default risk is the relevant one.

Two solutions are possible. First, if the risk premium of, for example, bankers' acceptances over Treasury bills is always 0.1 per cent in both markets, regardless of the absolute level of the interest rate, then the answer is that the interest-rate differential between London and New York is the same for all pairs of securities. Take for instance New York rates of 2 per cent and 2.1 per cent on Treasury bills and bankers' acceptances, respectively, and London rates of 5 and 5.1 per cent for the same types of securities: the Treasury-bill interest-rate differential and that of the bankers' acceptances are both 3 per cent.

---

* The investment officer of a large institution, interviewed by the author in 1960 about his awareness of foreign short-term investment opportunities, was willing to compare the yield on money-market paper issues by U.S. finance companies (in which he regularly invested) only with the yield on U.K. Treasury bills. The covered-yield margin of U.K. commercial paper over U.S. commercial paper did not interest him because of the lack of information on the soundness of the U.K. debtors.

Second, if the risk premium of one security type over the other is always 10 per cent of the current rate, and this is true in both markets, then there exists no unique interest-rate differential. Consider an example with the same Treasury-bill rates as before—2 per cent in New York and 5 per cent in London. Under the new assumptions, the rate for the bankers' acceptances would be 2.2 per cent in New York and 5.5 per cent in London. The international market differentials would thus be 3 per cent for Treasury bills but 3.3 per cent for the bankers' acceptances. In order to meet the analytical difficulties posed by these inequalities in differentials, we shall assume that the relevant rate differential for arbitrage purposes is an average of all existing differentials. For the purpose of empirical research or formulation of policy decisions, it may be convenient to assume that the differences are of a second order of smallness and can be neglected. Such an assumption is more reasonable the smaller the basic interest-rate differential and the smaller the percentage differences between the relevant securities and the security serving as the basis for comparison.

Maturity Structure of Forward-Exchange Rates

In today's developed exchange markets one can enter into contracts for the sale or purchase of foreign currency for delivery on the same day (cable), the following day (spot), or at any desired day in the future up to four years hence. The best-developed of these markets are the spot, 30-day, and 90-day markets, for which daily quotations are readily available. Quotations for odd days and long periods are made by dealers and banks on special request. The interesting relationship is that between the forward-exchange rates of different maturities at a given moment in time. The following analysis attempts to define this relationship.

The theory of forward exchange rate determination developed in the preceding chapters is generally valid for any maturity of the forward-rate contract or of the securities serving as the basis for interest arbitrage. The behavior of speculators and traders is the same in principle whether the forward exchange involved is for 30 days, 90 days, or a year, though there may be some empirically significant differences among contracts of different durations, with respect to the elasticities of the schedules we used in the model. Triangular arbitrage in forward exchange is similarly unaffected in principle by the maturity of the exchange involved. The various maturities have their greatest influence on the level of the parity forward rate, i.e., the forward rate at which covered interest arbitrage is zero and through which, in the central diagrammatic analysis, the arbitrage schedule is drawn.

It will be recalled that the parity forward rate X_t^* tends to take on a value such as to validate the equation

$$\left(\frac{X_t^* - X_0}{X_0}\right) \frac{360}{T} = \frac{R_d - R_f}{1 + R_f} \tag{8.1}$$

where the values of the spot rate X_0 and the domestic and foreign interest rates (R_d and R_f) are given exogenously. It will also be recalled that the interest rates are expressed as an annual rate of return, even though the maturity of the security may be 30 days, 90 days, or any other number of days hence. Because of this convention it is necessary to correct the simple percentage difference of the spot and forward rates on the left-hand side of the equation by an appropriate weight represented by the term $360/T$ (where T is time to maturity, in days). Thus, if the securities and the forward exchange have a maturity of 90 days, the exchange-rate premium or discount must be corrected by a factor of 4. This is accomplished by replacing T by 90 in the equation.

It may be worth explaining in somewhat greater detail why this correction factor is necessary. Assume for a moment that the securities to which the interest rates apply, as well as the forward rate, have a one-year maturity. In this case, interest-arbitrage equilibrium exists when the foreign center's interest advantage—say 2 per cent—is just wiped out by a forward-exchange discount also of 2 per cent; i.e., $(X_t^* - X_0)/X_0 = -0.02$. But now assume that the maturity of the securities and the forward rate is 90 days, and that the interest-rate differential expressed on an annual basis remains 2 per cent. The right-hand side of the equation remains unchanged. However, a 2-per-cent effective discount of the 90-day forward rate over the spot rate means a capital loss equivalent to 8 per cent per year, because 2 per cent of the initial foreign-exchange investment was lost in one quarter. This explains the need for the corrective factor, $360/T$.

We can disregard all problems of compound interest, since the interest-rate differential in Eq. (8.1) similarly neglects the compounding element. A U.S. Treasury bill of $10,000 paying $100 in 90 days is considered to be paying an interest rate of 4 per cent per year, even though reinvestment of the $100 quarterly receipts would raise the annual yield above 4 per cent.

By simple algebraic manipulation of Eq. (8.1), we obtain

$$X_t^* = \left[ID\left(\frac{T}{360}\right)X_0 \right] + X_0 \qquad (8.2)$$

which expresses the parity rate (X_t^*) as a function of the interest-rate differential $\{ID = [(R_d - R_f)/(1 + R_f)]\}$, the spot rate (X_0), and the weight $(360/T)$. From this equation we can see that for a given spot rate the parity forward rate for each maturity is equal to the spot rate plus the product of the spot rate, the interest-rate differential, and the weight.

If we assume that yield curves have nearly the same shapes in all countries and shift equidistantly with changes in the "interest rate," then it might be reasonable to assume that the interest-rate differentials at the various maturities are approximately the same, or that the differences are of a second order of smallness. Under this assumption, the parity forward rates show a distinct pattern: if we consider the one-year parity exchange rate to be one unit above the spot rate, then the half-year parity forward rate is one-half unit, that for three months one-fourth unit, and so forth, above the spot rate. This follows directly from Eq. (8.2), where the difference between equilibrium forward rates of alternative maturities is reflected only in the factor T.

To the extent that interest-rate differentials between financial centers are not the same at various maturities, the basic model must be modified. If, for example, the interest-rate differential is smaller the shorter the maturity, then the differences among parity forward rates will be more pronounced than they are under the previous assumption. Here again we shall arbitrarily make the premium for the one-year rate equivalent to unity. Thus at any given moment in time the 90-day parity forward rate will be less than one-fourth unit above the spot rate. This is demonstrated by Eq. (8.2), wherein the shorter maturity value is influenced by smaller values for both ID and T.

The theoretical relationship just outlined—that among forward rates with different maturities—represents only the expression of a tendency, for, as we know, the parity forward rate is rarely the equilibrium market rate. Entering the determination of the latter are speculative anticipations; it would be simply coincidental if expectations about the level of the spot-exchange rate 30 days hence were the same as for 360 days hence. Similarly, the elasticities of the relevant schedules in the real world are likely to be quite different for the two maturities.

One last problem remains, with respect to the maturity structure of forward-exchange rates: Is it possible to arbitrage among forward rates with different maturities? If arbitrage is defined as the act of purchasing a commodity in one market and selling it in another in order to profit from price differentials in these markets,* then arbitrage is not possible because 30-day and 90-day currencies are not the same commodity, differing in the essential respect of time of delivery. It is quite obvious that if an investor believes the current 30-day forward rate to be too low, and the 90-day rate to be too high, relative to what the spot rates are expected to be at the maturity dates, then he will not "arbitrage" by buying 30-day currency and selling 90-day currency. What would be involved here is double-barreled speculation. First there is speculation that in 90 days spot can be bought at a rate lower than the rate at which it is to be delivered. If this guess turns out to be wrong, it will not have helped that two months earlier the investor had accepted delivery of foreign currency under a forward contract for which payment could be made by selling it spot. This second speculative transaction is independent of the 90-day sale.

Arbitrage involving forward currencies *would*, on the other hand, be profitable and possible if, on a given day, three-month contracts with one month remaining to maturity sold at a different price than one-month contracts. But this "arbitrage" does not involve forward rates with different maturities.

There is only one indirect way in which arbitrage in the relevant sense can take place, but it does not involve the simultaneous purchase and sale of the same commodity. It occurs when a speculator with given resources and the desire to speculate must choose a maturity to speculate on; clearly, he will choose the maturity that appears to be the most profitable. This action will tend to equalize profits among various maturities, and if the expected spot rates are all approximately the same, the equilibrium forward rates will in turn tend to move toward their interest parities and to conform to the pattern we have analyzed above.

---

* See Kenneth Boulding, *Economic Analysis*, Third Edition, New York: Harper and Brothers, 1955, p. 76.

Part II

Empirical Evidence and the Model

To provide an adequate test of the theoretical model presented in Part I, and to use the model for the prediction of capital flows and the consequence of certain policies, it would be desirable to estimate statistically the most important parameters of the functions constituting the model. Unfortunately, we are prevented by a lack of data from preparing such estimates through empirical research. Of all the information required for such a study—spot and forward exchange rates, interest rates, quantity and type of forward commitments, and rate expectations—the unavailability of data on quantity and type of forward commitments presents the biggest stumbling block. The absence of statistics on this variable severely limits the scope and precision of empirical work on forward exchange.

Until such information is gathered and published, the data now available can be used to test the validity of some of the theoretical considerations in our model, but in a less rigorous, less general fashion than is desirable for the achievement of complete confidence in the model's usefulness as a description of reality. In the following chapters, empirically testable hypotheses, each hypothesis adjusted to the available data, are developed, and results are reported for the tests undertaken. The first chapter presents a general discussion of the data used, and is followed by four chapters of description and analysis of the various tests and their results.

9. Data Sources and Limitations

Past empirical studies of forward-exchange models have been limited to the analysis of relationships between pairs of countries, and have used data from but one financial center. The empirical studies in the following chapters extend the model to more than two countries, and employ data gathered from more than a single international money market. The principal motivation for both extensions arises from the important theoretical implications that triangular arbitrage in forward exchange has been shown to have for the model. Triangular arbitrage has become especially relevant because of the trend in recent years toward greater importance of European currencies in international finance. Furthermore, the newer markets, though less perfect and less deep than the extensively studied New York–London market, make it possible to accumulate additional evidence for the testing of relevant hypotheses.

Interest rates, spot rates, and forward rates were obtained for the several markets between New York, London, Paris, Ottawa, and Frankfurt, for the period July 1955 to July 1961. This period was chosen because it subsumes periods of relative stability in the exchange markets, as well as strong speculative activity both before and after the introduction of convertibility among European currencies during the last week of 1958.

In all cases the raw exchange data were daily observations. The data have been averaged (to a simple mean) for the weeks used as the bases for most of the computations undertaken in the detailed analysis. Interest rates are also weekly observations. Weekly data, rather than monthly or quarterly data, were used because the computation of triangular-arbitrage margins would be rather meaningless for the longer periods. In the computation of interest-arbitrage margins weekly observations are, moreover, likely to reveal developments that would be lost in averages covering longer time periods.

Such detailed and broad study has involved many computations and the processing of large numbers of observations. The availability of an electronic computer has made the project feasible, and the presumably greater reliability of the results has made the extra effort seem worthwhile.

Spot Rates, Forward Rates, and Interest Rates

It was assumed that the most prevalent form of arbitrage—that involving a single exchange rate but two markets—works sufficiently well that it was unnecessary to obtain both rates (dollar–sterling as well as sterling–dollar, for example). The validity of this assumption was tested and found to hold. (The test is described below.) Because of this assumption it was possible to limit the collection of exchange-rate quotations to three markets and yet obtain the exchange rates connecting four centers; quotations obtained from New York, London, and Frankfurt provided data for these three centers plus Ottawa. It was necessary to exclude Paris from some of the computations, for reasons that will be explained.

In New York the exchange-rate data were taken from the internal books of the Morgan Guaranty Trust Company. These data covered the dollar–sterling and dollar–Canadian dollar markets. Opening-day buying rates, which I was able to obtain, seemed the most appropriate choice, since they were quoted while the European markets were still open. The London exchange rates came from *Samuel Montagu's Review of Foreign Exchanges*, a biweekly publication of a leading British foreign-exchange dealer. The specific rates taken from this source, those for London–Ottawa and London–Paris, were midpoints of the reported daily ranges at which transactions had taken place. The Dresdener Bank of Frankfurt made available its internal books for the Frankfurt–London, Frankfurt–New York, and Frankfurt–Ottawa exchange rates. In this study I used midpoints between the buying and selling rates quoted in the source. It is interesting to note that the difference between buying and selling rates in the Frankfurt forward quotations was relatively large during times of crisis and speculation, and was small during normal times. The range of London rates exhibited analytically analogous behavior. No use was made of these variations in the computation of weekly averages.

Spot, 30-day, and 90-day rates for Frankfurt–London were the basis for tests of a hypothesis concerning time structure in forward-rates. The interest rates on 90-day securities were easy to obtain for New York, London, and Ottawa. For all three centers I used the rates on 90-day Treasury bills. Various rates were used in testing interest-rate structure: rates on bankers' prime acceptances and finance paper were obtained from New York, and rates on bankers' prime acceptances, prime commercial paper, and day-to-day money were obtained from London.

The Frankfurt money market is not as deep and well developed as the London and New York markets. The German Bundesbank has, however, since the mid-'fifties created a market for 90-day government securities, which it sells at prices that I have assumed reflect the opportunity cost of short-term funds.*

The problem of finding a meaningful interest rate for the underdeveloped Paris money market was more difficult. The French Treasury-bill rate, which remained almost unchanged during the period under observation, presents a distorted opportunity cost because these bills are used as legal reserve by French banks and special tax provisions make them especially attractive bank assets. Their yield was close to 3 per cent with very little variation throughout the period under consideration. The most meaningful market-determined rate obtainable was that on day-to-day money secured by private securities. For this reason computations involving the French franc were limited to a single special relationship involving the pound sterling and London day-to-day money.

Both the exchange-rate and the interest-rate data contain certain imperfections. Exchange rates do not reflect the difference between buying and selling rates. Similarly, a single interest rate has been employed, although the market's borrowing interest rates usually differ from its lending interest rates. Neither the exchange rates nor the interest rates can in any way take into account variations in price during the day or week, nor special discounts given to customers making large purchases or deserving such favors for some other reason. Such imperfections in data are typical in economics and are handled here in customary fashion. Some are taken into account in the statistical

---

* The interest rates were obtained from the following sources: *Monthly Reports of the Deutsche Bundesbank*, Frankfurt; *Bank of Canada, Statistical Summary, Financial Supplements*, Ottawa; *The Economist*, London; *Federal Reserve Bulletin*, New York; and an internal listing of the Bank of France, Paris.

TABLE 9.1

Balance-of-Payments Data: Minus Signs Denote Outflow; Plus Signs Denote Inflow.

Capital Movements

Year	Quarter	Germany* (millions of Deutsche marks) long-term capital	short-term capital	errors and omissions	United Kingdom† (millions of pounds sterling) long-term capital	short-term capital	errors and omissions	United States‡ (millions of Dollars) portfolio investment — Western Europe	portfolio investment — £ area in W. Europe	private and bank short-term capital — Western Europe	private and bank short-term capital — £ area in W. Europe	errors and omissions — Western Europe	errors and omissions — £ area in W. Europe	Canada§ (millions of Canadian dollars) other capital movements
1956	I	-94	-86	37	190 (entire year)	-70 (entire year)	47 (entire year)	0	6	-13	37	50	-105	206
	II	-105	460	106				-23	-23	-6	-31	113	165	93
	III	290	311	532				-25	-57	-68	-3	-261	311	-103
	IV	43	209	-121				38	-19	-70	-17	-49	-158	-48
1957	I	11	16	412	-160 (half year)	-20 (half year)	77 (half year)	-29	12	-44	-61	-113	108	111
	II	25	-149	758				38	-67	-11	8	-119	70	115
	III	238	927	1,415	-120 (half year)	30 (half year)	48 (half year)	-6	-8	-13	46	-210	302	-120
	IV	-35	-797	-832				-112	10	-21	-1	-171	-223	-11
1958	I	41	-735	209	-25	-2	77	-44	4	-3	17	-173	-211	131
	II	-164	-122	213	-65	17	53	-48	4	7	-10	-182	-51	19
	III	-35	-237	-83	-60	8	-9	-113	12	-36	-41	-585	98	-137
	IV	-360	357	-739	-40	9	-32	-128	22	-4	-1	-298	46	109
1959	I	-449	-1,365	33	-20	6	-29	-2	30	70	53	125	6	112
	II	-452	-382	-206	-50	-16	16	-12	17	49	-22	-89	25	201
	III	-175	-438	431	-60	-18	-23	-1	38	13	-52	-301	-6	41
	IV	-76	992	-332	-70	2	123	-19	19	13	12	-6	-334	-4
1960	I	-460	154	260	-31	-11	60	-64	37	55	-12	149	-197	-71
	II	93	1,760	1,058	-63	-29	115	-89	-19	-32	-144	-145	-167	162
	III	359	587	1,156	-36	-2	66	-80	-1	-12	-96	-163	-195	-39
	IV	1,000	408	-775	175	-17	72	-77	-2	-87	-84	-648	33	191
1961	I	796	-1,454	442	-83		25		-1	-40	94	64	-480	309
	II	135	-98	1,003	-83		125			-47	27	-847	318	207
	III	-77	-5	-624	-69									

* Source: *Monthly Report of the Deutsche Bundesbank*, Frankfurt, July 1963, Vol. 15, No. 7, p. 122. Figures include private capital only, i.e., the capital of the German party to the transaction in each case. Net errors and omissions are mainly due to changes in the terms of payments, computed as the difference between (a) change in monetary reserves of the Bundesbank and (b) balance of transactions in goods, services, donations, and capital.

† Source: International Monetary Fund, *Balance of Payments Yearbook*, Washington D.C., various issues. From 1958 on, column 2 is "UK banking acceptances" (extended:—); and column 3 is "Other miscellaneous short-term capital."

‡ Source: Same as for United Kingdom. The column headings shown apply to the period after 1960, I. Before 1960, column 1 is "Long-term private and bank assets (other than direct investments)"; column 2 is "Short-term private and bank assets"; column 3 is "Net errors and omissions."

§ Source: *The Canadian Balance of International Payments*, Ottawa, 1959, p. 42. The main components of the item shown are: bank balances and other short-term funds abroad (excluding official reserves); borrowings by Canadian finance companies; and net errors and omissions.

hypotheses and the interpretations of results presented below; others are asssumed to be insignificant.

Information about Speculation

For the interpretation of some of the series computed, we must have some general information about the direction and vigor of speculative activity during the period of consideration. This information, plus some analysis, is contained in some of the writings on forward-exchange markets found in the Bibliography. The true flavor of the events, however, is best reflected in contemporary articles in such publications as *The Economist, The Banker, Business Week, The New York Times,* and *The Wall Street Journal,* and in such official publications as the *Federal Reserve Bulletin, Survey of Current Business,* and the *Monthly Report of the Deutsche Bundesbank.* These sources were searched thoroughly and the information obtained is introduced at relevant points below. Since it is methodologically invalid to search for indications of speculative activity only during those periods when the data hint at their existence, I was careful to examine the journal and newspaper indexes for references to unusual happenings in the exchange markets during times when the data suggested there were none.

This more general information about speculation was buttressed by the collection of quarterly balance-of-payments estimates on private capital movements among Germany, Canada, the United States, and the United Kingdom. Table 9.1 presents balance-of-payments data to be used in the interpretation of the computations. In general, the minus signs in the table imply an outflow of funds from, and the plus signs an inflow into, the country named. Similarly, a plus sign in the item "errors and omissions" signifies unrecorded capital inflows into the country, accompanied by a speedup in payments for exports and a slowdown in payments for imports. Although other elements, such as nonreported transactions in goods and services, are also contained in these "errors and omissions," it is customary to attribute large variations to the two main factors most relevant for this study.* I have included the item "long-term capital movements" under the assumption that in

---

* See *Monthly Report of the Deutsche Bundesbank,* Frankfurt, October 1960, for a detailed analysis of the major capital flows that are not reflected in the balance-of-payments statistics and that therefore do not show up in "errors and omissions." For a warning about the possible dangers of such an analysis, as in the case of England, see the notes to the United Kingdom statistics in the *Balance of Payments Yearbook* published annually by the International Monetary Fund, Washington, D.C.

many instances these movements are in reality speculative short-term investments in bullish stock markets.

The Canadian balance-of-payments statistics contain as the most relevant item for this study "other capital movements," which includes, under this single heading, short-term funds abroad, borrowing by Canadian finance companies, changes in terms of payment, and errors and omissions. For the United Kingdom, the item "private short-term capital" is divided into two parts: acceptance credits extended and short-term funds proper.

One of the great disadvantages of these statistics is their global nature: the single figure conceals the individual component movements between a country and each of its partners. This reduces greatly the ability of these data to indicate the manner in which capital flows are correlated with interest-arbitrage margins that during nonspeculative periods often differ from one pair of countries to another. During speculative times, however, covered-arbitrage margins in one country usually move together in the same direction with respect to all countries. Under these circumstances, the capital-movement statistics indicate whether arbitrage margins are in the theoretically expected direction, and allow some limited inference about the influence of margin size on the size of these flows.

U.S. balance-of-payments statistics, available for Western Europe excluding the sterling area, and for the European sterling area itself, illustrate some of the difficulties associated with global figures. For example, during the first two quarters of 1961, there was an *outflow* of American short-term capital to Western Europe (40 + 47 million dollars) and a simultaneous *inflow* from the European sterling area (94 + 27 million dollars). Global figures, the only type of data available for the other countries, would have completely hidden these developments.

One of the most valuable aids in understanding and controlling short-term capital movements in the future would be the construction and periodic publication by some international institution of a matrix tracing the multilateral, multichanneled flow of international private money.

10. Covered Interest Arbitrage

In this chapter we test the interest-arbitrage model of forward exchange rate determination in three ways: the first consists of the computation and visual interpretation of plotted interest-rate differentials, implicit interest rates, and covered-arbitrage margins; the second interprets evidence on the interest sensitivity of short-term funds; and the third correlates statistically the changes in interest-rate differentials and implicit interest rates.

Covered-Arbitrage Margins

The following hypothesis, based on the theoretical model of forward exchange rate determination developed in Part I, is to be tested: Whenever expectations of future spot rates do not involve a revaluation of par, the intersection of the arbitrage and trader–speculator schedules occurs within the elastic range of the arbitrage schedule shown in Figs. 10.1 and 10.2. Empirically this means that during "normal times" we should find covered-interest-arbitrage margins "very near to zero." Both concepts—"normal times" and "very near to zero"—must be made operational.

"Normal times" is defined as periods when the sources of information on speculative activity mentioned above indicate no market sentiment anticipating a revaluation of the parity forward rate.

The concept "very near to zero" is more difficult to make precise. Past empirical studies of forward-exchange theory have been based on a theoretical model having as its central determinant of the forward rate the condition that in equilibrium all incentives for covered interest arbitrage are zero, i.e., the equilibrium condition of Eq. (2.4), in Chapter 2.* Although the theoretical considerations of such a model

---

* See John Maynard Keynes, *A Tract on Monetary Reform*, London: Macmillan, 1923; and Paul Einzig, *The Theory of Forward Exchange*, London: Macmillan, 1937.

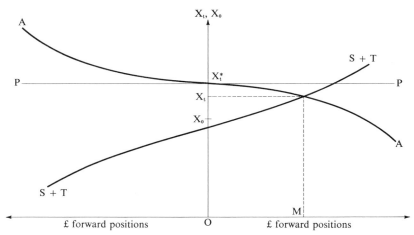

FIG. 10.1. Normal market situation: expected spot near current spot rate, parity rate above current spot rate.

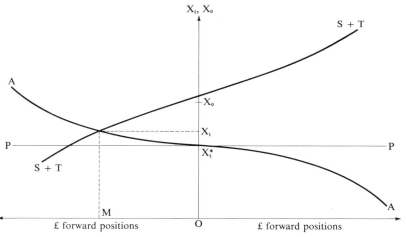

FIG. 10.2. Normal market situation: expected spot near current spot rate, parity rate below current spot rate.

lead to a predicted equilibrium-arbitrage margin of zero, the operational and testable hypothesis assumes that measured arbitrage margins of one-half per cent on either side of par are within the range of deviation predicted by the theory. Informed observers of pre-World War II financial markets* explained the justification for the one-half-per-cent

---

* Keynes, *ibid.*, p. 128; Einzig, *ibid.*, pp. 172–73.

margin as a demand by investors that the higher transactions costs involved with international arbitrage operations be reflected in such a minimum premium of the foreign investment over the domestic investment. The explanation is theoretically weak, however, since the lumpy transactions costs (the cost of a cable, for example) become effectively smaller, as a percentage of the value of the funds invested, the greater the quantity of these funds becomes. Thus nothing relevant can be said about the percentage cost of transactions unless the quantity involved is also specified. Transactions costs could in principle be proportional to the value of the funds transferred, but in this case they are not; they are absorbed by the differences in the foreign-exchange buying and selling rates, which are in turn fully reflected both in the prices and in computations of investors considering covered interest arbitrage. In a recent survey of market behavior after World War II, Einzig found that margins considerably smaller than one-half per cent were sufficient to induce some owners of short-term funds to pursue covered interest arbitrage.†

In our theoretical model the equilibrium condition would lead us to expect a nonzero measured arbitrage margin because of the generally less-than-perfect elasticity of the arbitrage and speculators' schedules. Although this is an important theoretical improvement upon earlier studies, we are still faced with the necessity of establishing a proposition stating precisely the point at which we consider a measured margin to be a violation of the hypothesis. Unfortunately, several characteristics of the data introduce considerable random elements and biases of an unknown direction into the measured magnitudes. For both the exchange rates and the interest rates, there are measurement errors due to averaging of the daily and weekly variations, the use of buying or selling rates, the disregard of quantity discounts, and so forth. There are the conceptual difficulties mentioned in Chapter 8 in choosing an interest-rate differential (whether that on Treasury bills or that on bankers' prime acceptances) and in determining the effects of investors' purchasing one type of security in one market and another type in the second market. Finally, there is the influence of triangular arbitrage involving forward rates alone, which could result in the appearance of covered-arbitrage margins even when there is no speculation in progress between the two currencies investigated. In the absence of empirical

---

† Paul Einzig, "Some Recent Changes in Forward Exchange Practices," *Economic Journal,* September 1960, pp. 485–96.

facts on which to base the choice of a measured arbitrage margin
that could be expected to result from these complicating factors, I have
settled on the value of one-half per cent used in previous empirical
studies. This value seems to be in the ballpark of intuitive judgments on
the size of measurement errors, if only because of its traditional use.

In practice there is still another complication with this figure: it
cannot be expected to be the same in all markets because the degree
of competition among exchange dealers and bankers, and the size of
turnover in a currency, are different from market to market and
influence decisively the size of profit margins, i.e., margins between
buying and selling exchange rates. The same reasoning applies to
interest rates. How much such factors may have affected the accuracy
of the recorded observations and therefore the appropriateness of the
one-half-per-cent margin must be considered for each series separately,
in the analysis of the computational results.

The available data permitted computation of the six covered-
interest-arbitrage margins among New York, London, Ottawa, and
Frankfurt. The six pairings in Fig. 10.3 exhaust the possible combinations. (The arrows are made directional simply to indicate the sources
of the exchange-rate data used in the study; thus Frankfurt is the
source for three sets of data, Ottawa for none.)

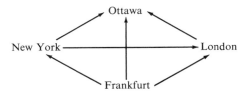

Fig. 10.3. Relationships among markets.

The computed, precise, implicit interest rates and actual interest-rate
differentials, as well as the resultant covered-interest-arbitrage margins,
have been plotted (Figs. 10.4 through 10.9) for visual interpretation.
The behavior of each arbitrage margin will be analyzed in detail,
with reference to major periods of speculation. The background
supplied for the New York–London speculative periods is used for the
interpretation of the other series as well.

New York–London. Because the money and exchange markets in
New York and London are the best developed in the world, the behavior

of the arbitrage margin between these two centers is a significant test of the quality of the data and the validity of the theory.

The most striking feature of the graph is the almost perfect correlation, over a wide range, between the interest-rate differential and the implicit interest rate. This correlation in itself may be considered a rough indication of the validity of the theory presented in Part I. Since throughout the period interest rates were set primarily for the achievement of domestic policy objectives in London as well as in New York, it can be inferred that the implicit interest rate is adjusted to the autonomous movements of the interest-rate differential in an almost perfect fashion. The net result of these correlated movements is the covered arbitrage for Treasury bills between New York and London.

The arbitrage margin fluctuated within a very narrow band until November 1956. Britain's balance of payments was favorable throughout this period, up to the month of June 1956. Despite several reports in *The Economist* that rumors of sterling and Deutsche mark revaluations were circulating, the balance-of-payments accounts showed no adverse movements in the relevant accounts. There seems to have been no actual speculation during this time, and arbitrage margins were near zero.

The Suez crisis made headlines from July 1956, when the Suez Canal Company was nationalized by Egypt, through the end of 1957. In its wake, sterling was subjected to two major waves of bear speculation. As expected, these waves appear clearly in the graph, and produce a striking contrast with the preceding period of stability.

One of these waves occurred after the armed intervention in Egypt. *The Economist** reported large British losses of gold and reserves during the fourth quarter. These were blamed on the flight of capital from London that occurred even while the current accounts showed a favorable balance. Behind this capital flight was a fear of general war and the expectation that sterling might be devalued once the war demand caused prices to rise and an unfavorable balance of trade to develop. Speculation also occurred in forward-exchange markets, and a large arbitrage margin that opened in favor of New York shows up very strongly on the graph.

It would be interesting to know what became of the capital that left London during the fourth quarter, but the global British figures

---

* *The Economist*, London, April 6, 1957, pp. 61–62.

PER CENT

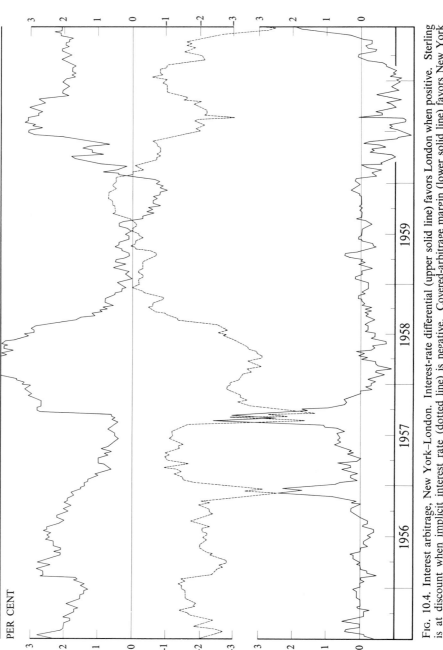

Fig. 10.4. Interest arbitrage, New York–London. Interest-rate differential (upper solid line) favors London when positive. Sterling is at discount when implicit interest rate (dotted line) is negative. Covered-arbitrage margin (lower solid line) favors New York when positive, London when negative.

conceal this information. The United States would seem a likely destination, but surprisingly enough the U.S. balance of payments during the fourth quarter shows no extraordinary capital inflows from the sterling area. The explanation may be that interest arbitrage by British subjects was illegal and that U.S. owners of funds in Britain had reduced their foreign working balances to a minimum during the 1955–57 U.S. boom. Thus no substantial repatriation of working balances was possible, and exchange restrictions then in effect made it difficult to return long-term investments to the U.S. within a short period. This explanation of why the large covered-arbitrage margin was not accompanied by a correspondingly large flow of funds into New York finds some support in later developments; in the first quarter of 1957, after the Suez crisis had calmed, substantial sums of short-term funds moved from New York to London, as shown in the short-term capital account (Table 9.1).

Hot money that had earlier left England for places other than the United States also returned to London in the first quarter of 1957. Britain's official reserves increased during March. The covered-arbitrage margins returned to a normal level of about one-half per cent in favour of New York during the first five or six months.

But then came the second major crisis, again shown clearly in the graph. Its roots lay in the slow deterioration of Britain's payments position on current account throughout the first half of 1957. Underlying these events were prolonged strikes, a sharp rise in prices, and renewed trouble in the Middle East, this time in Kuwait. Reserve losses occurred for the first time in July, and sterling was weak thereafter.

Bear speculation was very strong during the third quarter. During that period the U.S. balance-of-payments accounts show a large rise in capital inflows on short-term accounts, a rise reflected also in the "errors and omissions" item. Some of the speculation was on forward exchange. These dealings opened up the spectacular margins favoring New York shown in Fig. 10.4. Undoubtedly, a large part of the capital that moved to New York was induced to do so by the unusually large and safe profit opportunities this wide arbitrage margin represented.* Speculation was rampant when the franc was devalued August 12 and the September meeting of the International Monetary Fund drew close. It was firmly expected that sterling would be devalued and the Deutsche

---

* John Spraos, "Speculation, Arbitrage and Pound Sterling," *Economic Journal*, March 1959.

mark would be appreciated during this meeting. The largest arbitrage margins occur during this period.

Speculation finally collapsed when British authorities reasserted their determination to maintain the exchange rate they considered to be realistic from a commercial point of view. On September 15, the bank rate was raised to 7 per cent, its highest level in 15 years, and severe restrictions on bank lending were imposed. A week later the Washington meeting of the International Monetary Fund adjourned with no actions taken on currency adjustments, signaling the end of the second wave of bear speculation against sterling. Spot exchange rates improved, even surged, during the month of November when speculative forward contracts purchased in August matured and caused large spot purchases of sterling.

In keeping with our theoretical predictions, this return to normalcy with respect to expectations of future sterling exchange rates is accompanied by the closing of arbitrage margins. These margins remained small and fluctuated within narrow limits around zero from November 1957 through December 1959. Spot sterling was strong throughout the period and the overall increase in Western Europe's liquid reserves made it possible to reestablish convertibility of the currencies at the close of 1958.

But the events that allowed this return to convertibility also explain the third major period of instability, a period again reflected in the behavior of the arbitrage margin. The increases in reserves of the Western European countries were the result of heavy U.S. balance-of-payments deficits—deficits that had grown so large that the stability of the dollar came to be questioned. Fears of devaluation after the November 1960 elections were widespread. As expected, speculation also worked through the forward exchanges and a sizable arbitrage margin favoring London persisted all through 1960 and early 1961.

Although bear speculation in the dollar continued in 1961, the second quarter brought another major development in the dollar and sterling exchange markets. Sterling itself now came under bear attack and the arbitrage margin turned heavily in favor of New York. The U.S. and U.K. balances of payments reflect this change—borrowing in London via acceptance credits was unusually high, and the U.S. showed capital inflows from the U.K. for the first time since 1959.*

---

* The figures of the last quarter of 1960 and the first quarter of 1961 are somewhat distorted by the purchase of the stock of the English Ford Motor Company by Ford of Detroit, which involved a very large sum in a one-of-a-kind transaction.

In general, the behavior of the series exhibits a remarkable agreement between empirical evidence and theoretical considerations. Whenever outside information discloses no hints of speculation, arbitrage margins are smaller than one-half per cent. Periods of speculative activity coincide with large margins. Premiums and discounts are consistently in the appropriate directions.

London–Ottawa. The London–Ottawa market (Fig. 10.5) also shows a striking correlation between interest-rate differential and implicit interest rate. The net effects of these movements, however, do not cancel out as neatly as those in the New York–London market.

The periods known for stability between London and the North American Continent, 1955 through part of 1956, and 1958 through 1959, show up clearly again in this series. They are characterized by small arbitrage margins around zero, and only occasional short-lived deviations larger than one-half per cent.

The 1-per-cent margin favoring London that persisted during much of 1956 and 1957 must be explained by the heavy inflow of long-term capital into Canada.* These long-term capital inflows caused heavy purchases of Canadian spot currency, which drove the rate up to as high as 5 cents premium above the U.S. dollar. These forces were stronger than those engaged solely in covered short-term interest arbitrage, and the demand for forward cover from commercial quarters in Canada was also probably rather large. An excess demand for forward sterling and dollars, caused by a sizable commercial deficit, had a depressing effect on the forward rate while spot exchange remained in heavy demand. Speculative short-term capital movements added to the demand for spot currency and reduced the quantity of funds available for covered arbitrage. These speculative funds moved into Canada under the expectation of a further rise in the price of the Canadian dollar.†

In spite of the strong forces acting on the spot and forward rates, arbitragers kept both the margin (at around 1 per cent) and the interest-rate advantage in favor of London.

We have seen that bear speculation against sterling had produced large margins in the last quarter of 1956 and the third quarter of 1957 in the New York–London market. These periods of speculation are noticeable also in the London–Ottawa series. Interestingly enough,

---

* An inflow of C$1,431 million was recorded in 1956. This was C$783 million more than in 1955. For 1957, C$941 million in the first half and C$442 million in the second half were recorded.
† *Bank for International Settlements, Annual Reports,* Basel, 1958, p. 191.

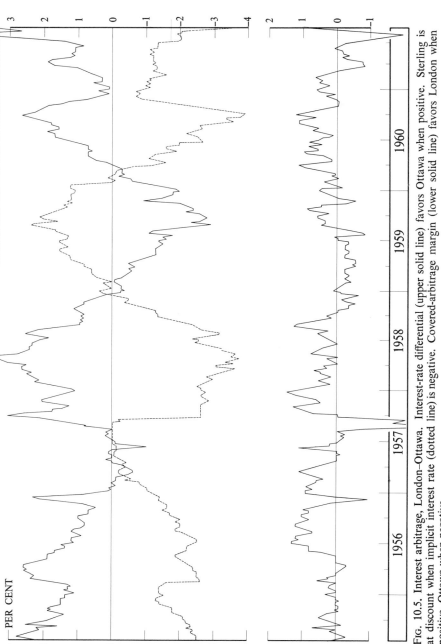

FIG. 10.5. Interest arbitrage, London–Ottawa. Interest-rate differential (upper solid line) favors Ottawa when positive. Sterling is at discount when implicit interest rate (dotted line) is negative. Covered-arbitrage margin (lower solid line) favors London when positive, Ottawa when negative.

however, the margins during these periods did not exceed 2.5 per cent in favor of Ottawa but reached 4.5 per cent in favor of New York. This disparity can be explained by the fact that while speculators drove up the Canadian forward rate, the freely adjusting spot rate also rose. As a result, the difference between spot and forward rates remained smaller than it would have been had the spot rate been denied further increase through central bank intervention after it reached an official peg.

During 1960, arbitrage margins fluctuated around 0.75 per cent in favor of London, where the interest rate was above that of Ottawa. This relatively large margin may have been due as much to a rather inelastic arbitrage schedule resulting from the smallness of the Ottawa money market, as to the persistent weakness of the U.S. dollar already discussed. The third period of bear attack on sterling, that during July 1961, is seen in the appearance of a large arbitrage margin in favor of Ottawa, which theoretical considerations would lead us to expect.

New York–Ottawa. Canadian and U.S. economic developments are highly interdependent, as shown in Fig. 10.6. The interest-rate differentials proper rarely exceed 1 per cent and are closely correlated with the interest rate implicit in forward-exchange premiums or discounts over the spot rate. Throughout the period under discussion the margin pierces one-half per cent occasionally, but only for very short durations. There are two notable exceptions to this pattern. One is from the middle of 1956 to the end of 1957, when the very heavy capital inflows into Canada mentioned above occurred. During this time the arbitrage margin remained near 1 per cent in favor of New York despite an Ottawa interest advantage. This phenomenon is also explained by the price of Canadian spot exchange, which was driven high by the demand from long-term investors, while the forward rate was under downward pressure from commercial circles. A heavy import surplus on trade accounts tended to create an excess of supply over demand for forward exchange as a cover for the exchange risk.

The second prolonged period of disturbance occurred during the second and fourth quarters of 1960 and the first quarter of 1961—the times when the bear speculation on the U.S. dollar was heavy. The large short-term capital inflows into Canada during these three quarters (C$162 million, C$191 million, and C$309 million, respectively) support this view. The substantial margin in favor of Ottawa encouraged riskless arbitrage and undoubtedly contributed significantly to the size

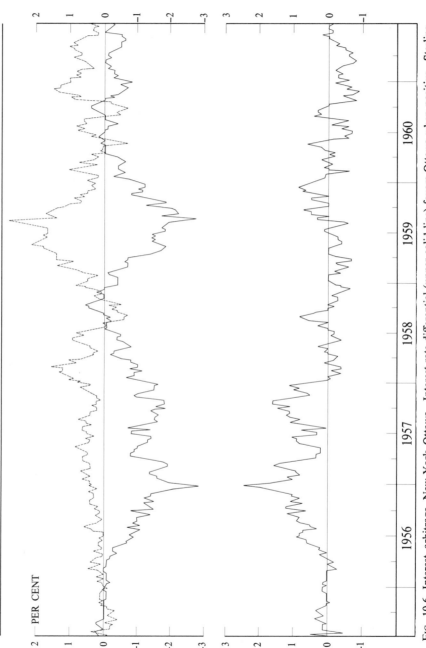

FIG. 10.6. Interest arbitrage, New York–Ottawa. Interest-rate differential (upper solid line) favors Ottawa when positive, Sterling is at discount when implicit interest rate (dotted line) is negative. Covered-arbitrage margin (lower solid line) favors New York when positive, Ottawa when negative.

of these figures. In addition, of course, large sums of uncovered speculative funds moved into Canada.

The largest arbitrage margins occurred during the two bear attacks on sterling in 1956 and 1957. One may ask why these margins appeared in the exchanges between the U.S. and Canada. As we have seen, the covered-arbitrage margin between Ottawa and London was smaller than that between New York and London. Triangular arbitrage in forward exchange, using this inconsistency, can theoretically have caused the margin to appear between New York and Ottawa.

Frankfurt–London. Throughout the period under consideration, Frankfurt attracted bull speculators during major exchange disturbances. During the 1956–57 and 1961 weaknesses of sterling discussed earlier, press articles consistently reported Germany as the largest single gainer of foreign exchange. The balance-of-payments statistics support these reports. As the figures show, the gains were not only on short-term capital account, and in changes in terms of payment (i.e., "errors and omissions"), but also very clearly on long-term capital account. The latter, of course, represents foreign investment in the booming stock market, often made as a speculative short-term venture, but recorded in the statistics as long-term.

This outside information explains the sizable covered-interest arbitrage margins vis-à-vis London during 1956–57 and 1961, which favored Frankfurt, as the theory suggests. Similarly, during 1958 and 1959, when the London interest rate was above the Frankfurt rate (as shown in Fig. 10.7), but when no abnormal events occurred, the arbitrage margin remained consistently in favor of London, fluctuating well within the range of expected measurement errors, given the relative shallowness of the Frankfurt money market.

Frankfurt–New York and Frankfurt–Ottawa. The large trends in the Frankfurt–New York series (Fig. 10.8) and the Frankfurt–Ottawa series (Fig. 10.9) are almost identical. It is therefore convenient to discuss them together.

The outstanding events of the period with respect to these three markets are again the bull speculations on Deutsches marks in 1956–57 and 1961. The arbitrage margins at these times strongly favor Frankfurt. Peaks appeared during July and August 1956 and again in the same months in 1957. During the period of stability from the middle of 1958 to the end of 1959 the margins remained in favor of New York and Ottawa, fluctuating within ranges explainable by measurement errors if

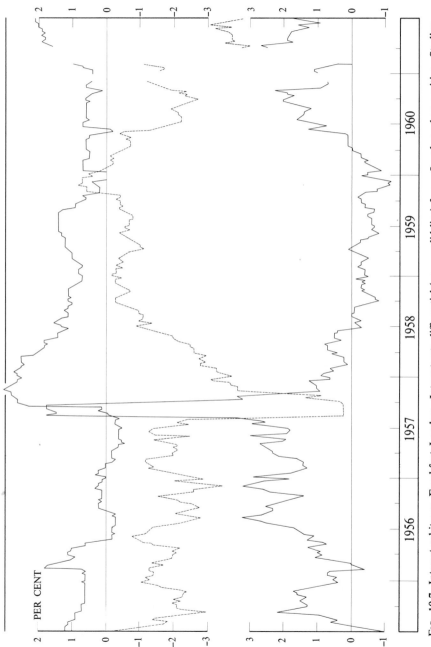

FIG. 10.7. Interest arbitrage, Frankfurt–London. Interest-rate differential (upper solid line) favors London when positive. Sterling is at discount when implicit interest rate (dotted line) is negative. Covered-arbitrage margin (lower solid line) favors Frankfurt when positive, London when negative.

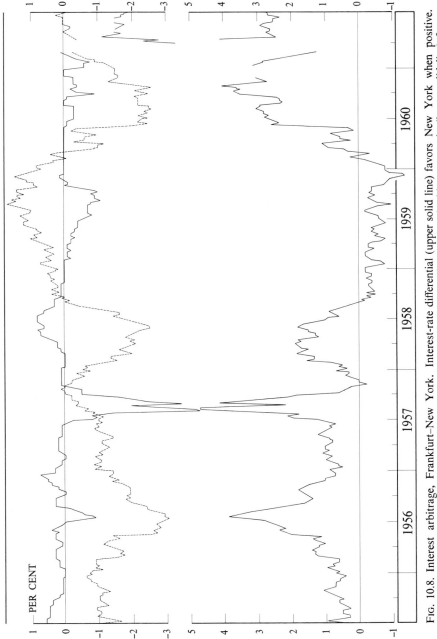

FIG. 10.8. Interest arbitrage, Frankfurt–New York. Interest-rate differential (upper solid line) favors New York when positive. Sterling is at discount when implicit interest rate (dotted line) is negative. Covered-arbitrage margin (lower solid line) favors Frankfurt when positive, New York when negative.

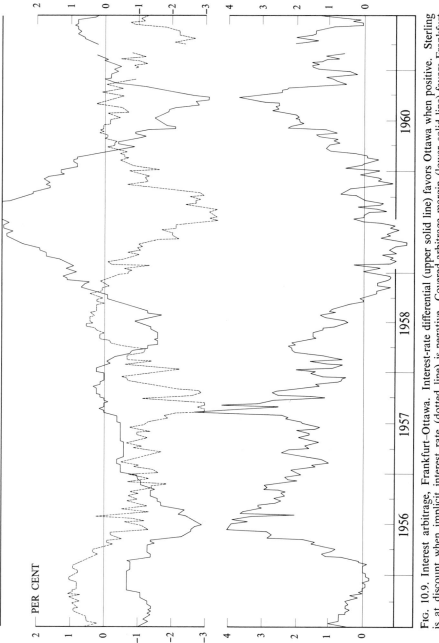

FIG. 10.9. Interest arbitrage, Frankfurt–Ottawa. Interest-rate differential (upper solid line) favors Ottawa when positive. Sterling is at discount when implicit interest rate (dotted line) is negative. Covered-arbitrage margin (lower solid line) favors Frankfurt when positive, Ottawa when negative.

due weight is given to the lack of depth of the Frankfurt money and currency markets. It should be noted that the fluctuations during this period were consistently less dramatic for the Frankfurt–New York market than for the Frankfurt–Ottawa market. This represents evidence in support of our depth-of-market contention, since Frankfurt dealings in U.S. dollars greatly exceeded and still exceed Frankfurt dealings in Canadian dollars. Throughout the six-year period, the directions of fluctuation were as expected by theoretical considerations. And because North American interest rates were higher than those in Germany, the margin generally favored New York and Ottawa.

As we have seen, the German balance-of-payments figures confirm more informal reports of heavy capital inflows. The Canadian balance-of-payments statistics are dominated too heavily by Canada–U.S. relations to show outflows during bull speculation in the mark. The U.S. data relating to Western Europe indicate very heavy outflows in "errors and omissions" as well as in short-term capital accounts during the third quarter of both 1956 and 1957. The figures for the fourth quarter of 1960 and the second quarter of 1961 exceed those of any previous period.

The persistence of a large arbitrage margin in favor of Frankfurt, and the continued flow of funds into Germany during 1960–61, are of great interest because of the several measures undertaken by the Bundesbank during that time to stem the tide of capital inflows. In June 1960 the discount rate was raised to 5 per cent in order to curb a strong domestic boom. Accompanying this move were regulations forbidding payment of interest on foreign sight and time deposits, and prohibiting the sale of money-market paper to foreigners. On August 24, 1960, the Bundesbank offered German commercial banks dollar swaps for periods of up to six months on terms equivalent to a premium of the forward dollar over the spot rate of 1 per cent per annum. This swap rate was raised to $1\frac{1}{2}$ per cent on September 26. From November 11 on, the swaps were to be used only for money-market transactions, whereas previously they had also been usable in commercial transactions. The swap offers were reduced after January 20, 1961, and were finally withdrawn on February 13, 1961.*

It is impossible to judge precisely the effects of these measures because we will never know what the levels of capital inflow would have

---

* See *Bank for International Settlements, Annual Report*, Basel, 1961, for the details of these policies.

been without them. It is a fact, however, that the German "errors and omissions" item changed from +DM1,049 million in the third quarter of 1960 to −DM783 million in the fourth quarter. This change seems to indicate a shift of financing in the desired direction. On the other hand, the short-term and long-term capital accounts remained heavily positive, and there appears to have been a substantial shift from short-term to long-term foreign investment, the former declining from DM572 to 425 million between the third and fourth quarters, and the latter surging from DM356 to 995 million in the same period. The Bank for International Settlements reported that in spite of these measures Germany received DM5.5 billion in credits from abroad in 1960 through such routes as credits taken by German firms in foreign countries, influx of foreign funds into the capital market, and the leads and lags in commercial payments.*

Important for present purposes is the fact again that in these two series the covered-arbitrage margin differed significantly from zero whenever special events stirred the exchange markets, and that it was sufficiently and consistently near zero when no such special events took place.

Conclusions for the hypothesis. The empirical evidence embodied in the computations just discussed is quite convincing in an intuitive way but unfortunately is not very precise; there is no critical level of confidence leading to the acceptance or rejection of the basic hypothesis. As was discussed earlier, this shortcoming is the result of employing data that, although the best available, is not entirely adequate for a scientifically acceptable test. The next section of this chapter, however, analyzes a set of correlations computed from highly aggregate data on short-term capital movements and interest-rate differentials, covered and uncovered. The final section of the chapter presents the results of a regression analysis involving the data used in plotting one of the series just discussed.

Evidence on Interest Sensitivity of Short-Term Funds

After my empirical studies for this book had been completed, some new evidence on the sensitivity of international short-term capital movements was published. This evidence, based partly on previously unpublished data, is quite general in nature but some aspects of it are of special interest to the theory of forward exchange.

---

* *Ibid.*, p. 16.

TABLE 10.1

FINDINGS REGARDING U.S. SHORT-TERM CAPITAL MOVEMENTS*

[Code: Statistically significant relationship (r^2 and estimates of β): with trade (T), with covered interest-rate differentials (I), with Euro-dollar–United States interest-rate differentials (E). Not consistent (NR); not examined (NE).]

Short-Term Capital Movements	Geographic Area			
	United Kingdom	Europe	Canada	Rest of World
Bank loans to foreign official institutions	NE	NE	NE	NE
Bank loans to foreign banks	†NE	NE	NE	NE
	‡NR	NR	NR	NR
Bank loans to all other foreigners	†NR	NR	NR	T
	‡NR	I	NR	NR
Bank collections outstanding	†NR	NR	NR	T
	‡I	NR	NR	NR
Other bank dollar claims	†T	T	NR	T
	‡NR	E	NR	E§
Nonfinancial dollar claims	†NR	NR	NR	NR
	‡I	I, E	I, E	NR
Bank foreign-currency claims	†I	I	NR	NR
	‡NR	NR	I	NR
Nonfinancial foreign-currency claims	†I	I	NR	NR
	‡I	NR	NR	NR

* Source: Benjamin J. Cohen, *loc. cit.*, p. 199.
† Readings on this line "Bell."
‡ Readings on this line "Kenen."
§ Japan.

The studies of Bell, Kenen, and Cohen* broke down U.S. short-term capital movements into the eight categories shown in Table 10.1. The data were in turn divided geographically, distinguishing the United Kingdom, Europe, Canada, and the rest of the world. Relationships were examined for quarterly periods from 1957 through 1962, for interest-rate differentials, covered and uncovered. The findings of the two studies are summarized in Table 10.1.

* Phillip W. Bell, "Private Capital Movements and the U.S. Balance of Payments Position," *Factors Affecting the United States Balance of Payments*, Compilation Studies Prepared for the Subcommittee on International Exchange and Payments of the Joint Economic Committee, Washington, 1962, pp. 395–482; Peter B. Kenen, "Short-term Capital Movements and the U.S. Balance of Payments," *The United States Balance of Payments*, Hearings before the Joint Economic Committee, Part I, *Current Problems and Policies*, Washington, 1963, pp. 153–91; Benjamin J. Cohen, "A Survey of Capital Movements and Findings Regarding Their Interest Sensitivity," *ibid.*, pp. 192–208.

The most significant aspect of these findings is that short-term capital flows are more often sensitive to the size of the covered-interest-arbitrage margins than to the size of the simple interest-rate differentials. This phenomenon is especially apparent in the relationships with the United Kingdom and continental Western Europe, as we would have expected it to be, on the strength of our knowledge of the nature of these markets.

Cohen, in the text of his paper, summarizes the evidence relating to covered arbitrage as follows: "Professor Bell did find that the outflow of bank and nonbank funds to Europe was significantly related to the covered United Kingdom–United States differential; since about 75 per cent of the outflow to Europe was into sterling, the relationship probably reflects covered interest arbitrage between London and New York."* "Professor Kenen found that flows between the United States and continental Europe demonstrated the greatest degree of interest sensitivity, in particular to the covered United Kingdom–United States differential."†

The results suggest the correctness of our theoretical model, not only in the general sense that covered interest arbitrage is a potent force in the market but also with respect to a specific aspect of our model. The arbitrage schedule in Fig. 10.10 shows that the covered-arbitrage margin, defined as the difference between the parity forward rate X_t^* and the market forward rate X_t' or X_t'', is functionally related to the quantity of forward commitments Q_1 and Q_2. If triangular arbitrage is not large, the quantity of forward commitments is approximately equal to the amount of short-term funds moved. As the diagram shows, the greater the covered-arbitrage margin $(X_t^* - X_t)$, the greater the quantity of forward commitments and stock of short-term capital, which is exactly what the empirical results imply. Results equivalent to those shown in Fig. 10.10 could also have been obtained by shifts in the AA schedule with the SS schedule held constant.

It should be noted that the simple parity theory of forward exchange developed in the first part of Chapter 2 does not explain these results. According to that theory, interest arbitrage should always bring the forward rate to parity, and measured covered-arbitrage margins are not functionally related to the size of actual capital flows.

---

* *Op. cit.*, p. 203.
† *Op. cit.*, p. 207.

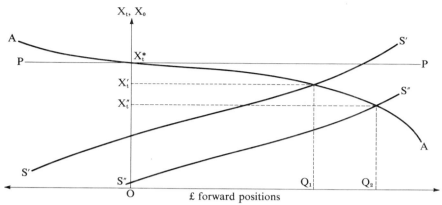

FIG. 10.10. Quantity of funds and size of margin.

Correlation of Interest-Rate Differential and Implicit Interest Rate

All of the charts presented in the first section of this chapter suggest a strong correlation between the implicit interest rate and the actual interest-rate differential. The following part of this chapter is an analysis of a test of correlation for the New York–Ottawa market.* This market was chosen for the test because during the period of observation the Canadian spot exchange rate was officially free to fluctuate. The uncertainty accompanying such a lack of official intervention brought about an especially strong need to cover commercial and exchange transactions in the forward market. Furthermore, the U.S.–Canadian market has the advantages of being well-developed and integrated and of having had no exchange restrictions during the period of observation.

The most simple statistical hypothesis about forward rates issuing from the model developed in Part I of this book is the following:

$$X_t = f(X_0, R_f, R_d) \qquad (10.1)$$

The three-month forward rate X_t is a function of the spot rate X_0 and the foreign R_f and domestic R_d interest rates on three-month short-term funds. The first part of this book is in fact devoted entirely to a formulation of the precise functional relationship among these variables. As an

---

* The computations were carried out by Hans Stoll, University of Chicago Graduate School of Business.

approximation of this complicated model, we can use the simple interest-arbitrage model of forward exchange rate determination. As we have seen, this model states that the three-month forward rate adjusts so as to make the implicit annual interest rate

$$IR = \left(\frac{X_t - X_0}{X_0}\right)4 \qquad (10.2)$$

equal to the actual annual interest-rate differential on three-month securities

$$ID = \frac{R_d - R_f}{1 + R_f} \qquad (10.3)$$

Given these concepts we should expect to find a high degree of correlation between ID and IR.

That the hypothesis does not suggest a perfect correlation is precisely because the simple arbitrage model represents only an approximation of the more complete model, which itself falls short of incorporating all real-world forces acting on the market. Only instantaneous adjustment of the forward rate to its parity value following a change in the actual interest-rate differential would produce a perfect correlation. But market-equilibrium forward rates were found to be rarely equal to the parity rate on theoretical grounds. In addition, the imperfections of the data mentioned above in the first section of this chapter are likely to introduce errors of measurement, which would tend to reduce the measured correlation coefficient. Our more complicated portfolio theory of forward exchange permits us to formulate an additional hypothesis about the correlation of ID and IR: since during periods of speculation the intersection of the arbitrage schedule with the speculators' schedule is likely to occur along the inelastic part of the former, the correlation should be higher for data covering nonspeculative "normal" times than for data from speculative periods.

These simple hypotheses about the relationships between ID and IR are supported by the computations. For the 299 weekly observations covering the period from the first week of July 1955 to the third week of March 1961, the correlation coefficient is $r^2 = 0.3230$, a value found to differ from zero at the 0.01 level of significance. The correlation coefficient for observations excluding the period from the second week in November 1956 through the second week in November 1957 (the period of speculation surrounding the Suez crisis) is $r^2 = 0.5316$, a notable improvement over the previous correlation. For the number of observations in the data (246), the result again differed from zero at the 0.01 level of significance.

In addition to these correlation coefficients we have computed a set of regression equations of the form

$$IR = a + bID + u \qquad (10.4)$$

where u is the error term assumed to be normally distributed around a zero mean. We shall again use the simple interest-arbitrage model as a starting point for the formulation of a hypothesis. Figure 2.2, reproduced here as Fig. 10.11, differs from the original in Chapter 2 in

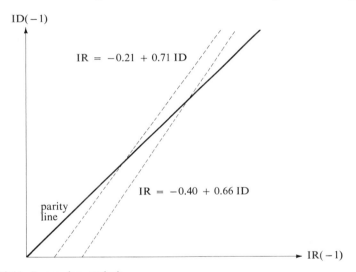

FIG. 10.11. Regression analysis.

that we have plotted what would normally be the southwest quadrant as the northwest quadrant in order to have the observations and the regression line in the positions customary in other econometric studies. Thus the horizontal axis to the right of the origin measures a discount from the New York point of view, and the vertical axis north of zero measures an Ottawa interest advantage. Because during the period under observation the Ottawa interest rate nearly always exceeded the New York rate, and the Canadian dollar nearly always sold at a forward discount, a scatter diagram puts nearly all points in the first quadrant.

According to our model we should find that during "normal times" observations are scattered randomly but within a narrow band around the parity line. This follows from the fact that during these "normal times" the determination of the forward exchange rate is dominated by the highly elastic part of the arbitrage schedule, regardless of whether the speculative schedule intersects to the right or to the left of the zero vertical coordinate in our central diagram (Fig. 6.1) in Chapter 6. The width of the band around the parity line is determined by the elasticity of the arbitrage schedule. It must also be noted that the size of the basic interest-rate differential does *not* normally influence the shape of the arbitrage schedule, so that the band of observations should not be wider at large interest-rate differentials; i.e., the scatter diagram should not take on a conical shape.

During times of speculation we would expect to find observations at greater distances from the parity line than under normal conditions. How far away depends of course on the size of the speculative sentiment and the inelasticity of the arbitrage schedule over the relevant range. If we include speculative periods in our total set of observations, the scatter diagram should show a conical shape if it is true that large interest-rate differentials are typically associated with speculative periods.

From these theoretical considerations we can formulate the statistical hypothesis that the regression line should be close to the parity line over the relevant observed range of interest-rate differentials, but its slope should not necessarily be unity. The regression line should be steeper and should have a smaller intercept for data excluding the periods of speculation than it has for data including these speculative periods.

The calculations for the full set of data produce the following regression equation (standard errors of estimate in parentheses):

$$IR = -0.4027 + 0.6647 \, ID \qquad (10.5)$$
$$(0.0449) \quad (0.0559)$$

For data excluding the speculation surrounding the Suez episode, we find

$$IR = -0.2075 + 0.7060 \, ID \qquad (10.6)$$
$$(0.0362) \quad (0.0425)$$

The estimates are all statistically highly significant, and the relative magnitudes of the coefficients of the two estimates are in agreement with the statistical hypothesis. Eighty-five per cent of all observations of interest-rate differentials lie within 1 per cent, and only seven times was the differential greater than 2 per cent, so that the regression line for the normal period is very close to the parity line over the relevant range of interest-rate differentials.

Lagging of variables produced no significant improvement of the results. The residuals of the regression equations (10.5) and (10.6) are serially correlated, which comes as no surprise from the point of view of forward-exchange theory; speculative sentiments and expectations change gradually and tend to persist for some time. Thus we would expect long runs of observations above or below the computed regression line. The importance of this serial correlation is that the computed standard error of estimate is too small. But in our computations the standard error could be much larger and yet remain statistically significant, so that serial correlation has no effect on our basic findings. In sum, the regression analysis leads us to accept our statistical hypothesis and therefore lends strong support to the predictive value of our theoretical model.

11. Triangular Arbitrage

In this chapter we shall attempt to measure the extent to which spot and forward cross-rates have been consistent in a sense to be defined. The same computations allow us to make inferences about the reliability of the exchange-rate data underlying all of our empirical work. No comparable earlier studies have come to my attention, presumably because the importance of triangular-arbitrage operations for the theory and policy of forward exchange has not been realized.

Formulation of the Hypothesis

Formulation of our hypothesis begins with the basic theoretical consideration that in equilibrium, and disregarding transactions costs, the price of dollars in terms of Deutsche marks (DM · $) is equal to the product of the price of sterling in terms of Deutsche marks (DM · £) and the price of dollars in terms of sterling (£ · $). In symbols: (DM · $) = (DM · £)(£ · $). As defined in Chapter 1, the algebraic difference between the two sides of the equation is the triangular-arbitrage margin. The concept of triangular arbitrage will be recalled to be applicable equally to spot rates and to forward rates of the same maturity.

On theoretical grounds we would expect these triangular-arbitrage margins to be always near zero, because the market for currencies, dealing as it does in a homogeneous commodity with low transactions costs and well-functioning channels of information, is highly perfect. Foreign-exchange dealers are known to watch carefully for profit opportunities that might arise when prices for the same currency differ in two markets, and their simple bilateral arbitrage returns the prices to equality. Triangular arbitrage, similarly cheap and speedy, keeps prices in three or more markets mutually consistent, and thus tends to wipe out all opportunities for further profitable arbitrage operations.

In practice, measurement errors and transactions costs explain why we should not expect computations from the available data to show consistently zero profit opportunities. Furthermore, exchange restrictions in effect before Christmas 1958 prevented effective arbitrage between European currencies, and it seems plausible to allow for the appearance of profit margins on these grounds.

The question arises, however, which types of behavior in these arbitrage margins can be interpreted as showing the effective working of triangular arbitrage and which cannot. To determine whether triangular arbitrage was actually keeping forward rates consistent, the following null hypothesis was tested: Deviations from the median triangular-arbitrage margins are random.

Deviations from the median value of the margin are employed for the basic test because the use of buying rates rather than selling rates (or midpoints between the two) results in a bias between actual and observed market rates that is assumed to remain constant over time. Thus even if triangular arbitrage has been working perfectly, this type of measurement error would cause the recorded margin to be of a constant, nonzero size.

The use of midpoints of daily ranges in computing the weekly averages used here produces two types of error. One occurs when a trend during the day has caused a price above or below the midpoint to prevail for the longer part of the day, so that the midpoint is not a truly representative price. This type of measurement error tends to be canceled out in weekly averages. Trends lasting throughout the averaging period cause a bias that is assumed to be small. In computations such as ours, involving more than one such series of exchange rates, the biases associated with the various series are assumed to cancel each other out. Remaining errors are likely to be randomly distributed around the true value. The second type of error is caused when quantity and special customer discounts shift the midpoint to a rate that is descriptive of only a few transactions. Errors of this type are also assumed to contribute to randomness in deviations of the observed rate from the true rate.

These measurement errors explain why actually computed triangular-arbitrage margins may differ randomly from a median nonzero value even when triangular arbitrage is an active force in the market. On the other hand, when triangular arbitrage is inactive the forward rates are likely to be out of mutual equilibrium in the triangular sense for prolonged periods of time, or for however long bilateral speculation and other unusual events prevail. The alternative hypothesis is therefore that triangular-arbitrage margins appearing for extended periods of time and in distinct patterns must be attributed to the working of triangular arbitrage in a manner theoretically less than perfect. For this hypothesis, then, outside knowledge of speculation or other unusual conditions must be called in for consideration in the interpretation of the data.

The statistical hypothesis also provides us with some information about the general reliability of the exchange-rate data used. Because there are such strong a priori reasons for expecting triangular arbitrage to be effective in the spot markets, at least since convertibility was restored, a rejection of the null hypothesis in the case of spot rates would throw serious doubt on the quality of the data. In order to gain understanding of the significance of convertibility, which occurred in the last week of December 1958, the empirical tests were carried out for two periods, 1955–61 and 1959–61, and for both spot and forward rates. Comparisons of these four series permit inferences to be drawn in two areas: the influence of exchange restrictions on arbitrage, and differences between spot and forward exchange markets.

The statistical test used is nonparametric and involves both number and runs of deviations from the median. It is based on the following rationale: If a set of numbers is drawn randomly from a stable population, each successive drawing must be either equal to, greater than, or less than the median of that sample. Let us call the number of times the observations in the series of drawings switch from one side of the median to the other u (runs). If we were then to repeat the same experiment an infinite number of times, mathematical considerations dictate that we should obtain a distribution of u with the mean

$$\mu_u = \frac{2n_1 \cdot n_2}{n_1 + n_2} + 1$$

and standard deviation

$$\sigma_u = \sqrt{\frac{2n_1 n_2(2n_1 n_2 - n_1 - n_2)}{(n_1 + n_2)^2(n_1 + n_2 - 1)}}$$

where n_1 and n_2 are the total numbers of observations above and below the median.[*]

---

[*] Paul G. Hoel, *Elementary Statistics*, New York: Wiley, 1960, p. 170, and Table IX.

It is interesting to note that because of the way this test is organized, the acceptance of the hypothesis that triangular arbitrage works does not depend on the randomness of measurement errors, for if measurement errors are nonrandom, the null hypothesis will be rejected. Acceptance of the null hypothesis, on the other hand, means that measurement errors are random *and* that triangular arbitrage is at work.

The available exchange-rate quotations made it possible to compute triangular-arbitrage margins for weekly averages of five combinations of rates, both spot and forward:

Frankfurt–New York, Frankfurt–London, London–New York, i.e., $(DM \cdot \$) - (DM \cdot £)(£ \cdot \$)$, hereafter referred to as the Frankfurt–New York–London series.

Frankfurt–New York, Frankfurt–Ottawa, Ottawa–New York, i.e., $(DM \cdot \$) - (DM \cdot C\$)(C\$ \cdot \$)$, hereafter referred to as the Frankfurt–New York–Ottawa series.

Frankfurt–London, Frankfurt–Paris, Paris–London, i.e., $(DM \cdot £) - (DM \cdot F)(F \cdot £)$, hereafter referred to as the Frankfurt–London–Paris series.

Frankfurt–London, Frankfurt–Ottawa, Ottawa–London, i.e., $(DM \cdot £) - (DM \cdot C\$)(C\$ \cdot £)$, hereafter referred to as the Frankfurt–London–Ottawa series.

New York–London, New York–Ottawa, Ottawa–London, i.e., $(\$ \cdot £) - (\$ \cdot C\$)(C\$ \cdot £)$, hereafter referred to as the New York–London–Ottawa series.

Interpretation of the Evidence

The interpretation of the statistics is divided into two parts. The first takes up the randomness hypothesis and the number of runs. The second concerns the visual interpretation of the five computed series.

The results of the computations testing for the randomness of deviations of the triangular-arbitrage margins from the median are shown in Table 11.1. The table lists the values for u, μ_u, and σ_u for the ten series covering the period 1959–61, and in the last row shows whether the statistics dictate acceptance or rejection of the null hypothesis at the 0.05 level of significance, by two-tailed t test.

Inspection of the table reveals that the deviations from the median triangular-arbitrage margin involving spot rates are indeed random, with one exception. With forward rates, however, factors other than random measurement errors seem to have influenced the pattern of profit margins.

TABLE 11.1

RESULTS OF TESTS FOR RANDOMNESS OF DEVIATIONS FROM
TRIANGULAR-ARBITRAGE MEDIAN, 1959–61

| | Triangular–Arbitrage Market | | | | | | | | | |
| | Frankfurt–New York–London | | Frankfurt–New York–Ottawa | | Frankfurt–London–Paris | | Frankfurt–London–Ottawa | | New York–London–Ottawa | |
Statistic	Spot	Forward	Spot	Forward	Spot	Forward	Spot	Forward	Spot	Forward
u	61	46	63	40	61	10	60	5	48	8
n_1	66	65	65	62	65	58	63	59	66	65
n_2	66	65	65	62	65	58	63	59	66	65
μ_u	67	66	66	63	66	59	64	60	67	66
σ_u	5.73	5.68	5.68	5.54	5.68	5.36	5.59	5.41	5.73	5.68
accept or reject null hypothesis	acc.	rej.	acc.	rej.	acc.	rej.	acc.	rej.	rej.	rej.

Tests for randomness for the entire period 1955–61, not shown in the table, lead to a rejection of the null hypothesis in both spot and forward markets for all series, with the exception of the Frankfurt–London–Paris spot market. However, most important, all series for spot and forward rates show a marked reduction in amplitude and length of arbitrage-margin runs after convertibility. This tendency, apparent in the computed statistics, can be seen quite clearly in the graphic representation of the series (Figs. 11.1 to 11.3), in which we have plotted the triangular-arbitrage margin, i.e., the simple algebraic value of the difference between one exchange rate and the product of two related others, as, for example, $(DM \cdot \$) - (DM \cdot £)(£ \cdot \$)$. For the purposes of our analysis it is indifferent whether the computed values are negative or positive, since this distinction indicates only the directions in which arbitrage transactions are profitable. Our prime concern is with the magnitude of the arbitrage margins' deviations from zero and the length of time such deviations persisted. In the interpretation of the series we shall be drawing on the information concerning speculation that was presented in the second section of Chapter 9 and used in the interpretation of interest-arbitrage margins.

Frankfurt–New York–London. In the Frankfurt–New York–London series (Fig. 11.1) peaks in spot and forward arbitrage opportunities appear during the 1955–56 speculative crisis as well as during the 1957 Suez crisis. The reduction of these margins occurs the week after the introduction of convertibility.

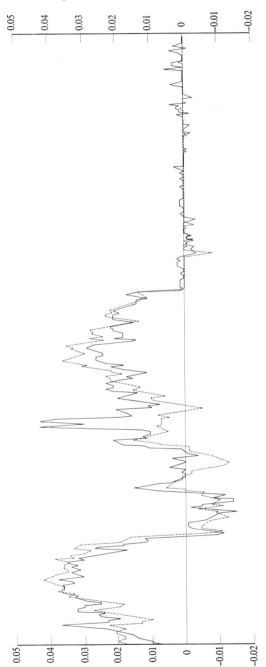

FIG. 11.1. Triangular-arbitrage margins: Frankfurt–New York–London. Spot rates dotted, forward rates solid.

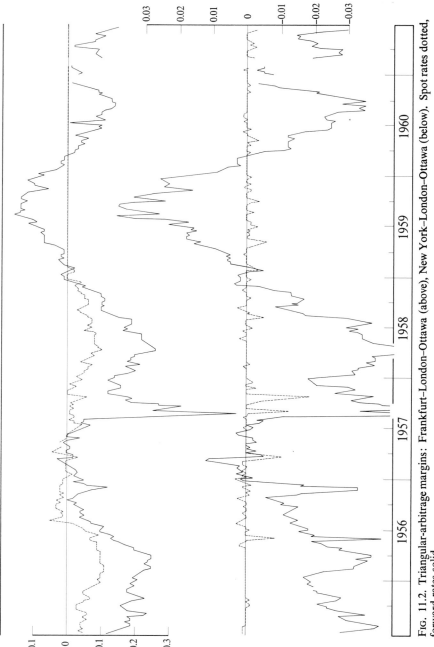

FIG. 11.2. Triangular-arbitrage margins: Frankfurt–London–Ottawa (above), New York–London–Ottawa (below). Spot rates dotted, forward rates solid.

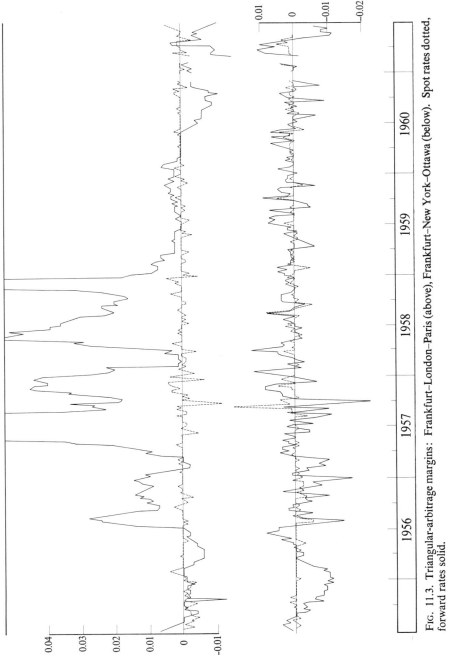

FIG. 11.3. Triangular-arbitrage margins: Frankfurt–London–Paris (above), Frankfurt–New York–Ottawa (below). Spot rates dotted, forward rates solid.

Frankfurt–New York–Ottawa. Casual inspection of the Frankfurt–New York–Ottawa graphs might lead one to believe that both series show random fluctuations. The test for randomness, however, suggests that this is not the case. Only the spot rates after convertibility pass the test. With respect to forward rates, a comparison of the two periods shows that the deviations from the expected median margin are relatively more random after convertibility than during the period as a whole.*

Frankfurt–London–Paris. The Frankfurt–London–Paris series shows spot margins behaving in the theoretically expected manner throughout the period 1955–61. This may be interpreted to mean that although exchange restrictions *can* interfere with the smooth operation of the markets, the high turnover in the currencies of these three countries and their close commercial and banking ties did not in fact prevent them from functioning properly. So much more astonishing is the contrast with the forward margins, which have been scaled down to one-tenth of their value to permit comparison with the spot rates on the same graph. Again, however, the large margins coincide with speculative attacks on the franc in 1957 and 1958, and recede with the devaluation of the spot currency. Moreover the size of the margins has diminished greatly since convertibility.

In general, the large margins may be explained by the absence of suitable Paris money-market securities for foreigners to invest in. The absence of this money market also makes it impossible for potential Paris lenders to compute their own opportunity costs. These two effects explain the existence of a relatively thin market in forward francs. Nevertheless, the great reduction in margins after the introduction of convertibility indicates that the market became deeper, and that some mechanism, perhaps triangular or interest arbitrage, was integrating the market with other money markets.

Frankfurt–London–Ottawa. The Frankfurt–London–Ottawa series exhibits a striking movement toward perfection of the spot market after 1958, but the forward market shows no such trend. Rather, the forward margins continue to describe long sallies above and below zero in a way that suggests a cyclical influence, as they did before convertibility. This cyclical pattern is repeated in the series next described, and will be discussed in greater detail there.

---

* The observed value of u was seven standard deviations from the expected μ_u in the period 1955–61, whereas the difference was only four standard deviations for the period 1959–61.

New York–London–Ottawa. New York, London, and Ottawa have well-developed money markets, and the turnover in currencies, both spot and forward, is large with respect to most of the currencies already discussed. Because exchange restrictions have never existed for American or Canadian citizens, one might expect the markets for foreign exchange to be rather perfect. It is therefore disappointing to find that the test for randomness in the spot margins for both periods leads to a rejection of the randomness assumption. Other, more intuitive, criteria, however, lead one to believe that the profit margins reflect the operation of triangular arbitrage. The number of positive and negative margins is practically equal (160 and 153) and the fluctuations, except those that occurred in the Suez and 1957 crises, are relatively small. But even if one remains skeptical about the general quality of the data, forward rates are subject to the same measurement errors, and the difference between the relative sizes of the spot and forward margins and their behavior over time remains meaningful.*

The forward-arbitrage margin fluctuates around zero in a pattern closely resembling that of the Frankfurt–London–Ottawa series. Considering that both series have in common only the sterling–Canada exchange rate, the explanation of the pattern must be sought in this rate. The sterling–Canada rate in turn is determined principally by the interest-rate differential between London and Ottawa and the spot rate, as was discussed in connection with the interest-arbitrage model in Part I. But an inspection of the covered-interest-arbitrage margin reveals no comparable cyclical pattern. Rather, there is a striking correlation between the absolute London–Ottawa interest-rate differential and the profit margin throughout the period, in direction as well as amplitude. This correlation cannot now be explained and requires further research.

Conclusions for the hypothesis. In general, the data support the following conclusions. Since the introduction of exchange convertibility, the cross-spot rates examined can be considered consistent. It is suggested that triangular arbitrage is the major force bringing about this consistency.

Fluctuations in arbitrage margins for forward rates appear to be nonrandom. In an analytical framework this would mean that triangular arbitrage is not the major force determining forward exchange

---

* As Table 11.1 reveals, for the shorter period the number of standard deviations in the difference between expected and observed values is three for the spot and ten for the forward series.

rates. But it should be noted that during the last two years under examination the arbitrage margins decreased in size and became more random with respect to the earlier period. This may imply a tendency toward perfection of the forward-exchange markets, including more extensive triangular-arbitrage operations.

12. Profits from Forward-Exchange Speculation

Whether speculation in forward exchange is profitable or not is an important question for forward-exchange theory and policy. Since direct evidence on this question is not available it is necessary to search for it indirectly. This chapter develops one such method of indirect search and applies it to empirical data.* In essence the approach involves the measurement of a rate of return that a speculator could have earned if he had followed certain simple rules of behavior during a period of approximately six years, from July 1955 to May 1961. I have been careful to use only information available to the speculator at the time he would have made his decisions. The results do not prove that speculators actually did earn the computed rate of return, but they do suggest that following these simple rules would have yielded consistently high profits. From this follows certain conclusions that are developed below.

The Model of Speculative Behavior

The forward-exchange speculator's per unit profit P arises from the difference between the price at which he commits himself to deliver (or accept delivery of) a unit of forward (let us say) sterling 90 days hence X_t and the actual price of sterling on the day his contract matures X_0^t, i.e.,

$$P = X_t - X_0^t \qquad (12.1)$$

More specifically, if he sells sterling forward and $(X_t - X_0^t) > 0$, then $P > 0$; if $(X_t - X_0^t) < 0$, then $P < 0$. On the other hand, if he buys

---

* This chapter has benefited from comments by Jacques Dreze, Milton Friedman, and Harry G. Johnson on an earlier draft. It draws heavily on my article of the same title published in the *Quarterly Journal of Economics*, May 1965.

forward sterling the relationships are reversed: if $(X_t - X_0^t) > 0$, then $P < 0$; if $(X_t - X_0^t) < 0$, then $P > 0$.

If the number of pounds forward sterling bought or sold on day i is equal to k_i, then total profits for the year P_T are

$$P_T = \sum_{i=1}^{n} P_i k_i \tag{12.2}$$

where n is the number of working days during the year and P_i is the per unit profit on day i.

The average capital required to finance such speculative activity is equal to the yearly sum of the daily investments $X_{ti}k_i$ divided by 40. The division by 40 is necessary for two reasons. One is that in the 90-day forward market investigated here, capital is tied up for only one quarter and can be invested four times a year. The second reason is that today foreign-exchange dealers or banks can easily be found who are willing to accept forward commitments for a 10-per-cent margin deposit.* The average amount of capital invested K therefore comes to†

$$K = \frac{\sum_{i=1}^{n} X_{ti}k_i}{4 \cdot 10} \tag{12.3}$$

The annual rate of return from speculation R is thus

$$R = \frac{P_T}{K} \tag{12.4}$$

Foreign-exchange dealers charge no commissions; they obtain payment for their services by buying and selling at different rates. Since competition among foreign-exchange dealers is keen, the difference between buying and selling spot rates is very small, typically $2.7980 buy and $2.7983 sell, i.e., $0.0003 per pound sterling.‡ The data underlying the computation in this study are buying rates. The earnings have been adjusted to account for these transactions costs in the following way. Each complete transaction consists of one forward

---

* Clearly, rates of return depend on the size of the margin deposits. The rate of 10 per cent was used in the computations because the author was quoted this rate by a large New York bank in the summer of 1961.
† To minimize computations, sums were taken for the whole period, and simple annual averages were then derived. Year-to-year changes can be analyzed on the basis of the data in Fig. 12.1.
‡ The margin between buying and selling rates is somewhat larger for forward rates and tends to widen during periods of speculative activity. No account was taken of this phenomenon since precise information is lacking. Profits are slightly overstated as a result.

sale (or purchase) and one spot purchase (or sale). The profits computed on the basis of buying rates thus overstate the profits (or understate the losses) by 0.0003 k_i per day, or

$$\sum_{i=1}^{n} 0.0003 \, k_i \qquad (12.5)$$

per year of n days,* and have been corrected appropriately. Other transactions costs, such as telephone calls and time required to gather information and make the transactions, are assumed to be zero.

Moreover it is assumed that the opportunity cost of the balances invested is zero, and that we may neglect the costs arising from the need to hold additional funds in liquid form as a precautionary balance from which to meet demands for higher deposit margins on short notice, should the price of the spot currency decline. The rates of return quoted are therefore not adjusted to reflect these costs.

The speculator is assumed to be prepared to speculate every working day. He must make two decisions:

1. Whether to buy forward, sell forward, or refrain from entering a contract.

2. Given that he decides to speculate that day on the basis of decision rule (1), how much money to commit.

The rules guiding the speculator's decision (1) are rather simple. The current (today's) forward rate is given in the market, and his decision depends on the spot rate expected to prevail 90 days hence $E(X_0^t)$. Specifically, if $[X_t - E(X_0^t)] > 0$, sell; if $[X_t - E(X_0^t)] < 0$, buy forward sterling. If $E(X_0^t) = X_0^t$, enter no transactions. Three different models of expectation formation are presented below.

Decision (2) depends on the speculator's confidence in the correctness of his $E(X_0^t)$ forecast. The models described below incorporate two different, simple methods of deciding how much to commit to the speculation.

It is quite clear from the analysis so far that the speculator's success depends on his ability to form a good judgment of the shape of the expected future spot-rate probability distribution, especially the mean and variance of the distribution. The formation of such expectations is a purely personal matter. The inability of the investigator to know ex post facto either what a speculator's estimate of the shape of the

---

* At a commitment of £100 per day the yearly transactions costs come to about $7.50.

TABLE 12.1

PROFITS FROM SPECULATION

$E(X_0^t)$ = expected future spot rate; K = average annual dollar investment; P = average annual profits in dollars; R = average annual rate of return on investment.

(See text for further explanation.)

Expectations Models	Period I						Period II						Period III					
	Investment Rule A			Investment Rule B			Investment Rule A			Investment Rule B			Investment Rule A			Investment Rule B		
	K	P_T	R	K	P_T	R	K	P_T	R	K	P_T	R	K	P_T	R	K	P_T	R
(i) $E(X_0^t) = 2.80$	1,612	256	16	8,380	2,198	26	1,612	235	15	8,104	1,885	23	1,612	282	18	8,831	2,625	30
(ii) $E(X_0^t)$ = moving average	1,612	267	17	8,380	2,270	27	1,612	247	15	8,104	1,964	24	1,612	291	18	8,831	2,666	30
(iii) $E(X_0^t)$, by complex rule	1,612	276	17	8,380	2,363	28	1,612	264	16	8,104	2,059	25	1,612	290	18	8,831	2,679	30

distribution has been or on the basis of what information it was formulated makes it impossible to discern from the available data with any meaningful degree of reliability whether speculators have actually profited during the period under consideration.* This study addresses itself therefore to the more limited purpose of determining how well a speculator in forward exchange would have done had he used only the information embodied in past exchange and interest-rate data in the process of formulating his expectations of future spot exchange rates. It may not be unreasonable, moreover, to assume that a real-world speculator could have improved on that performance had he had access to other pertinent information.

Table 12.1 summarizes the results of the computations carried out. Each row in the table represents a different hypothesis of the speculator's rationale in arriving at his estimate of the expected future spot rate $E(X_0^t)$. The division of columns into three main groups involves a distinction (about which more will be said) between "normal" periods and periods when the par value of the exchange rate was suspect. These periods were identified on the basis of the studies in Chapter 10. The columns headed "Rule A" and "Rule B" under each time period show the alternative rates of return to be had from using two different rules (to be defined) on how much to commit on each day. The three figures in each column in turn are the average annual dollar investment (K), average annual profits (P_T), and the annual rate of return on the invested capital (R). Altogether there are 18 rates of return; each is the outcome of a different combination of the behavioral assumptions. Before turning to an interpretation of these findings I shall explain in detail the meaning of the alternative assumptions that have been made.

Expectations models. The expected value of the future spot rate is established by one of three approaches (shown in the left-hand column of Table 12.1):

(i) The simplest guess the speculator may make is that the expected future spot rate is equal to its par value, $2.80.

(ii) A more sophisticated but still rather simple method of arriving at an estimate for the expected future spot rate is that it is equal to a 50-week moving average. This rule allows for prolonged deviations from the par value.

---

* See Jerome L. Stein, "The Nature and Efficiency of the Foreign Exchange Market," *Essays in International Finance*, No. 40, October 1962, Princeton: Princeton University Press, for a method of identifying ex post facto whether speculators have pursued bull or bear behavior.

(iii) The third, most complex, method of forming an expectation of the future spot rate assumes that spot rates often move in clearly discernible cycles with definite upper and lower bounds (the intervention points), resembling sine waves with rates of change slower the greater the proximity to the intervention points. If we define

$$WA_t = \text{weekly average spot rate at time t}$$
$$WA_{t-1} - WA_{t-2} = D_1$$
$$WA_{t-2} - WA_{t-3} = D_2$$

the third decision rule states that if

$$WA_{t-1} > WA_{t-2} > WA_{t-3}$$

and $X_0 < 2.79$ then $E(X_0^t) = X_0 + 2(D_1 + D_2)$

$2.81 \leq X_0 \leq 2.79$ then $E(X_0^t) = X_0 + D_1 + D_2$

$X_0 > 2.81$ then $E(X_0^t) = X_0 + (D_1 + D_2)/2$

in which the upper limit of $E(X_0^t)$ is 2.82. The mirror image states that if

$$WA_{t-1} < WA_{t-2} < WA_{t-3}$$

and $X_0 > 2.81$ then $E(X_0^t) = X_0 - 2(D_1 + D_2)$

$2.81 \geq X_0 \geq 2.79$ then $E(X_0^t) = X_0 - D_1 + D_2$

$X_0 < 2.79$ then $E(X_0^t) = X_0 - (D_1 + D_2)/2$

in which the lower limit is 2.78. All other relationships of WA_{t-1}, WA_{t-2}, and WA_{t-3} result in an $E(X_0^t)$ of X_0.

Periods for speculation. Three separate time periods, based on three different behavior assumptions, were employed for the calculation of profits from speculation listed in Table 12.1. It should be noted that all three expectations periods imply that the speculator did not anticipate a coming revision of par values.

For Period I, the decision rules were applied to the entire period from July 15, 1955, through April 24, 1961.

For the Period II group of models, the speculator ceased to speculate whenever the data informed him that other speculators and traders were betting on a change of the par value of the exchange rate. He is assumed to have obtained this information by computing the covered-interest-arbitrage margin between London and New York based on the spot rate, the 90-day Treasury-bill rates in the two countries, and the forward rate. Whenever the forward rate failed to establish interest parity, he withdrew from the market. The periods when he thus dropped out of the market were the Suez crisis and sterling bear episode of November 13, 1956, through November 12, 1957, and the dollar bear attack after February 15, 1960. The critical value for the existence of extraordinary speculation on par values was a covered-interest-arbitrage margin in excess of $\frac{1}{2}$ per cent per annum.

The rationale for concentrating on the "normal" periods is that great interest attaches to the elasticity of supply of speculative forward exchange during these periods, for, as was mentioned above, it is this supply of forward exchange that determines what quantity of covered spot arbitrage funds can flow in response to any given interest-rate differential. Furthermore, such behavior might also appeal to classes of speculators who dislike high-risk, high-return situations.

The Period III group of models shows the profitability of speculating only during periods when par exchange values have become suspect.

Choice of quantity invested. Two rules were formulated for determining the amount of each investment, for each of the time periods shown in Table 12.1.

The first, very simple, rule (A) requires that the speculator commit himself to £100 each working day. The maximum potential capital requirement is equal to the average, about $2,000 on the basis of 70 working days per quarter and a 10-per-cent margin requirement.

The second rule (B) is more complicated. It assumes that the frequency distribution of spot rates is approximately bell-shaped, with the mean at par 2.80 and extreme limits at the intervention points, 2.78 and 2.82. An explanation for the shape of such a distribution would be that exchange-rate policy, as carried out by exchange-equalization accounts and central governments, aims at keeping the rate at par without always succeeding, but uses ever more effective and more powerful tools to change trends once the rate has moved close to the intervention points.*

Given the assumption that spot rates behave in the way described, it follows that the closer the forward rate moves toward the intervention points, the greater is the probability that the spot rate will differ from the forward rate in a predictable direction. Therefore the speculator

---

* For the period under consideration the distribution of spot rates was:

| 2.782 to 2.7859: 141 | 2.796 to 2.8059: 424 | 2.816 to 2.8199: 122 |
| 2.786 to 2.7959: 256 | 2.806 to 2.8159: 572 | |

Neither 2.780 nor 2.820 was ever recorded.

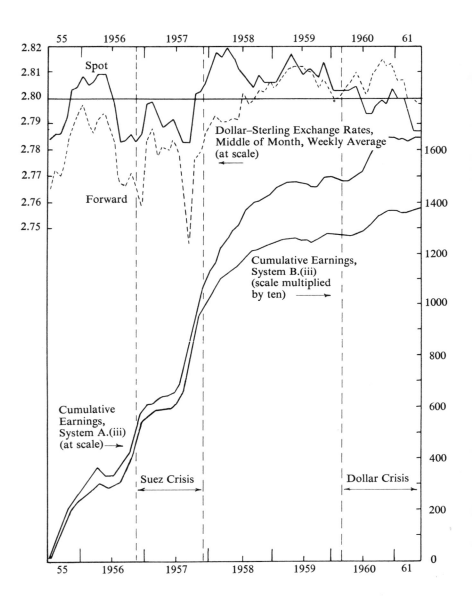

Fig. 12.1. Exchange rates and cumulative earnings.

varies the quantity of his commitment according to the following schedule:

Forward Rate	Commitment
below 2.785	£1,000
2.786 to 2.790	500
2.791 to 2.795	300
2.796 to 2.805	100
2.806 to 2.810	300
2.811 to 2.815	500
above 2.816	1,000

Under this scheme, the maximum capital requirement at any given moment in time is about $20,000—the amount required if there were a daily commitment of £1,000 during each of the 70 working days of an average quarter and an exchange rate of £2.80. The actual average capital requirement was much lower, of course, as the table of profits shows.

Interpretation of Computations

Five interpretations of the data are particularly worth noting:

1. From the table of profits (Table 12.1) it can be seen that the more recent the information used by the expectations model the greater the returns, though the differences are rather small. How well these models worked in an absolute sense was determined by computing how much a speculator could have earned if he had known precisely whether to buy or sell but had continued to invest only £100 per day. The average annual rate of return under these assumptions was found to be 19 per cent, as compared with the 17 per cent earned under the comparable model I.A.(iii). The small difference between the simple models and the perfect foresight model is rather surprising. For an interpretation the accompanying graph (Fig. 12.1) was made. The graph shows cumulative profits from two of the models and the behavior of spot and forward rates during the period. The striking fact is that the forward rate was very consistently below the spot rate, a phenomenon explained by the interest-rate parity theory as having occurred because the London interest rates exceeded the New York rates. During a short stretch in 1959, in fact, when the interest rates diverged very little, and the spot and forward rates were therefore very close, the calculations for cumulative earnings indicate losses. We may

generalize that during such periods the simple expectations models used here can be expected to yield poor results; and that the high rates of return we computed for the period under investigation were due largely to the large and one-sided interest-rate differentials that consistently kept the forward rate well below the spot rate.

2. The difference in earnings under amount-to-invest rules A and B is quite large. What is especially significant is that this is so even during "normal" periods. Changing the weights in the direction of making even heavier commitments (than had been done in the model) the closer the forward rate is to the intervention points would clearly have returned even greater profits. The resulting average investment for the period could conceivably be the same as it was under the alternative assumptions. This result could be achieved by lowering some of the weights around the center of the spot-rate frequency distribution.

3. The rate of increase in total earnings was greatest in the last months of the Suez crisis but was rather small during the dollar bear episode after February 1960. During "normal" periods the greatest rate of increase in earnings occurred in the last half of 1955 and in the first half of 1958. Both of these periods are characterized by abnormally high interest-rate differentials and correspondingly wide spreads between spot and forward rates. During 1955–56 the average interest-rate differential was 2 per cent; early in 1958 it centered around 3.5 per cent.

4. The longest period of zero or negative earnings was seven months. The greatest cumulative losses were $50 under the A model, $300 under the B model.

5. The rates of profit are based on a 10-per-cent margin requirement and are very sensitive to changes in the margin. Thus a 20-per-cent margin would cut profits in half, whereas a 5-per-cent margin would double them. If a speculator maintains large deposits with his bank for other purposes he may quite conceivably speculate with less than 10 per cent down.

Implications for Forward-Exchange Theory

The foregoing considerations suggest that speculation in forward exchange during the period 1955 to 1961 could have been very profitable, especially since the computed rates are probably conservatively low figures which speculators with "inside" information could likely have improved upon rather easily.

Within the larger framework of the theory of forward exchange three interpretations of these findings are possible. The first is that the high rates represent a risk premium and that the market has remained in equilibrium while demanding such high rates of return. Although this proposition cannot be tested empirically, some data are available that permit an intuitive estimate of the relative risk of the activity.

The greatest risk facing the speculator is that of devaluation. Thus a 10-per-cent devaluation means the loss of the entire equity; at a 30-per-cent rate of return this is equivalent to three years' profits. Off-setting this possibility, of course, is the chance of an equally large gain should the speculator anticipate correctly the direction of the revaluation. In principle, the fact that periodic revaluations can be expected to occur makes the rates of return highly uncertain.

However, devaluations do not occur randomly; they can usually be anticipated by changes in reserves and spot rates. A speculator should be able to improve on the statistical odds of "one devaluation every n years" and on the losses thus implied. This problem was met by separating out earnings during "normal" periods; the probability of a revaluation during such periods is not zero, but it is very small. The rates of return even during these normal periods were about 25 per cent per annum. It seems reasonable to conclude, therefore, that the risk does not adequately explain the high rates of return that could have been earned by speculators behaving in the way hypothesized.

Second, if speculators did not on the average behave as the simple rule suggests, their earned rates of return were actually lower than those we have computed. Some scanty information about the behavior of speculators is available and should be compared with the behavior of the speculator in the model.

There are indications that some speculators have not earned these high rates of return; independent evidence drawn from the financial press indicates that general speculative behavior was at odds with that underlying the model during bear episodes against sterling and the dollar in 1957 and 1960, respectively.* In both episodes the real-world speculators must have lost money, whereas the type of behavior suggested in this model would have been profitable.

However, this second interpretation is consistent with our third. It is not unreasonable to believe that the market's system of rewards and punishments has led and will continue to lead to the selection of a core

---

* See various articles in *The Economist*, London, for the years 1957–58 and 1960–61.

of speculators who are successful because they follow behavior rules of the type this study has shown to have been consistently profitable for such a long period. Because of the high rates of return, this core of perhaps professional speculators is likely to increase its own resources and to attract new members.

There is some evidence supporting the view that this process has been at work during recent years. The increase in elasticity of covered interest arbitrage since 1957 can be explained, in our model, by the increased supply elasticity of forward exchange. One indirect piece of pertinent evidence is the recent greater concern the central bankers have shown for the international coordination of interest-rate policies and the ex post facto handling of large, disturbing, short-term capital flows. Reference need be made only to the discussions about world monetary reform, such recent institutional innovations as the Basel Agreements, and the regular monthly meetings of European and North American central bankers. Further evidence is the significant relationships that statistical studies have found between covered interest-rate differentials and short-term capital flows.* There has been a large increase in short-term dollar movements by U.S. nonfinancial corporations and in foreign-currency claims of U.S. banks between 1957 and 1962, with most of the increase concentrated in the period since 1960. Most of the interest sensitivity of these funds "probably reflects covered interest arbitrage between London and New York."† (See Chapter 10, third section.) Some of the increased sensitivity of short-term capital may be due to a greater perfection of markets caused by the convertibility of European currencies in 1958. However, American dollar holders had never been subjected to exchange controls, so that some of their greater readiness in recent years to shift funds abroad can reasonably be attributed to the greater earnings opportunities opened up by speculators in forward exchange.

Whether or not interest-rate differentials between London and New York have narrowed already is not clear from the statistics, especially since the statistics are likely to be distorted by Britain's efforts to attract funds during the 1961 bear pressures on sterling. But during the last two years the average differential has been smaller than during any period of equal length since 1956.

---

* See the footnote on p. 83, with reference to the work of Benjamin J. Cohen, and to that of Philip W. Bell and Peter B. Kenen.
† Ibid., p. 203.

Following are the *Federal Reserve Bulletin* data on monthly interest-rate differentials (absolute values) on U.S. and U.K. Treasury bills, averaged for calendar years:

1956	2.31	1960	2.04
1957	1.58	1961	2.71
1958	2.75	1962	1.41
1959	0.45	1963	0.58

The most important conclusion that can be drawn from this study is the following: Unless interest-rate differentials narrow, earnings from forward-exchange speculation are likely to remain high and to attract further resources into this activity. One consequence of such a development will be an increase in the interest sensitivity of covered international short-term capital flows, which can be expected to cause further reductions in the ability of countries to pursue independent interest-rate policies.

13. Different Pairs of Securities and Time Structure of Forward Rates

This chapter deals briefly with two subsidiary problems of forward-exchange theory: whether empirical evidence offers any help in determining which pair of interest-rate differentials is relevant for arbitrage; and whether the data allow us to make generalizations about the maturity structure of forward exchange rates.

Different Pairs of Securities

In our theoretical discussion in the first section of Chapter 8, we argued that if the difference in the default risk between London Treasury bills and London bankers' acceptances is equal to the difference in the default risk between New York Treasury bills and New York bankers' acceptances, then the interest-rate differential between the London and New York Treasury bills should be approximately equal to the differential between bankers' acceptances in the two centers. From this same theoretical model it follows also that where the difference in risk between two securities in one country is not equal to the difference in risk between two comparable securities in the other country, the inter-country differentials on these pairs should show an approximately constant margin. This means in fact that one security in at least one of the pairs is not "equivalent" in risk to its foreign counterpart. Unfortunately, the question of what constitutes equivalent securities in different international markets is unexplored, and we have no outside information we may draw upon for the study.

However, the computations themselves can be expected to shed some light on these problems. We have computed covered-arbitrage margins for three pairs of 90-day securities: New York and London Treasury bills; New York finance paper and London prime commercial paper; and New York and London bankers' prime acceptances. The margins are plotted in Fig. 13.1. It should be noted that the actual interest-rate

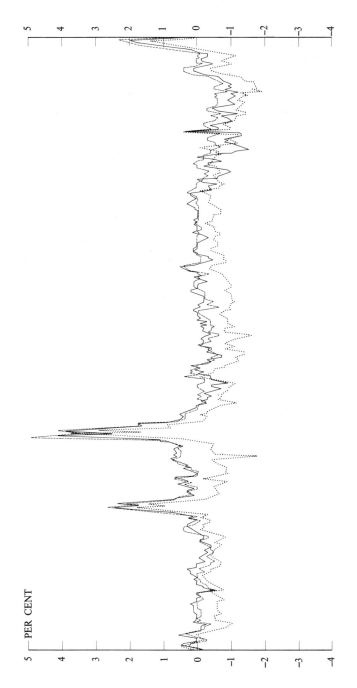

Fig. 13.1. Interest-arbitrage margins for New York–London pairs of securities. Solid line is for Treasury bills; dotted line is for New York finance paper, London prime commercial paper; crossed line is for bankers' prime acceptances.

differential each week and for each pair was subtracted from the implicit interest rate computed from exchange rates for that week, so that the same relative movements of the series would have been found if we had simply plotted the interest-rate differentials.

The graph shows a great degree of correlation among the three series. Two of the lines move together quite markedly, intersecting frequently. And although the difference between these two series and that for bankers' prime acceptances is comparatively large, the observed distance is constant over wide ranges of observation, especially during periods when there was no speculative activity in the markets (as so defined by the outside information presented earlier). These phenomena lend strong support to our theoretical considerations. If we assume the theory to be correct, we can infer from the graph that the risk of New York finance paper and London prime commercial paper relative to the two respective Treasury bills is approximately equal in the two markets, whereas the same relative risk does not hold for the bankers' prime acceptances.

For purposes of computing covered-arbitrage margins and making policy decisions concerning forward-exchange policy, it is important to know which of the three series best predicts the level of the forward rate. In other words, it is important to know which of the three series maintains the smallest average arbitrage margin. For this purpose we summed the absolute deviations of the arbitrage margin from zero. On these grounds the finance-paper/prime-commercial-paper series with a value of 122.1 is superior to the Treasury bill series (142.4) and the bankers' prime acceptances (233.2).

Time Structure

The lack of data makes it impossible to formulate a hypothesis that would test the theory of the time structure of forward rates presented in the second section of Chapter 8. Although businessmen can obtain market quotations for practically any forward-exchange maturity up to at least one year, only the 30-day and 90-day markets are sufficiently deep and developed to generate prices subject primarily to the influences developed in our model. Prices for forward exchange involving maturities beyond one year are usually made by banks and dealers more by way of accommodating the special wishes of customers than in response to genuine demand and supply conditions. That this is so probably explains why long maturity rates are not published.

The interest rates for 30 and 90 days are of little use to our investigation in this context because the two rates are in such close mutual proximity on the yield curve that effective variations in rate differences are likely to be swamped by the relatively large measurement errors discussed in earlier chapters. It is therefore primarily for purposes of illustration that we have assembled some statistics using rates with different maturities. The upper part of Fig. 13.2 shows the covered-interest-arbitrage margin between London and Paris, differing from the customary form only in that the actual interest-rate differential is that for day-to-day money, whereas the implicit interest rate is based on 90-day forward exchange. It is surprising to find that during periods when there was no speculation (i.e., from the beginning of our data to early 1956, and from early 1959 to early 1961) the computed arbitrage margin shows the kind of random fluctuations exhibited by other series discussed earlier; the oscillations rarely exceed a range of 1 per cent, though the entire series lies consistently below the zero line for 1959–60. The explanation of this phenomenon is that the correlation between interest rates on day-to-day and 90-day funds was great, with the rate differential on the longer maturity somewhat larger than that on the shorter maturity. A one-half per cent upward shift of the line tracing the arbitrage margin in 1959–60 would make the graph look like what we would have expected it to had we used 90-day maturities for both series. Unfortunately, the unavailability of 90-day interest rates for Paris makes it impossible to check the correctness of this interpretation.

The two lower series in Fig. 13.2 are the implicit interest-rate differentials computed on an annual basis for 30- and 90-day forward rates for Frankfurt–London. More precisely, the 30-day series plotted represents the value of weekly averages of the 30-day forward rate X_{30} minus the spot rate X_0, divided by the spot rate X_0, multiplied by a factor of twelve (360/30):

$$IR_{30} = \left(\frac{X_{30} - X_0}{X_0}\right) 12$$

The computations for the 90-day series are analogous:

$$IR_{90} = \left(\frac{X_{90} - X_0}{X_0}\right) 4$$

The two series display no mutual consistency throughout the period, the lines crossing frequently during normal times. There appears to be

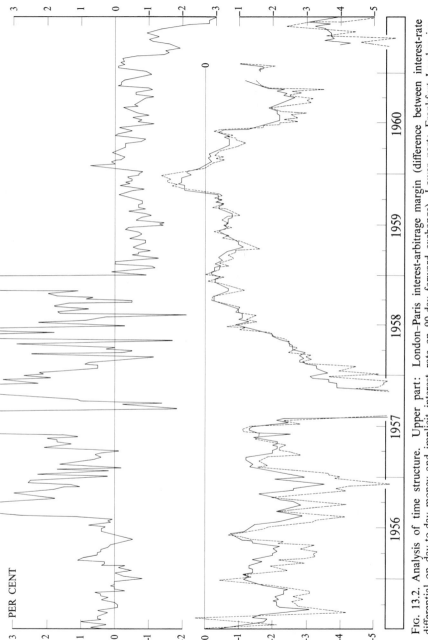

Fig. 13.2. Analysis of time structure. Upper part: London–Paris interest-rate margin (difference between interest-rate differential on day-to-day money and implicit interest rate on 90-day forward exchange). Lower part: Frankfurt–London implicit interest rates (dotted line for 30-day, solid line for 90-day forward exchange).

a tendency for the shorter maturity to exhibit a greater amplitude in its fluctuations. This phenomenon is consistent with our theory of forward exchange rate determination, since the shorter-maturity interest rates actually fluctuated more widely than the longer-maturity rates.

Clearly the two topics of forward-exchange theory discussed in this chapter require further empirical work.

Part III
The Theory of Forward-Exchange Policy

The third part of this book considers how forward exchange policy can be used to deal with short-term capital movements, one of the great, nagging problems of international monetary control. The first chapter analyzes the nature and causes of international short-term capital flows in order to establish explicitly where forward-exchange policy can be useful and to what extent it deals in practice with causes rather than with effects of such flows. The subsequent chapters employ the theoretical apparatus presented in Part I in analyzing the rationale, cost, operating procedures, and general problems of forward-exchange policy. To facilitate the exposition we shall at first assume that neither triangular arbitrage nor official gold points exist. In Chapter 18, we shall then modify the earlier analysis to take account of these two phenomena. Some conclusions are presented in Chapter 19.

14. The Nature of International Short-Term Capital Flows and Forward-Exchange Policy

Capitalist economies are constantly subject to instability in price levels, employment, and balance of payments. The causes of this instability are numerous, as are the policy tools with which governments can combat them. In this chapter we shall analyze precisely that source of instability in the balance of payments that can be neutralized by forward-exchange policy.

Hot-Money Flows

Much confusion about the subject of international short-term capital movements is caused by the failure to distinguish between two broad types of such capital movements. One type, that we shall do well to call "normal" capital movements, is characterized by flows in the direction of statistically observable advantages in earnings opportunities. The second type, generally called "hot moneys," has been described by Nurkse as "erratic and unresponsive to interest rates, massive, unpredictable and unproductive."* Although all large-scale short-term capital flows are frequently referred to under the label "hot money," especially in the financial press, it is advisable to limit the term to those with the characteristics described by Nurkse.†

Frequently underlying such hot-money flows are forces outside the sphere of economic analysis, such as political instabilities and mass

---

* Ragnar Nurkse, *International Currency Experience*, League of Nations, Geneva, 1944, p. 80.
† Another classification of short-term capital movements depends on whether they are equilibrating or disequilibrating, i.e., whether they flow into the country with an otherwise unfavorable balance of payments or whether they aggravate the prevailing imbalance. See: Arthur I. Bloomfield, "Postwar Control of International Capital Movements," *American Economic Review*, 1946, p. 688; Charles P. Kindleberger, *International Economics* Homewood: Irwin, 1953, pp. 333–36; Stephen Enke and Virgil Salera, *International Economics*, third ed., New York: Prentice-Hall, 1958, p. 153. For the purposes of the present analysis, the alternative classification we formulated is more useful in that it focuses on causes rather than effects of short-term capital movements.

psychosis. In the past, some of these flows may have had their roots in economic maladjustments, but their significance arose out of their having aggravated what might otherwise have been only a minor disturbance from equilibrium. Thus, they may force the devaluation of a currency, through depletion of a country's reserves, between the time a balance-of-payments deficit first arises and the time when remedial actions become effective.

Short of outright controls, such money flows cannot be prevented with tools generally available to the economic policymaker. Their prevention is largely a matter of politics and the maintenance of an atmosphere of stability and confidence in Western economies. Success in dealing with them effectively *after* they have occurred depends on the extent to which central banks and their governments cooperate and trust each other's integrity. But this, too, is a matter more of politics than economics.

As I shall argue below, the main problems with international short-term capital movements in the future may arise not from such autonomous hot-money flows but rather from normal movements of funds seeking a statistically observable higher earning opportunity. In the following section we shall analyze the nature and cause of such "normal," but nevertheless disequilibrating, money flows.

International Short-Term Capital Movements in the Classical Model

In the classical gold-standard model, private international short-term capital movements play an important role. When business cycles or random disturbances such as bad harvests or wars cause an excess of imports over exports, the country is assumed to pay for the excess with gold. But not all of the excess need be paid in gold; some will be adjusted by short-term capital flows. These are brought to bear when the initial loss of gold causes interest rates to diverge, raising them in the gold-losing country and lowering them in the gold-gaining country.

The size of the trade deficit and the elasticity of supply of short-term funds determine how far the interest rates must diverge. Thus, as the trade deficit develops, *some* gold leaves the country. However small that gold movement, interest rates in the countries involved tend to change. If the elasticity of supply of short-term funds is great enough, the minute interest-rate differential thus created may attract enough funds to obviate the need for further gold movements.

But how does this help the adjustment of the basic disturbance, which can be achieved in real terms only by a change in price levels or income effects? Doesn't the inflow of funds sustain the domestic demand and thus prevent the adjustment? The answer to these questions is that short-term capital movements do not prevent the adjustment from taking place, but simply slow down its progress. Income effects continue to exert their influence, and however little the interest rate rises from its initial equilibrium rate caused by the gold loss, this higher rate will somewhat reduce the aggregate demand. Eventually prices will fall, and a logically equivalent development in the gold-gaining country will bring about the adjustment.

But it is clear that the reduction in demand will be smaller and the price changes slower the less the interest rates move from their original equilibrium position. Therefore, in order to call forth a given reduction in demand, the less the interest rates depart from equilibrium, the longer they must remain at their new level. Short-term capital movements thus impose the dimension of time on the adjustment process in an essential way.

In a world where adjustments are not instantaneous, the time element is important. A lengthening of the adjustment process means fewer and less-severe disruptions of the ordinary course of business, because prices and wages are more flexible in the long run, and because unemployment and misallocation of resources are reduced. In general, then, international short-term capital movements, in the classical model, can be said to serve as a beneficial cushion protecting the domestic economy from excessive stresses and strains that might otherwise be caused by disturbances originating in foreign countries. Such movements also reduce the need for gold and reserves in each country. What, then, explains the current concern with international money flows and the search for methods to control them?

Real-World Imperfections and Policy Conflicts

There are some important ways in which the real world differs from the theoretical model just presented, and it is these differences that lie at the heart of today's difficulties with international short-term capital movements. For one, there has probably never been a direct and complete relationship between gold losses and interest rates, even in the absence of conscious national interest policies. Cyclical or institutionally determined variations in the circulation velocity of money may have stronger influences on rates than changes in the quantity of money, leaving us simply with a tendency for interest rates to shift in the proper direction. Most important of all, however, is a characteristic of prices and wages that the classical model fails to take into account: they are downwardly rigid to an extent making efforts to lower them exceedingly costly in terms of unemployment and growth. This factor is probably most to blame for the reluctance of many countries to accept domestic price changes when one trading partner experiences some unique shock to his stability. This is especially so because external stability requires, with certainty, a subsequent re-adjustment of the price level. And since the quantity of short-term flows is determined solely by the supply elasticity of short-term funds in the market, these adjustments may have to be very rapid if elasticities are low.

Countries are today unwilling to have external events and unimpeded markets forces exert much pressure on domestic conditions. Since the end of World War II, it has become the declared national economic policy objective of most Western countries to maintain price stability and full employment of resources. The traditional and most widely used tool for achieving these objectives is monetary policy and changes in interest rates. If each country were to set its interest rate at a level ensuring a maximum degree of internal stability, then interest-rate differentials between countries would be uniquely determined.

Given these interest-rate differentials between countries, the supply elasticity of international short-term funds determines the size of the capital movements—just as in the classical model, with freely adjusting interest rates, this elasticity determines how great the differential will be. And here lies the conflict: it is impossible to set both the interest rate differential *and* the size of the flows. But as long as countries are preoccupied with domestic stability, they will continue to set interest rates for this purpose. And the result is the problem of international short-term capital flows.*

The supply elasticity of these funds is crucial in determining the size of the flows and the magnitude of the problem. Rather inelastic supply

---

* Currently, various economic policies are being tested and discussed, such as a greater reliance on fiscal policy or attempts to change the shape of the yield curve of securities. These are aimed at reducing the dilemma associated with the use of interest-rate policies. These tools will be listed later, but detailed analysis of them goes beyond the scope of this study. Instead, we shall focus on forward-exchange policy, the potential of which has been the initiating force for this study, and which is just one of the methods for dealing with the problem just analyzed.

schedules are not too burdensome; their implication is that countries must forego the benefits of equilibrating flows and meet balance-of-trade deficits (plus long-term capital flow imbalances) with previously accumulated reserves. More burdensome, however, is the situation in which the supply of funds is so elastic that even small interest-rate differentials result in massive shifts of funds, and thus tend to tax the existing reserves. The world has been moving rapidly from the first situation to the second. Immediately after World War II, exchange restrictions prevented effective interest arbitrage. But, with the re-establishment of convertibility at the end of 1958, these restrictions were removed. The expansion of international trade, increasing confidence in the stability of Western economies, improved methods of communication and warfare techniques (making Paris as safe as New York), and the growth of worldwide manufacturing and banking enterprises have been important contributing factors to the increase in the elasticities of supply of internationally mobile funds. These developments can be expected to continue in the future and may make this problem of the conflict between internal and external balance one of the greatest facing the Western world in the next decade.*

The Pure Case of Conflict

The preceding analysis thus pinpoints the most basic cause of disturbing international short-term capital movements during normal times—the use of interest rates in the pursuit of national policies at the expense of external balance. However, this is not always so. There exists a situation not envisaged in the classical model in which international short-term capital movements are disequilibrating even without pegging of the interest rates. This situation develops from the possibility that business cycles may be generated purely domestically, and that they may be accompanied by either import or export surpluses. Table 14.1 illustrates the possible combinations for a two-country case, where country D is assumed to experience an excess of imports over exports and country S an excess of exports over imports.

---

* "The most important economic problems of the decade may well be. . . the limitation on massive international shifts of short-term funds." Theodore O. Yntema, "Economic Adjustments Among Nations," *The Journal of Finance*, March 1961, p. 5. The same point is made by several expert witnesses in *International Payments Imbalances and Need for Strengthening International Arrangements*, Hearings before the Subcommittee on International Exchange and Payments of the Joint Economic Committee, Congress of the United States, May 16, June 19, 20, and 21, 1961, Washington: U.S. Government Printing Office, 1961; see especially the testimony by Bernstein, Dillon, Hayes, Heller *et al.*

The meaning of the table can best be explained by examining case 4: country D, having an import surplus, is assumed to face domestic overemployment. The right-hand part of the table shows that for the achievement of both external and internal balance, it is necessary for country D to raise its interest rate. Country S, with an export surplus and underemployment, must lower its interest rate for both reasons. Case 4 is the classical case, causing no conflicts in the interest-rate adjustments of the two countries.

TABLE 14.1

INTEREST-RATE POLICY AND THE ACHIEVEMENT OF INTERNAL
AND EXTERNAL BALANCE

Case	Country D		Country S	
	External	Internal	External	Internal
1. Overemployment in both countries	raise	raise	lower	raise
2. Underemployment in both countries	raise	lower	lower	lower
3. Underemployment in country D and overemployment in country S	raise	lower	lower	raise
4. Overemployment in country D and underemployment in country S	raise	raise	lower	lower

Nor do the first two cases, although not completely classical, present absolutely insoluble problems. In case 1, when country D raises its interest rate, the interest-rate differential between the two countries remains free to increase as required by the external balance between the two countries, even though country S also raises its own rate (but somewhat less than country D) for the sake of internal stability. Analogous reasoning explains case 2. Case 3, however, presents the two countries with what may be called the pure case of conflict between external and internal stability. The combination of conditions causing this conflict is not simply the remaining outcome of a search for all possible combinations; these conditions have a nonzero probability of occurring in the real world.

If we are willing to accept the premise that the European currencies and the dollar were in long-run equilibrium at the existing exchange rates during the early 'sixties, then perhaps the dilemma in which the two continents found themselves is a case in point. Europe's domestic boom called for high interest rates, and thus attracted short-term capital investments, while at the same time a substantial surplus on current account persisted. Much of this capital came from the U.S., where interest rates were kept low to stimulate the domestic economy, while the trade surplus was not sufficient to meet long-term capital outflows and other foreign commitments. But this example demonstrates also the difficulty of judging the difference between a long-run disequilibrium and a mere cyclical disturbance of the type under discussion.

On the theoretical level, the following example represents a combination of circumstances that can be envisaged rather easily. Let us suppose, for example, that the export surplus and overemployment in country S and the underemployment in country D are due to booms in both S and D, with S being the supplier of machinery for investments in both countries, so that D does not reach full employment but S does. With respect to international short-term capital movements, the result is that the country needing to attract funds to protect its reserves can do so only at the expense of further restrictions on domestic demand.

Forward-Exchange Policy as One Solution

Many solutions to the problem of international short-term capital movements—both speculative and "normal"—have been proposed. They fall into two groups. One is centered around discarding interest-rate policy as a tool for the achievement of domestic stability. Insofar as this solution means discarding influence over the economy, it is not likely to be acceptable today to the Western world's politicians and policymakers, faced as they are with the challenge of rapid economic progress in Communist countries, increasing burdens of defense, and social needs requiring stability and sustained growth. Because of this resistance, the proposals involving a diminished role for interest-rate changes are usually coupled with recommendations for the use of other means for retaining influence over the economy. The most important of these is, of course, the recommendation to use fiscal policy more readily and more flexibly than in the past, in order to achieve the desired freedom for interest rates.*

Belonging partly to this group of solutions and partly to the next is the effort to change the yield curve on securities. This involves

---

* *Money and Credit*, *Report of the Commission on Money and Credit*, Englewood Cliffs: Prentice-Hall, 1961, p. 247.

changing long-term interest rates by means of open-market operations to suit domestic needs, while at the same time trying to set short-term interest rates in order to minimize disturbing international short-term capital flows.*

Solutions in the second group aim at retaining monetary and interest policy in its traditional use. These solutions envisage combating the impacts of burgeoning international money flows. The most important of these is the creation of sufficient international reserves to enable countries to weather the large losses in the wake of capital flows, or simply the provision of standby agreements between countries to help each other in cases of emergency.†

All of these methods and some others not mentioned are being considered by economists and politicians. Each of the methods has certain problems, advantages, and disadvantages associated with its adoption. Forward-exchange policy is one solution that has been recommended as a complement to the others. It has been claimed that this policy will contribute materially to a solution of the basic dilemma of one interest rate's influencing both internal and external stability, and that it will also help reduce the impact of speculative attacks on currencies. The following chapters of this book seek to discover the actions necessary to validate these claims.

---

* *Ibid.* See also *The Economic Report of the President*, *the Annual Report of the Council of Economic Advisers*, Washington: January 1962.
† See Herbert G. Grubel, ed., *World Monetary Reform*, *Plans and Issues*, Stanford: Stanford University Press, 1963.

15. The Basic Rationale for Forward-Exchange Policy

This chapter makes use of the theoretical model developed in Part I to analyze the basic rationale for forward-exchange policy. The rationale is presented first for the policy as it would be exercised under normal conditions, and second as it would be used as a tool to deal with speculative runs on currencies. As mentioned earlier, triangular arbitrage and official gold points are assumed not to exist.

The Rationale for Normal Periods

In Fig. 15.1, the intersection of the free-market speculator–trader and arbitrage schedules determines the forward rate X_t and the quantity of forward commitments OM, which in the assumed absence of triangular forward arbitrage is equal to the quantity of investment in the foreign market. More specifically, the graph indicates that speculators expect a spot rate in the future approximately equal to the current spot rate X_0. The London interest rate is assumed to be above that in New York, and the parity forward rate X_t^* in the graph is therefore below the current spot rate. The London interest advantage attracts OM funds from New York covered by OM sale of forward sterling, which investors need to convert the principal and interest of the London securities into dollars upon maturity. Speculators have bought these contracts at the low price, planning to sell the sterling at the higher price expected to prevail at the maturity of the contract.

Forward-exchange policy envisions influencing the held quantity of foreign securities by appropriately changing the forward rate. Thus, for instance, beginning with the forward rate X_t in Fig. 15.1, lowering the rate to X_t^a would cause a reduction in foreign net holdings of AM to OA. Raising the forward rate to X_t^b would cause an increase of MB to OB. If the forward rate were reduced to X_t^c, there would be an accumulation of funds in New York of OC in spite of the fact that

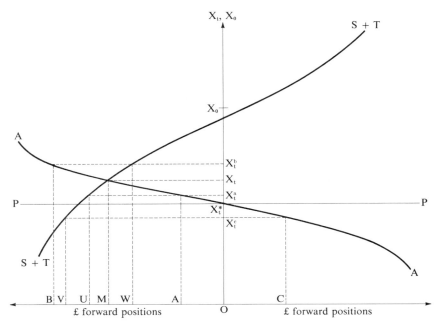

Fig. 15.1. Effects of forward-exchange policy: no revaluation expected.

persistence of the original spot rate, expectations, and interest-rate differential favoring London have been assumed.

Since investment in foreign securities means the exchange of spot currency against domestic currency, the rationale for forward intervention is obvious: a country's stock of foreign exchange can be increased or decreased at will, without requiring changes in the interest rate, thus leaving this instrument free for the achievement of domestic policy objectives.*

Forward-Exchange Policy and Speculation

Although the basic principle of forward-exchange policy just presented holds in general for all constellations of exchange and interest rates, one

---

* Forward-exchange policy had as its most prominent advocate John Maynard Keynes. See his *A Tract on Monetary Reform*, London: Macmillan, 1923, and "The Future of the Foreign Exchanges," *Lloyds Bank Monthly Review*, December 1935. Keynes' recommendations spawned a series of publications in the 'thirties that discussed the merits of such a policy. See Charles P. Kindleberger, *International Short-term Capital Movements*, New York: Columbia University Press, 1937. See also Paul Einzig, "The Theory of Forward Exchanges," *The Banker*, July 1936; "Some Theoretical Aspects of Forward Exchanges," *Economic Journal*, September 1936; and *The Theory of Forward Exchange*, London: Macmillan, 1937. The last-named work also contains a history of forward-exchange policies undertaken by governments.

case is sufficiently different to deserve special attention. This case, shown in Fig. 15.2, implies a bear speculation against sterling. The speculative sentiment is reflected in the fact that the S + T schedule intersects the ordinate at a rate well below the current spot rate X_0, at $E(X_0)$. At any current forward rate above $E(X_0)$, speculators are willing to sell sterling forward in quantities shown by the S + T schedule. With the interest-rate differential assumed to be in favor of London, as before, the parity forward rate is again below the current spot rate. At any forward rate below the parity rate, London's interest advantage is more than wiped out, and interest arbitrage in favor of New York is profitable. The intersection of the AA and S + T schedules results in a forward rate of X_t and forward commitments of ON, which in the absence of triangular arbitrage is also equal to the funds moved into New York.

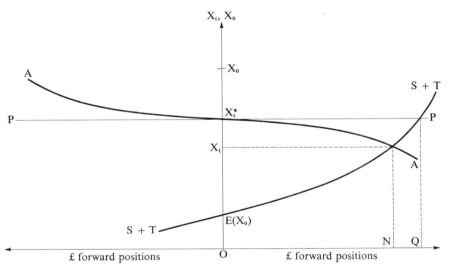

FIG. 15.2. Effects of forward-exchange policy: revaluation expected by speculators.

This example shows quite clearly how the effect of speculation in the forward markets is transformed into an effect on the spot currency markets, and how the size of the actual reserve losses accompanying speculation of this nature depends on the elasticities of the two schedules involved. Empirically, because of the great leverage forward-exchange speculation gives to speculators, and the normally large size of commercial transactions that can be turned to speculative purposes by forgoing the purchase of forward cover, there is every reason to believe that the

S + T schedule is very elastic. Increasing availability of information on foreign investment opportunities has given and will continue to give great elasticity to the arbitrage schedules.

As the graph shows, forward-exchange policy that pegs the forward rate at or near parity (X_t^*) can prevent an outflow of ON funds. According to our arguments about the elasticities of the two schedules determining the distance ON in the real world, the outflow of possibly very large funds can thus be prevented. In addition, of course, the policy might be to peg the forward rate above parity, thus actually inducing the inflow of funds into a country that otherwise would have suffered a loss of reserves through the combined influence of speculation and interest arbitrage.*

---

* The literature concerned with forward-exchange policy following World War II was focused on the problem of curbing speculative runs on sterling under the special conditions of exchange restrictions existing then. See the Bibliography for a detailed listing of the contributions by Anthony Egan Jasay, John Spraos, and Merlyn N. Trued. These authors concluded essentially that forward-exchange policy would be a useful weapon in the fight against speculators. Opposition to this view came mainly from an article by an anonymous author, "Case for the Status Quo," *The Banker*, April 1958. Jasay and Spraos recently had the opportunity to present their views in hearings before the Radcliffe Committee published in the *Report of the Committee on the Working of the Monetary System*, Command 827, London: H. M. Stationery Office, 1959, and *Memoranda of Evidence*, III. The *Report* failed to endorse the use of forward-exchange policy during speculative periods but suggested that it might be useful during times when speculative pressures were absent. See the Treasury memorandum, "The Forward Exchange Market – Policy," *Memoranda of Evidence*, I, pp. 121–22, for a point of view opposing the use of forward-exchange policy against speculation.

16. The Benefits and Costs of Forward-Exchange Intervention

The basic rationale for forward-exchange policy developed in Chapter 15 represents a rather simplified picture of the benefits accruing to a country from such a policy. Moreover, the chapter includes no discussion of the costs at which such benefits are acquired. A systematic analysis of the costs and benefits of forward-exchange policy must be pursued before conclusions about the advisability of its use can be reached. This chapter presents such an analysis.

We shall deal first with the purely financial costs of forward-exchange intervention, then the balance-of-payments effects of the policy, and finally the elements of real social gain that can be expected to follow from it.

Financial Costs of Intervention

Any discussion of the costs and benefits of government activity must distinguish between purely financial involvements, which are essentially transfer payments between citizens of the same country, and real costs and benefits involving the use of creation of actual resources.

The financial cost or gain of government intervention in the forward market arises out of the difference between the price at which currency is sold (or bought) forward and at which it must be purchased (or sold) in the spot market when the contract matures. If we ignore the possibility that the central bank serving as the intervening agency itself owns a stock of foreign exchange bought in the past at certain prices, then it is clear that the sale of forward exchange at a price known today and the uncertainty of the actual future spot rate at the time of maturity involves the bank in an act of speculation.

The relevant considerations determining the size of the involvement can best be seen by the following example, which is based on Fig. 15.1.

Given the elasticities of the S + T and AA schedules shown, and the shift of OM covered arbitrage funds, we shall assume that the policy objective is to increase the amount of funds in London from OM to OB. This requires pegging the 90-day forward rate at X_t^b. If it is expected that the need for the increased foreign funds of BM will last for six months, and that none of the parameters underlying the schedules in Fig. 15.1 will change during that time, the cost or profit P of keeping these funds for six months will be

$$P = [X_{90}^b - E(X_0^{90})](BM + MW)$$
$$+ [E(X_{90}^b) - E(X_0^{180})](BM + MW) \quad (16.1)$$

In terms of the example, this means that the cost or profit will be equal to the following: 90-day forward rate pegged at X_t^b minus spot rate 90 days hence multiplied by the quantity of funds to be attracted BM plus the quantity of forward contracts to be taken over from the reduced holdings of speculators MW. To this we must add the cost of repeating the process once more at the end of 90 days, at which time the forward rate will again be unknown, i.e., $E(X_{90}^b)$.*

From the above analysis, it should be clear that the magnitudes or parameters of none of these variables are actually known to the central banker. All he is reasonably sure of is the magnitude of the required capital inflow BM. Most important, he does not know whether the actual future spot rates will be greater or smaller than the forward rates and thus whether the two products in Eq. (16.1) will be positive or negative. Nor does he know the elasticities of the two schedules, the influence of triangular arbitrage, and whether and how the schedules will shift in response to the pegging operation. This makes it impossible to know precisely at what rate the pegging must occur, or how large MW will be. And, of course, the above assumptions about the constancy of the relevant parameters of the functions are unrealistic.

However, the analysis of forward-exchange policy summarized in the first part of Chapter 15 allows us to make some rough comparisons of the financial costs or benefits of forward-exchange policy under some frequently observed circumstances. The first situation used in our example, that based on Fig. 15.1, can be considered in some sense to be a normal situation. It will be recalled that the interest-rate differential favors London, that speculative sentiment expects the future spot rate

---

* This approach to the presentation of the cost and benefit of forward-exchange policy has been suggested to me by Professor Michael Lovell of Carnegie Institute of Technology.

to be about equal to the current rate, and that the market has produced a capital inflow into London. If the British policymakers share the market's expectation about the future spot rate and desire to attract *additional* short-term funds, they will do so in the expectation of a financial gain, since in order to satisfy the needs of interest arbitragers the intervening agency will buy forward sterling at, say 2.80, and expects to resell it in the spot market at a rate above 2.80, say 2.81, at the time of maturity.

Next let us turn to a situation where the same conditions prevail in the market as before, but where policy is designed to reduce the stock of foreign short-term capital in London from OM to OA. Pegging the forward rate at X_t^a will achieve this objective. At that price speculators are willing to buy OU sterling forward, and interest arbitragers will sell OA, thus leaving an excess demand for sterling of AU, which the intervening agency must supply. This sale results in a government loss if the spot rate 90 days later is above X_t^a.

A third interesting situation can also be illustrated by Fig. 15.1. Assume again that the same conditions exist in the market as before, and that officials believe the spot rate in the future will be X_0. However, let the policy objective now be the attraction of OC spot funds into New York by activities of the Federal Reserve Bank of New York. Since the interest-rate differential favors London, the forward rate now must be depressed below parity to X_t^c. The agency's involvement is now OB plus OC, since at that rate both the speculators and interest arbitragers will buy forward sterling. In this situation the intervening agency can again be expected to take a financial loss, since it is selling sterling at X_t^c, say 2.79, for delivery at a time when expectations are that it can be bought only at, say, 2.81. The reason why the cost of intervention in this case is so much higher is that the central bank is overcoming a natural interest-rate disadvantage and is taking a position against speculators even though knowing that the speculators' expectations are correct.

The fourth example of forward-exchange intervention and its cost lies in the speculative situation underlying Fig. 15.2. It will be recalled that in the example the interest-rate differential favors London (i.e., $X_0 > X_t^*$) but that speculators expect a devaluation of the currency to $E(X_0^t)$, well below the current spot rate X_0. Here the policy objective is to prevent a capital flow to New York of ON by pegging the forward rate at parity (X_t^*). As the diagram shows, only speculators are willing to engage in transactions at that price. Since forward sterling is priced higher than they expect it to be at the time of contract maturity, they are willing to sell OQ forward. It should be noted that a strong expectation of exchange-rate devaluation tends to make the $S + T$ schedule highly elastic, so that in real-world situations OQ may be a very large absolute sum. Whether the intervening agency will lose large amounts of money through this policy of buying forward sterling at X_t^* depends on the level of the spot rate at the time of maturity. If speculators are correct in their predictions, large losses will be sustained by the government. On the other hand, if the spot rate does not depreciate, the government will make large profits.

But whatever the outcome, the balance of payments at the time of intervention is improved by the once-and-for-all return of ON spot sterling from New York. Similarly, regardless of whether a spot-rate revaluation has taken place or not at the time of maturity, there will be only a negligible impact on the spot rate at that time since the speculators owning no spot funds will be forced to purchase (or sell) the foreign currency which they deliver (or receive) through their forward contracts. In the real world, speculators often balance their accounts simply by settling the difference between spot and their forward rates, without engaging in simultaneous sales and purchases. The spot rate can be influenced only by speculators' net profits and only if they are withdrawn in the form of foreign exchange.

In the literature* there is much argument about whether the government should stand by to sell unlimited quantities of sterling (presumably OQ very large) in situations such as that of Fig. 15.2. Our analysis provides a rather clear-cut answer to this problem. If the government's information about the basic strength of the currency is such that its officials are certain the spot rate will not depreciate, then such intervention in the forward market is an eminently rational and effective policy. If, on the other hand, the government expects the exchange rate should be given a basic downward adjustment, then the intervention is an expensive way to delay what is inevitable. Forward-exchange policy is never a substitute for devaluation. Because the consequences of devaluation are so clear, the act of intervention itself is a strong weapon in the hands of officials wishing to signal to speculators their determination not to devalue; by wielding such a weapon the officials can in fact bring about shifts in the $S + T$ schedule and

---

* See the contributions of Aliber, Auten, Goldstein, and Stein listed in the Bibliography.

speculators' expectations in a direction that reduces the need to take speculative positions. We shall analyze the impact of forward-exchange policy on the behavior of the market participants in the first section of Chapter 17.

The conclusions to be drawn from the foregoing analysis can be summarized by saying that forward-exchange policy limited to the *reinforcement* of an existing interest-rate differential, other things being equal, tends to be profitable for the government, and to be unprofitable where the policy is designed to *overcome* an existing interest-rate differential. In terms of commitments to speculators, wherever its position on future price forecasts opposes that of the speculators, the government will profit if the speculators are wrong and lose if they are right. The size of possible gains and losses is determined by the elasticities of the underlying functions.

Offsetting these types of financial gains and losses are some others. Forward-exchange policy is a substitute for interest-rate changes pursued for the sake of maintaining external balance. As such it affects the interest cost of holding the government debt, reducing this cost if interest rates can be set lower than they would otherwise have to be, and raising it in the opposite case. The financial effects devolving from these interest payments must be offset against the losses or gains from the forward-exchange dealings, in seeking an estimate of the financial cost.

Two other aspects of forward-exchange policy operations require comment at this point. First, our analysis makes clear that the activity is speculative in nature, because of the uncertainty of future spot prices. Speculation is often abhorred by conservative central bankers, regardless of the odds for gain or loss. The uncertainty aspect of the activity itself represents a great disutility for people trained to be trustees of others' funds, as many central bankers are. This phenomenon goes far toward explaining the official reluctance to engage more readily in forward-exchange policy than has been the case in the past.

Second, it should be noted that the profits or losses represent no more than a redistribution of income in society, to (or away from) speculators and from (or to) the general public, through the intervening agency as the representative of the public. Disregarding the probably minor resource cost of selling and purchasing exchange and the possibility that some speculators and asset holders may be foreigners, the forward policy's official profits or losses do not represent any use of productive resources.

Balance-of-Payments Effects

Forward-exchange policy influences the balance of payments by four analytically distinct routes: changes in the stock of short-term capital, interest payments to foreigners, speculation profits or losses by foreigners, and changes in the balance of trade.

The principal effect of forward-exchange policy—the effect discussed almost exclusively in the literature, and presented as the "basic rationale" in Chapter 15—is the change in the stock of foreign short-term investments in the market. This once-and-for-all change in stock becomes translated into a balance-of-payments flow item, and may be large or small, depending on conditions.

Next there are interest payments to foreigners. Assume that before the forward-exchange policy is instituted a certain quantity of domestic assets is held by foreigners, and thus requires interest payments that enter the balance of payments. Now if the forward policy attracts additional foreign funds, interest payments are increased; if the policy reduces the foreign-held assets, payments are reduced. This reasoning is to be contrasted with that for the situation where another policy is substituted for forward-exchange policy. For example, in the absence of forward-exchange policy, interest rates might have to be raised, which would result in increased interest payments to foreigners because of the higher rates both on assets already held and on those newly attracted. Balance-of-payments effects under this alternative would be greater than those under the forward-exchange policy. Both methods of reasoning are valid, and the choice between them rests on the circumstances surrounding policy actions.

Third, the activity of speculators affects the balance of payments to the extent that their profits or losses involve foreigners who must either buy or sell exchange to settle their accounts.

Fourth, exporters' and importers' behavior influences the balance of trade to the extent that these traders base their transactions on the level of the forward rate. Increasing the forward rate through policy, for example, tends to lower exports and increase imports, where normal trade elasticities are assumed.

The general effects just enumerated can be illustrated by referring to one of the examples presented in the first section of this chapter. (The example makes use of Fig. 15.1.) It will be recalled that in case 1 there was a capital inflow into London equal to BM. Also, it was assumed that there would be official profits, rather than profits by the speculators. Since some of the speculators are likely to be foreigners, their reduced profits decrease the demand for dollars. At the same time the capital inflow raises the spot demand for sterling. The increased short-term capital holdings by foreigners require additional interest payments, tending to increase the demand for dollars. Since in our first case the policy objective requires raising the dollar–sterling rate, British goods become more expensive relative to U.S. goods, thus leading to an increase in imports into the United Kingdom, a decrease in exports, and a net addition to the demand for dollars. We have, then, two factors tending to raise the dollar–sterling spot exchange rate and two factors tending to lower it.

For policymakers the important question is which of these influences can be expected to dominate. The answer depends on the elasticities of the relevant functions representing the forces of demand and supply and their behavior over time. Of predominant importance in the short run are the short-term capital flows, whereas the other three factors are likely to be of a second order of magnitude and can be neglected. Currently, and under normal conditions, the fraction of total trade based on forward-exchange quotations is not very large. Given typical price elasticities for exports and imports, and the usual range of forward-exchange variation, there is a fairly strong presumption that empirically, in the short run, the balance-of-trade effect is likely to be fairly small as compared with the size of the short-term capital flows. Over a longer period, however, the relative importance of the two effects could easily be reversed.

As the discussion of this example shows, the direction and quantitative balance-of-payments impact of forward-exchange policy under different conditions can be estimated in principle. What the officials responsible for setting the policy must establish more precisely is their estimate of the likely sizes of the various components.

Real Costs and Benefits

The real costs and benefits arising from the use of forward-exchange policy fall into three categories: changes in the transfer of resources to foreigners, the use of resources by operation of the policy itself, and, most important, the gains to be had by allowing the country to operate close to full employment.

As we have indicated, some of the forward-exchange speculators may be foreigners. Their profits (or losses) decrease (or increase) the country's command over real output. Similarly, resources are transferred to foreigners by the interest payments due them for the loan of their short-term capital. But it is clear that these interest payments are not a social loss, since the capital lent by the foreigners has added to the productivity of the receiving country, and this productivity is presumably somewhat more substantial than the interest due the foreigners. In addition, the taxation of these interest earnings represents an appropriation of part of the net productivity and therefore a net social gain for the taxing country. The reverse holds true for the case where forward-exchange policy reduces the amount of foreign short-term capital in the country.

The second category of resource use is one already mentioned briefly—the costs of pursuing the forward-exchange policy arising from selling and purchasing the exchange, gathering information, and making decisions. These costs are likely to be rather small, since the exchange markets are organized very efficiently and the productivity of one man and a telephone is very great.

The largest real benefits of forward-exchange policy provide its very rationale. As we have seen in Chapter 14, the use of interest-rate and monetary policy for purposes of domestic full employment and price stability under fixed exchange rates can easily conflict with the requirements for external balance. The choice is on the one hand either discarding or modifying the domestic policy objective when the disciplines of the balance of payments so require, and on the other hand using forward-exchange policy as a lever operating exclusively on the external balance. In the typical situation a certain domestic interest rate is required to maintain full employment but it is too low, relative to that prevailing in other countries, to attract the short-term funds necessary to tide the country over a temporary, perhaps cyclical, imbalance in its external payments. Raising the interest rate would attract the foreign funds but would cause underemployment of domestic resources. By the exercise of forward-exchange policy this loss of output can be avoided, and avoiding it represents the real gain from the policy. It is difficult, though, to make general statements about the size of these gains without knowledge of the specific circumstances surrounding the need for the exchange policy. However, it is clear that the impact of even small interest-rate changes in large countries such as the United States may be appreciable in real terms.

Forward-exchange policy also yields real gains to the economy when it reduces speculative pressures against domestic currency. Such speculation is capable of forcing payments restrictions or devaluations, with all of their disruptive impact on the economy, which would otherwise be unnecessary and may even have to be reversed subsequently. Such repeated adjustments of the economy to new prices and government regulations call forth shifts and reallocations of resources that in a world characterized by friction and widespread immobility are costly. In this sense a policy obviating the need for such restrictions and revaluations yields a positive gain. The size of the benefits is again hard to estimate but in the typical Western economy it is undoubtedly quite large.

17. Two Problems of Policy: Market Reactions and Choice of Technique

This chapter considers briefly two important aspects of forward-exchange policy. The first concerns the market's likely reaction to the act of forward-exchange intervention itself. The second is related to the problem of choosing appropriate techniques for bringing market forward rates to desired levels.

Market Reactions to Intervention

The reactions of interest arbitragers are most important to the effectiveness of forward-exchange policy aimed at changing the stock of foreign short-term capital held in the country. Other things being equal, the quantity of short-term capital moving at any given forward rate depends on market elasticity, i.e., on the elasticity of the AA schedule in our model (where, again, we assume that triangular arbitrage is not operating). As argued earlier, the people engaged in interest-arbitrage operations are most often conservative institutional investors. Their behavior is not likely to be influenced to any significant degree by the actions of the intervening agency. Investors seeking an advantageous rate of return free from exchange risk are likely to allot to the transaction the same quantity of funds, regardless of whether the forward exchange is made available to them by private speculators or by a central bank. Therefore, the conservative institutional investors, who represent a large component of the AA schedule under normal conditions, will probably not change their behavior pattern when forward-exchange intervention takes place.

On the other hand, a certain fraction of the investors who normally prefer to cover their foreign investments through purchase of forward exchange may be tempted during some speculative situations to move part of their funds without cover. Such situations would arise where adverse balance-of-payments and international-reserve developments are accompanied by speculation expecting a devaluation of the currency. Under these circumstances the probability for a substantial future rise in the country's spot exchange rate is negligible—though not zero— as compared with the chances for a depreciation. Therefore an uncovered outflow of funds will with high probability yield a capital gain and with much smaller probability no change or a loss in capital value. These are the conditions, as we argued in the first section of Chapter 7, under which some investors who are normally interest arbitragers will turn speculators and move funds without cover. In the context of this chapter the question is whether the intervening agency's actions are likely to change the expectations of these investors in a certain direction, and most important, whether in their mind the odds for a devaluation have increased.

The answer to this question depends on whether the would-be speculators believe the intervention to be a signal of the government's determination to maintain the current exchange rate, or whether they believe it to be equivalent to the government's admitting that there is a crisis and that the forward-exchange policy is only a delaying action before the unavoidable revaluation. In principle either of these two expectations or no change in expectations at all can occur. However, there is a strong argument that the government's willingness to intervene should be interpreted as a signal of its determination *not* to devalue. As we have seen in the preceding chapter, the act of intervention represents counterspeculation, which becomes very expensive if a devaluation ultimately takes place. It is extremely unlikely that any government would try to put off a required devaluation in this expensive way. Would-be speculators can be expected to know this, so that if a country does engage in counterspeculation in the forward market, it must have the resources and the determination necessary to prevent later devaluation. The acts of announcing and carrying out the policy may in fact be one of the strongest tools available to the authorities by which to demonstrate to the public the strength of their confidence in the current exchange rate.

It should be noted that of the three possible reactions to intervention, only one—a majority conviction that devaluation is inevitable—is positively harmful. If speculators do not, on the whole, change their expectations, the policy has done no harm on this account and will be successful on the other accounts analyzed in the last chapter. And, of course, if would-be speculators are, on the average, convinced that a devaluation is unlikely, the forward-exchange policy will have been doubly successful in relieving pressure on the spot exchange rate by reducing both covered interest arbitrage and speculative uncovered outflows of funds.

Moreover, it must be emphasized that all these considerations of the behavior of would-be speculators owning spot funds apply only where speculative sentiment in the market expects a drastic change in the exchange rate. If the markets are normal and exchange-rate variations are likely to be within a much narrower range and with less probability of being in but one direction, the quantity of funds the owners are willing to move without cover is not likely to reduce greatly the availability of funds responsive to covered arbitrage. Changes in expectations brought about by forward-exchange policy have, therefore, only a small leverage.

We turn next to the forward-exchange speculators and traders, whose behavior patterns are summarized in the S + T schedule of our model. In general their expectations are influenced by the same types of considerations that determine the expectations of the spot-fund owners just discussed. Once again, therefore, the act of intervening in the forward market can, under given circumstances, leave expectations unchanged or can lead to the collapse or intensification of a specific sentiment.

During times when a drastic change in the spot rate is not expected, sizable shifts of the S + T schedule are unlikely. For periods when revaluation is expected, forward-exchange speculators will again need no reminding of the logic of the argument that the cost to the government of intervention plus devaluation is prohibitively high.

The most damaging of the possible reactions is a conviction among speculators that the government will be unable to keep the spot exchange rate at its current level; when this occurs, an intervention strengthens their expectations. If the speculators are in fact mistaken, the result of this worst possible reaction is ultimately a larger government profit, though there may be some repercussions for the spot market arising from a large accumulation of forward obligations. Offsetting the latter influence is the direct effect of the policy-induced covered-interest-arbitrage flow on the spot rate. This effect is determined only by the shape of the arbitrage schedule and is essentially independent of shifts in the S + T schedule.

Summing up, we can conclude that the cost-benefit analysis presented in the previous chapter is not modified in any essential way by taking into account what appear to be the most likely market reactions to the act of official intervention in the forward market.

Alternative Methods of Market Entry

Discussion of methods of intervention in forward-exchange markets and the influence of these methods on exchange rates has been neglected in the literature. Most writers limit themselves to a brief description of the two basic methods available. Yet Einzig implies that they may entail different effects and that therefore in any discussion of the merits of forward-exchange policy it ought to be stated whether the use of one method or the other is contemplated.* The existence of triangular arbitrage, for example, represents a complication of forward-exchange policy that can be circumvented in part by the use of one technique in preference to the other. For these reasons we shall do well to analyze the nature and impact of the two basic methods of forward-exchange intervention.

In the simple pegging approach the official agency enters the market as a buyer or supplier of forward exchange to raise or lower the rate, respectively. Essentially, the authorities stand by to buy or sell forward exchange in unlimited quantities at a specified rate, say X_t^a, in Fig. 15.1. As the schedules show, speculators and traders want to buy OU sterling forward, whereas the arbitragers want to sell only OA sterling forward. The authorities will therefore find themselves holding contracts calling for the future delivery of AU sterling at X_t^a. This technique is very simple, since the market mechanism allocates the forward exchange unmindful of the categories of users, and the intervening agency therefore requires no information about the use to which the exchange is put. Because of this administrative ease the technique is very recommendable. It has, however, the disadvantage that it is likely to involve the agency in official losses under certain circumstances, as was argued in the first section of Chapter 16. It will be recalled that if the speculators are correct the spot rate at the maturity of the forward contract will be above the forward rate, thus causing an official financial loss equal to $(X_0 - X_t^a)AU$ sterling. Analogous reasoning applies to the case where the rate is pegged below parity; here, according to our

---

* Paul Einzig, *A Dynamic Theory of Forward Exchange*, London: Macmillan, 1961, p. 389.

earlier analysis, intervention at rates above X_t, say X_t^b, is likely to yield profits.

The losses likely under the first situation tempt governments to search for a method of intervention wherein speculators can be excluded from taking advantage of the officially available exchange rate, thus reducing the losses incurred by sales to them. The leverage whereby this can conceivably be achieved rests on the essential difference between the two types of market participants—the ownership of spot funds. The second basic method of intervention, the use of swap accommodations, is based on these considerations.

There are basically two situations for swap dealings, only one of which can succeed in attaining a stated objective. Both situations involve the offer to buy (or sell) spot exchange at a certain rate while simultaneously selling (or buying) forward exchange at another rate. The price difference between the two rates is chosen so as to realize the objectives of the policy with respect to the movement of funds. Thus the forward discounts may have to be made greater or smaller than those in the market, depending on the policy goal.

The first set of conditions under which swap dealings offer no advantage over direct sales can best be demonstrated with the help of the two diagrams presented in Chapter 15. It is recalled that the assumptions underlying Figs. 15.1 and 15.2 differ essentially in that, in the latter, speculators expect a depreciation of the dollar–sterling spot rate, whereas in the former they do not.

Swap dealings fail to offer an advantage whenever policy objectives require operating with forward rates that are on the same side of parity as the free market rate, i.e., above parity in Fig. 15.1 and below parity in Fig. 15.2. The reasoning underlying this conclusion is as follows. If, for example, British authorities wish to reduce the stock of capital held in London from OM to OA (Fig. 15.1), the swap offer would have to be sales of spot sterling at X_0, repurchased forward at X_t^a. But no investor will accept such a swap deal, since the market provides a more advantageous yield at the forward rate X_t. Thus if the swap offer is to be made attractive the forward rate offered must be above X_t. But above X_t the original policy objective of decreasing the funds held in London is defeated and, in fact, more investments are attracted. In addition, the forward commitments of the central bank will be equal to what they would have been under direct sales, because a swap offer at X_t^b will divert all owners of spot funds from the free market. With the supply curve for forward sterling thus shifted, the excess demand by speculators will drive the price of forward sterling up from X_t to the X_t^b rate offered by the official agency. At this point arbitragers become indifferent to their source of forward dollars and at a marginally higher price will purchase OA sterling from speculators. As a consequence, the overall London investments of OB are covered by BA forward contracts from the central bank and OA contracts from speculators. The official commitment here is identical to that which would have resulted from direct intervention.

Analogous reasoning applies to the situation shown in Fig. 15.2, but with the objective of the swap offers now being the attraction of additional funds into New York or the reduction of the quantity held there. Again, either the offers will not be taken or they will yield the same results as the alternative method of intervention.

It is theoretically possible to offer swap dealings that prevent speculators from dealing with interest arbitragers altogether, even under the conditions just discussed. This would occur if officials offered to sell spot sterling at a rate above X_0 and repurchase it forward at a rate such that the total yield would exceed the highest rate the market would be willing to provide. In our model, as described by Fig. 15.1, the greatest market rate of return is reached at the highest forward rate at which speculators will still purchase a pound sterling. Such a policy would in essence extinguish the free market for forward exchange. The difference between market and official spot rates could be large and could tempt abuses. It might therefore be difficult to administer.

Swap operations do produce results different from those under direct intervention whenever the policy objectives require a forward rate on the side of parity opposite that of the free market, i.e., forward rates below X_t^* and above X_t^* in the situations underlying Figs. 15.1 and 15.2, respectively. Presuming again the first set of conditions (Fig. 15.1), we find that offering a spot rate X_0 and a forward rate below X_t^*, say X_t^c, to investors attracts London owners of sterling funds, who under existing conditions would simply have left their funds invested in London at the local interest rate. The swap offer now raises the covered New York yield above the simple London rate of return.

As a consequence of such a policy, the left-hand sides of the arbitrage and speculative schedules are unaffected, and so also, therefore, is the profitability of keeping assets in London. The official intervention thus produces a flow of funds in the direction opposite that created by the market, opening up a difference between the official and the market forward rates.

The forward commitments and balance-of-payments effects accompanying outright pegging at X_t^c and swaps offering at X_t^c can be compared as follows. Under pegging the official forward sales of sterling are equal to $OV + OC$, whereas under swap arrangements they are equal to only OC. The balance-of-payments changes are equal to $OM + OC$ under pegging and OC under swaps. Since $OC/OC = 1$ and $OV + OC/OM + OC > 1$, the balance-of-payments effect is more direct and greater per unit of forward commitment under swaps than it is under pegging. Thus it follows that under certain conditions the swap technique of forward-exchange intervention is more efficient than its alternative.

18. Policy under Triangular Arbitrage and Official Spot Limits

So far, in Part III, we have ignored the effects of triangular arbitrage and the maintenance of spot rates within certain official limits about par. In the present chapter we shall analyze the implications these influences have for the effectiveness and usefulness of forward-exchange policy. The task is facilitated by using the theoretical tools developed in Part I.

Triangular Arbitrage in Forward Exchange

When the activities of triangular arbitragers in forward exchange are included in our theoretical model, the most important changes that result are the greater elasticity of the arbitrage schedule and the lack of a one-to-one relationship between the quantity of official forward-exchange commitments and the actual stock of short-term capital in the particular market in which the pegging action takes place. However, in terms of the overall quantity of short-term capital attracted from other countries combined, the one-to-one capital and forward-exchange relationship will most likely be unaffected. I have argued elsewhere* that the one-to-one relationship would probably be disturbed; the following extensive analysis demonstrates that it probably would not.

Triangular arbitrage keeps the three forward rates in equilibrium such that $(\$ \cdot \pounds) = (\$ \cdot DM)(DM \cdot \pounds)$. A numerical example for the condition is $3.00 = 0.30 \times 10.00$. Now assume that the dollar–sterling rate is pegged at 2.00. Arbitrage will tend to lower both the dollar–mark rate and the mark–sterling rate. To keep the discussion at this point free from one complication caused by this policy, we shall

---

* In "A Multicountry Model of Forward Exchange: Theory, Policy, and Empirical Evidence," *Yale Economic Essays*, Spring 1963; "A Neglected Aspect of Forward Exchange Theory and Policy," *Journal of Finance*, September 1963; and in the reply to a note in the same journal, September 1964.

assume that all of the equilibrating adjustment occurs in the dollar–mark rate. The new equilibrium will then be at the values $2.00 = 0.20 \times 10.00$.

In other words, if one of the dollar rates is established by pegging, market adjustments will change the other dollar rate in the equation by the same percentage and in the same direction. What this simultaneous lowering of the two rates means can be seen by considering the following example, based on Figs. 18.1 to 18.3.

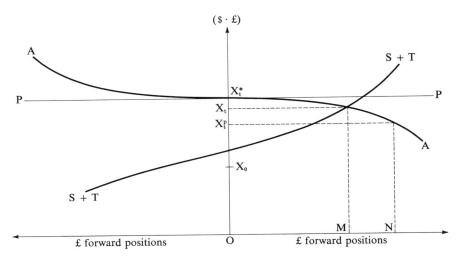

FIG. 18.1. Triangular arbitrage and capital flows: dollar–sterling market.

The first diagram (Fig. 18.1) shows the dollar–sterling spot rate below the parity rate, indicating a New York interest advantage. The position of the S + T schedule signifies that the market expects no drastic change in the spot rate in the future. The market forward rate X_t leads to OM investments in New York. The pegging objective is to increase the stock of investments in New York by lowering the forward rate to X_t^p. We have argued earlier that some of the additional sterling commitments MN are not accompanied by capital inflows from London but rather are held by triangular arbitragers. But how did these triangular arbitragers obtain the sterling they sold forward to the central bank against dollars? They must have obtained it by reselling the dollars for marks and using the marks to buy sterling. Now the question is: Who are the buyers of the forward marks?

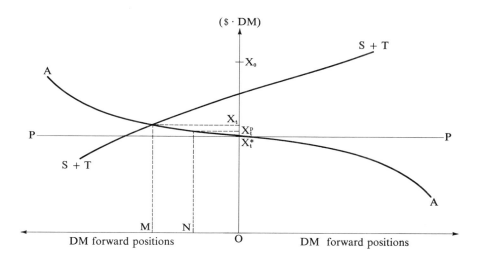

FIG. 18.2. Triangular arbitrage and capital flows: dollar–Deutsche mark market, Frankfurt interest advantage.

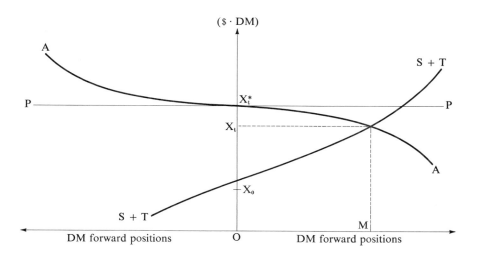

FIG. 18.3. Triangular arbitrage and capital flows: dollar–Deutsche mark market, New York interest advantage.

It is tempting to argue at this point that the mark buyers could be either interest arbitragers or speculators. If they are interest arbitragers, each pound forward sterling bought by the central bank produces a pound's worth of short-term capital inflow from Frankfurt, but if they are speculators this conclusion does not hold. Our theoretical model suggests that the buyers of the forward marks offered will be interest arbitragers, regardless of existing market conditions. For a proof, consider Figs. 18.2 and 18.3.

In Fig. 18.2, the relationships between the dollar–mark spot rate X_0 and parity forward rate X_t^* indicate a Frankfurt interest advantage, and the forward rate X_t causes a stock of short-term assets to be held in Frankfurt. The lowering of this rate caused by triangular arbitrage produces a return flow of funds to New York, since as investments mature the lower yield makes New York placement more attractive to the marginal asset holder.

Figure 18.3 describes the situation analogous to that of the New York–London market of Fig. 18.1, except that the currencies are marks rather than sterling and the interest rates relate to Frankfurt rather than London. Under these conditions the lower forward rates will again attract funds into New York. The conclusions would be the same if the S + T schedule had been such as to produce capital flows opposite those suggested by the simple interest-rate differential.

The systematic integration of triangular arbitragers into the other-market relationships of our model requires that the demand schedules of triangular arbitragers be added to the speculators' schedule. In the example just presented this addition would move the S + T schedules in Figs. 18.2 and 18.3 to the right, thus yielding the analytically required lower market forward rates and capital flows to New York.

The effectiveness of achieving the inflow of a given amount of capital by pegging one rate in a world of multilateral relationships does not seem to be destroyed by the existence of triangular arbitrage in forward exchange. Nevertheless some other important problems are raised. In the analysis just completed we assumed that triangular arbitragers do not influence the free mark–sterling market rate. This is clearly an unrealistic assumption. In the process of adjustment, and through the repeated forward sale of marks for sterling by arbitragers, this rate will tend to decline. If before the New York pegging operations the mark–sterling rate is in equilibrium, the lower rate will produce shifts of interest-arbitrage funds between Frankfurt and London. This may be undesirable for either or both of these countries. In the real world, where not only these two cities but also Milan, Paris, Amsterdam, Geneva, and many other money markets are affected in a similar way, at least some of the countries would find such capital moves among themselves embarrassing.

All these side effects will be accentuated if several countries engage in forward-exchange policy simultaneously. In the example where the U.S. tries to attract short-term capital from London through a lower peg on the dollar–sterling forward rate, if the German authorities simultaneously peg the mark–sterling forward rate, then triangular arbitrage will affect the dollar–mark forward rate and, as a result, spot funds may flow from New York to Frankfurt or vice versa.

There are two approaches to the solution of the third-country problems raised by pegging a single forward rate. One is to peg all forward rates; the other, appropriate in certain situations, is to use the technique of swaps rather than pegging.

The first solution requires that all forward exchange rates be pegged an equal percentage above or below their parity value, depending on the objective of the policy. In the example where New York tries to attract additional short-term funds, the pegging of the dollar–sterling rate at 2.00 and of the dollar–mark rate at 0.20 ends all problems of triangular arbitrage involving the mark–sterling market relationship. Similar peggings are required in all other dollar markets. However, this solution has itself some more or less important disadvantages.

Simultaneous pegging of all rates seriously complicates the administration of the policy. It is much easier to keep accurate track of interest-rate and spot-forward differentials for a pair of currencies than it is to do the same for as many as ten or fifteen major currencies. Elsewhere in the literature of forward-exchange policy, the examples run in terms of a single country, and their strong implication is that the tool influences only two markets at a time. This limited ramification of the policy could be a great advantage, since usually one country's temporary balance-of-payments difficulties are matched by some other country's unusually large surpluses.

When the U.S. engages in the type of intervention presented in our example by pegging all forward rates, other countries are faced with a pattern of forward rates they cannot alter. The mark–dollar rate, for instance, is pegged directly, and the sterling–mark rate is moved toward equilibrium by triangular arbitragers. Any effort by the German authorities to peg any mark rate in a way inconsistent with the rates determined in this fashion will involve the German or American authorities in very large losses as the triangular arbitragers exploit the rate inconsistencies. From this it follows that the worldwide co-ordination of forward-exchange policies is required, which would not be necessary in the absence of triangular arbitrage.

The analysis in Chapter 17 demonstrated that the various directions of pegging involve the intervening agency in losses with varying degrees of certainty. The prime determinant of these outcomes is the existing interest-rate differential. Because *all* forward rates must be pegged, it is impossible to choose a *particular* rate for which the likelihood of profits exceeds the likelihood of losses. Therefore, the cost of forward-exchange policy tends to be increased.

Let us turn now to the analysis of the second suggested solution to the problems raised by the existence of triangular arbitrage—the use of swaps as a method of market entry. According to the analysis in Chapter 17, swap operations are more efficient and lead to smaller official involvement than pegging if the policy objective is to create an outflow from the financial center having the free-market covered-interest advantage. Since under these circumstances the free-market equilibrium forward rate is not disturbed, triangular arbitrage is not induced. Because triangular arbitragers own no spot funds, they can take no advantage of the swap rates offered by the intervening agency. Therefore, under these conditions the swap technique is not only more efficient but also more selective in its impact than the technique of outright pegging.

The circumstances under which the swap technique produces the same results as pegging are in themselves such as to reduce the effective-ness of this form of market entry in dealing with the problems raised by triangular arbitrage. Consider Fig. 18.4, where the simple and covered interest advantage has led to a stock of sterling investments in New York equal to OL plus other currency investments induced by triangular arbitrage equal to LM. This follows from the fact that AA is the arbitrage schedule of interest arbitragers alone and A'A' is that of interest and triangular arbitragers combined. Now assume the policy to be the attraction of a total stock of ON funds from London. The offer to sell forward sterling at the pegged forward rate X_t^p only to owners of spot funds immediately creates an excess supply of forward sterling by speculators, which tends to lower the forward rate to X_t^p.

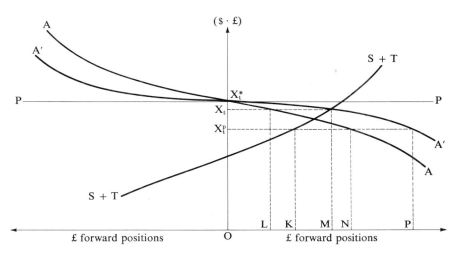

FIG. 18.4. Swaps and triangular arbitrage.

This pegged rate is the floor for the market rate since, at the price, interest arbitragers are indifferent to whether they buy their forward contracts from the central bank or in the free market.

In equilibrium at X_t^p the following relationships hold. Total sterling forward contracts outstanding are OP, of which NP are triangular-arbitrage contracts held by the speculators. We presume OK to be greater than NP, so that speculators hold (OK − NP) in contracts with interest arbitragers. The quantity (OK − NP) subtracted from the total of sterling spot funds moved to New York ON is equal to the quantity of forward swaps consummated by the intervening agency. The important conclusion from this analysis is that NP triangular-arbitrage contracts are induced by the policy, which leads to the type of undesirable side effects discussed above. Thus swaps offer no advantage over direct pegging under these and similar circumstances.

The most general conclusion to be drawn from this analysis of the influence of triangular arbitrage on the effectiveness of forward-exchange policy is that triangular arbitrage is a force tending to complicate the administration of given policies by making it nearly impossible to effect capital flows between two countries only. Above all it increases the necessity for international multilateral coordination of forward-exchange policies, and under certain circumstances calls for the use of special techniques of market entry. The need for multi-lateral agreements is of a rather special nature. Ad hoc negotiations are usually slow and cumbersome when large numbers of countries are involved. Yet to be really effective, forward-exchange policy must be exercised promptly and in fine gradations, depending on local market developments. Therefore, unless international agreements can be reached and channels of communication institutionalized *in advance* of actual need, the usefulness of forward-exchange policy is likely to be limited.

Official Spot-Intervention Limits

Our analysis of the influence that the existence of official intervention points exerts on the basic model of forward exchange has produced several conclusions, some of which are important for forward-exchange policy.

First, when the spot rate is near the lower intervention point and the interest-rate differential favors the country with the relatively weak currency, then the relevant covered-arbitrage schedule is distorted and inelastic at small quantities. Under these conditions (and in the logically analogous situation for the spot rate at the upper inter-vention point) the quantity of funds that can be induced to move by forward-exchange policy is smaller than in the basic model.

Second, whenever the policy objective requires pegging of the forward rate and entering contracts with speculators and traders, the greater elasticity of the S + T schedule around the intervention points is likely to lead to larger forward commitments than under the simple case.

Clearly these implications are quantitative rather than qualitative. Any recommendations based on either implication require empirical estimates of elasticities that are hard to measure. In the real world, however, officials responsible for forward-exchange policies are likely to have some idea of the size of relevant parameters of the functions serving as the basis for their decisions.

There is one more dimension policymakers can examine in deter-mining appropriate policies for a given objective—the maturity of the forward contracts they select as their entry into the market. This choice is examined here because it may carry the means for solution of some of the problems associated with the existence of official inter-vention points.

We know from the analysis in Chapter 8 that the equilibrium condition for a forward rate of maturity T is

$$X_T^* = \left(ID\,\frac{T}{360}\,X_0\right) + X_0$$

The difference between the spot and forward rates is therefore

$$X_0 - X_T^* = -\left(ID\,\frac{T}{360}\,X_0\right)$$

Assuming an equal annual interest-rate differential for 30- and 90-day maturities, we find the absolute difference between spot and 30-day forward rates to be one-fourth of that for the 90-day maturity. From this it follows that a spot rate at the official IMF points will yield a parity forward rate closer to this limit the shorter the maturity, and officials would do well to choose to intervene in maturities that require pegging at rates least subjected to the problems raised by the IMF points.

Another promising method of dealing with the difficulties arising from the existence of intervention points stems from the fact that the covered-arbitrage margin—the size of which determines the magnitude of the capital flows—is a function not only of the forward exchange rate but also of the spot rate and the domestic and foreign interest rates. Insofar as central banks are willing to influence the spot rate through purchases or sales of foreign exchange, they can achieve the desired arbitrage margin with a forward rate pegged away from the critical region. Often it may be convenient to adjust the interest rate *somewhat* in the direction that would restore the usefulness of forward-exchange policy. The interest-rate adjustment required for external stability is still likely to be smaller than it would have to be in the absence of forward-exchange policy.

To summarize, intervention points and confidence in their mainte-nance can be considered complicating factors in the administration of forward-exchange policy under certain circumstances, but they do not substantially reduce its overall usefulness if accompanied by approp-riate and complementary policies.

19. Forward-Exchange Policy: Summary and Conclusions

In the Preface to this book I mentioned that my interest in the study of the forward-exchange markets was aroused by the alleged usefulness of forward-exchange policy as an instrument for the control of international short-term capital flows. Now, after a lengthy and often intricate theoretical analysis, and an examination of large volumes of data, it is appropriate that I close the study by returning to the question of forward-exchange policy, and that I present my own judgment on its usefulness in the real world.

I shall not begin this last look by repeating all the qualifications and limitations of the model of the forward-exchange market set out in great detail in the previous eighteen chapters, but clearly the generalizations I shall make must be considered in the context of the entire book. Really serious students of the subject, reading this summary in isolation, could in fact be expected to consider my remarks frivolous and irresponsible.

With these caveats in mind I am willing to argue that forward-exchange policy is a potent and useful tool in the preserve of officials responsible for orderly functioning of the international monetary system. Exercising the policy can reverse or neutralize short-term capital flows by creating profitable investment opportunities—free of exchange risk to the asset holder—that produce counterflows of direction and magnitude dictated by policy objectives of the moment. In principle, the exercise of the policy is discreet, quick, and immediately effective. The policy can be applied in large or small doses, and can be reversed or eliminated, without great difficulty. Because of these attributes it is vastly superior to the unwieldy direct control of capital movements, and also to changes in the discount rate, which may be undesirable from the point of view of domestic price and employment objectives.

Our analysis has distinguished two situations in which forward-exchange policy can be applied. In the first, the covered interest-rate differential is very close to zero, whereas there may or may not be a yield differential on uncovered assets. As I have argued, such "normal" conditions tend to prevail when a revaluation of the currency is not expected. The sets of information required for carrying out forward-exchange policy under these conditions are clearly identified by our model—that the model does so must be considered one of its attractions. The sets of information thus identified are the elasticities of the forward-exchange demand-and-supply-schedules for interest arbitragers, triangular arbitragers in forward exchange, speculators, and traders. Obviously, the analytical functions cannot be observed directly in the real world, and much of the skill of foreign-exchange dealers consists of piecing together bits of evidence in deriving a useful estimate of the relevant parameters. The difficulties surrounding the fitting of clues and the making of right decisions at the actual trading desk of central banks should not be underestimated, though the flexibility of the tool itself leaves room for error and experimentation without serious consequence.

If the trend toward perfection of the forward-exchange markets and toward integration of international money markets continues, the interest elasticity of covered-arbitrage funds may well become very high, so that even small changes in interest-rate differentials will lead to very large shifts of funds—shifts so large relative to the other balance-of-payments components as to be felt distinctly disturbing. At such a time it will be necessary either to harmonize interest-rate policies more effectively, or, alternatively, to use forward-exchange policy more aggressively, in order to mitigate these influences.

The second set of conditions under which forward-exchange policy is useful is characterized by expectations of a revaluation of the currency. I am in agreement with most other analysts in the view that forward-exchange policy used to combat speculation in forward exchange is desirable only when currency devaluation can in fact be avoided—that is, only when the government believes firmly that forces at work in the economy are strong enough or the support provided by other countries or international organizations sufficient to permit the maintenance of the exchange rate that has come under attack. As I have argued, the financial and real losses accruing from a pegged forward rate and subsequent devaluation may be staggering. One sympathizes with the decision-maker in his agony in having to assess the world about him and having then to make up his mind whether devaluation is necessary or not. It does not ease his agony to realize that the implementation of forward-exchange policy may make it possible to conclude a critical time period with a reasonable rather than an untenably low level of international reserves, thus influencing the probability of devaluation itself.

The lesson to be drawn from this analysis is that in speculative situations forward-exchange policy should be exercised only in clear-cut cases of temporary, reversing, balance-of-payments disequilibria. The act of intervention can be a useful and powerful signal to speculators that the government is able and willing to take them on and practically to guarantee the maintenance of the exchange rate. In doubtful situations, when the government itself is uncertain about its ability to weather the exchange and balance-of-payments crisis without devaluation, the decision-maker is well advised to forego the immediate benefits of forward-exchange policy.

The analysis in this book has produced clarifications of several issues directly relevant to the administration of forward-exchange policy. The first is that the concern for the "proper" interest-rate differential in computing the covered-arbitrage margin is largely misplaced. The interest-rate differential on a pair of securities, one domestic and one foreign, with equal maturity and default risk is likely to be equal to or only negligibly different from the differentials on other pairs of domestic and foreign securities having equal maturities and default risks. The comparison of such "equivalent" pairs is relevant for investors and serves as a basis for their calculation of the covered-arbitrage margin. For practical purposes it is therefore irrelevant which pair of equivalent securities serves as the policy guideline for the intervening agency.

Second, we showed in our analysis that arbitragers who operate on forward exchange alone (a group that has been largely neglected in previous studies of the forward-exchange markets) are an important factor complicating the administration of forward-exchange policy. If official intervention occurs in only one currency, well-functioning triangular arbitrage will tend to change covered-arbitrage margins with respect to all other money markets for which forward-exchange trading exists. In the process, third markets are likely to be disturbed, and capital flows of undesired nature and magnitude are likely to take place. Forward-exchange pegging may alternatively be undertaken in all of the important currencies. This procedure, although avoiding third-market effects, is much more difficult to administer than pegging a single currency, and may involve lengthy negotiations with numerous countries. In general, the existence of effective triangular arbitrage in forward exchange tends to wipe out the opportunity to influence capital flows between just two countries, except under one condition I shall discuss shortly.

The third area in which our analysis has clarified issues important for forward-exchange policy is the method of market entry. Pegging and the offer of swaps sometimes fail to produce equal capital flows, and under one set of circumstances may in fact induce only bilateral capital flows. The latter possibility arises when a country initially attracts a certain quantity of foreign investments because it has the interest advantage, so that speculators and traders are willing to sell forward exchange at the prices necessary to affect the shift of funds. Because of the relative attractiveness of the center the normal market forces do not induce domestic asset holders to move their funds abroad. However, swap offers at attractive rates can cause these investors to shift funds abroad, funds flowing actually *against* the market-directed stream. Swaps can, in effect, tap a segmented part of the market, and their influence on prices in the free market is negligible. Because swap operations can exclude speculators from obtaining the rate offered by the intervening agency, whereas pegging operations cannot, the former may well become the favorite official method of market entry. Our analysis in the text shows, however, that under many plausible circumstances the exclusion of speculators from the market is only apparent, and that in these circumstances swaps are equivalent to pegging in every relevant sense.

The analysis of the preceding chapters has served also to point up the availability and usefulness of an added dimension of forward-exchange policy—intervention in different maturities. By choosing appropriate maturities for forward contracts it is possible not only to attract funds for shorter or longer periods, or to exploit favorable demand or supply elasticities, but also to avoid the problem otherwise brought on when given interest-rate differentials and the spot rate require that the forward rate be pegged outside the official intervention points. However, taking full advantage of the flexibility afforded by operating in more than one maturity presupposes a clear understanding of the maturity structure of forward rates and the maturity structure of interest rates in different countries. In my judgment, such an understanding has not yet been reached, and in fact cannot be, without further research.

Finally, I would like to draw attention to the importance of the kind of cost/benefit analysis presented in Chapter 16. Such an analysis is necessary before a rational decision on the usefulness of forward-exchange policy in a given situation can be arrived at. It is well to distinguish in such calculations between true social costs and benefits, on the one hand, and such costs and profits as are merely transfer payments, on the other. There is no question that many consequences of forward-exchange policy are nowhere reflected in the books of the intervening agency, and may in fact be impossible to trace by any means. Yet, certain other costs or profits are likely to show very distinctly on the books of the institution carrying out the forward-exchange policy. Although it is tempting to try to balance the account books, such motives tend to leave the social accounts unbalanced, most often to the detriment of the economy. Official exchange-market managers should pursue forward-exchange policy that maximizes social welfare and not the profits of the central bank or treasury.

Appendixes

Statistical Appendix A

Weekly Exchange Rates: July 4, 1955, to June 12, 1961

This appendix lists weekly spot and three-month forward exchange rates for eight exchange markets. All rates are expressed as the number of domestic-currency units required to purchase one unit of the foreign currency, except for the £ · C$ and £ · F rates, which are presented in terms of the number of foreign-currency units required to purchase one domestic unit.

All quoted rates were obtained by computing a simple mean of daily observations for each week. More specifically, the daily Frankfurt rates, taken from the internal books of the Dresdener Bank, Frankfurt am Main, are midpoints between buying and selling rates; the basic London rates, drawn from *Samuel Montagu's Review of Foreign Exchanges*, London, are midpoints of daily ranges; and the New York rates, taken from the internal books of the Morgan Guaranty Trust Company, New York, are opening-day buying rates.

The very extensive daily recordings on which the weekly exchange-rate data reproduced here are based are stored on a magnetic tape that can be duplicated and will be made available at cost to anyone writing to the author.

DATE	UK L	– FFR	UK L	– CAN $	US $	– UK L	US $	– CAN $
YR M DAY	SPOT	3-M FORW	SPOT	3-M FORW	SPOT	3-M FORW	SPOT	3-M FORW
55 −7 −4	9.7518	9.7318	2.7441	2.7585	2.7848	2.7717	1.0152	1.0155
55 −7-11	9.7441	9.7241	2.7420	2.7584	2.7844	2.7699	1.0151	1.0156
55 −7-18	9.7315	9.7215	2.7384	2.7577	2.7844	2.7654	1.0162	1.0167
55 −7-25	9.7359	9.7301	2.7424	2.7619	2.7882	2.7691	1.0166	1.0168
55 −8 −1	9.7366	9.7366	2.7436	2.7615	2.7888	2.7711	1.0166	1.0168
55 −8 −8	9.7368	9.7384	2.7450	2.7602	2.7874	2.7727	1.0156	1.0159
55 −8-15	9.7311	9.7361	2.7465	2.7615	2.7867	2.7729	1.0144	1.0149
55 −8-22	9.7302	9.7375	2.7468	2.7621	2.7867	2.7724	1.0144	1.0149
55 −8-29	9.7294	9.7435	2.7453	2.7563	2.7854	2.7704	1.0146	1.0149
55 −9 −6	9.7297	9.7447	2.7475	2.7650	2.7854	2.7682	1.0137	1.0140
55 −9-12	9.7321	9.7454	2.7511	2.7668	2.7859	2.7707	1.0125	1.0126
55 −9-19	9.7598	9.7598	2.7527	2.7659	2.7866	2.7735	1.0122	1.0122
55 −9-26	9.7757	9.7757	2.7572	2.7694	2.7877	2.7759	1.0111	1.0111
55−10 −3	9.8125	9.8125	2.7626	2.7740	2.7889	2.7772	1.0099	1.0099
55−10-10	9.8310	9.8310	2.7730	2.7832	2.7913	2.7813	1.0072	1.0071
55−10-17	9.8187	9.8187	2.7872	2.7986	2.7921	2.7810	1.0020	1.0020
55−10-24	9.8279	9.8329	2.7900	2.8036	2.7957	2.7821	1.0020	1.0020
55−10-31	9.8301	9.8401	2.7951	2.8081	2.8004	2.7876	1.0026	1.0026
55−11 −7	9.8263	9.8355	2.8002	2.8140	2.8028	2.7888	1.0010	1.0010
55−11-14	9.8177	9.8235	2.8021	2.8152	2.8026	2.7896	1.0002	1.0002
55−11-21	9.8147	9.8247	2.8016	2.8126	2.8021	2.7904	1.0002	0.9998
55−11-28	9.8155	9.8255	2.8025	2.8130	2.8022	2.7903	0.9997	0.9994
55−12 −5	9.8235	9.8335	2.8004	2.8113	2.8021	2.7905	1.0005	1.0000
55−12-12	9.8324	9.8424	2.8015	2.8118	2.8043	2.7931	1.0008	1.0005
55−12-19	9.8246	9.8346	2.8008	2.8112	2.8031	2.7918	1.0007	1.0004
55−12-27	9.8369	9.8469	2.8016	2.8094	2.8037	2.7927	1.0009	1.0007
56 −1 −3	9.8430	9.8530	2.8021	2.8124	2.8051	2.7941	1.0008	1.0005
56 −1 −9	9.8471	9.8504	2.8032	2.8126	2.8075	2.7976	1.0014	1.0012
56 −1-16	9.8516	9.8516	2.8037	2.8129	2.8084	2.7980	1.0015	1.0010
56 −1-23	9.8498	9.8498	2.8033	2.8121	2.8076	2.7966	1.0015	1.0010
56 −1-30	9.8361	9.8361	2.8037	2.8135	2.8072	2.7954	1.0011	1.0008
56 −2 −6	9.8299	9.8299	2.8035	2.8150	2.8066	2.7941	1.0011	1.0008
56 −2-14	9.8257	9.8307	2.8034	2.8180	2.8058	2.7906	1.0006	1.0003
56 −2-20	9.8281	9.8398	2.8049	2.8218	2.8077	2.7905	1.0007	1.0004
56 −2-27	9.8297	9.8472	2.8051	2.8215	2.8085	2.7915	1.0010	1.0009
56 −3 −5	9.8306	9.8506	2.7996	2.8170	2.8044	2.7863	1.0015	1.0013
56 −3-12	9.8404	9.8604	2.8012	2.8197	2.8059	2.7869	1.0015	1.0012
56 −3-19	9.8456	9.8690	2.8015	2.8194	2.8061	2.7873	1.0014	1.0010
56 −3-26	9.8422	9.8672	2.8010	2.8197	2.8048	2.7845	1.0013	1.0008
56 −4 −2	9.8465	9.8715	2.8021	2.8210	2.8063	2.7866	1.0015	1.0010
56 −4 −9	9.8509	9.8759	2.8019	2.8199	2.8082	2.7892	1.0023	1.0017
56 −4-16	9.8531	9.8781	2.8016	2.8174	2.8097	2.7926	1.0027	1.0021
56 −4-23	9.8521	9.8771	2.7917	2.8054	2.8084	2.7916	1.0060	1.0050
56 −4-30	9.8524	9.8774	2.7929	2.8063	2.8079	2.7909	1.0055	1.0045
56 −5 −7	9.8533	9.8783	2.7895	2.8030	2.8111	2.7952	1.0070	1.0060

DATE	DM – UK L		DM – US $		DM – FFR		DM – CAN $	
YR M DAY	SPOT	3-M FORW	SPOT	3-M FORW	SPOT	3-M FORW	SPOT	3-M FORW
55 -7 -4	11.6857	11.6768	4.2136	4.2205	1.1984	1.1940	4.2776	4.2833
55 -7 -11	11.6817	11.6613	4.2136	4.2205	1.1989	1.1932	4.2773	4.2830
55 -7 -18	11.6765	11.6422	4.2138	4.2205	1.2002	1.1933	4.2834	4.2858
55 -7 -25	11.6987	11.6472	4.2142	4.2205	1.2017	1.1945	4.2833	4.2888
55 -8 -1	11.7033	11.6502	4.2142	4.2205	1.2024	1.1957	4.2826	4.2880
55 -8 -8	11.6940	11.6517	4.2143	4.2205	1.2012	1.1960	4.2802	4.2865
55 -8-15	11.6862	11.6400	4.2146	4.2205	1.2015	1.1960	4.2772	4.2840
55 -8-22	11.6918	11.6345	4.2148	4.2205	1.2018	1.1964	4.2758	4.2833
55 -8-29	11.6878	11.6240	4.2146	4.2205	1.2015	1.1963	4.2762	4.2842
55 -9 -6	11.6795	11.6033	4.2148	4.2205	1.2006	1.1956	4.2730	4.2828
55 -9-12	11.6807	11.5907	4.2150	4.2210	1.2004	1.1938	4.2687	4.2787
55 -9-19	11.7095	11.6425	4.2151	4.2210	1.1997	1.1937	4.2659	4.2750
55 -9-26	11.7137	11.6510	4.2151	4.2203	1.1984	1.1931	4.2608	4.2708
55-10 -3	11.7255	11.6637	4.2151	4.2200	1.1952	1.1895	4.2559	4.2643
55-10-10	11.7220	11.6612	4.2151	4.2185	1.1928	1.1857	4.2436	4.2537
55-10-17	11.7208	11.6560	4.2152	4.2175	1.1938	1.1873	4.2234	4.2342
55-10-24	11.7260	11.6653	4.2152	4.2175	1.1931	1.1877	4.2237	4.2313
55-10-31	11.7305	11.6638	4.2152	4.2168	1.1935	1.1980	4.2233	4.2346
55-11 -7	11.7367	11.6692	4.2152	4.2165	1.1946	1.1888	4.2196	4.2297
55-11-14	11.7484	11.6782	4.2152	4.2165	1.1967	1.1902	4.2161	4.2260
55-11-21	11.7543	11.6832	4.2152	4.2165	1.1978	1.1915	4.2151	4.2238
55-11-28	11.7580	11.6933	4.2152	4.2165	1.1978	1.1923	4.2147	4.2240
55-12 -5	11.7480	11.6955	4.2153	4.2165	1.1960	1.1907	4.2170	4.2257
55-12-12	11.7415	11.6940	4.2153	4.2165	1.1944	1.1895	4.2180	4.2270
55-12-19	11.7308	11.6864	4.2154	4.2165	1.1943	1.1916	4.2188	4.2300
55-12-27	11.7178	11.6848	4.2153	4.2172	1.1915	1.1877	4.2189	4.2300
56 -1 -3	11.7298	11.6907	4.2152	4.2162	1.1916	1.1885	4.2200	4.2300
56 -1 -9	11.7275	11.6917	4.2152	4.2160	1.1911	1.1885	4.2221	4.2317
56 -1-16	11.7358	11.6933	4.2153	4.2160	1.1913	1.1875	4.2219	4.2310
56 -1-23	11.7337	11.6910	4.2154	4.2163	1.1913	1.1875	4.2218	4.2310
56 -1-30	11.7307	11.6873	4.2156	4.2173	1.1924	1.1885	4.2202	4.2302
56 -2 -6	11.7255	11.6847	4.2157	4.2185	1.1924	1.1887	4.2201	4.2300
56 -2-14	11.7162	11.6780	4.2157	4.2185	1.1922	1.1885	4.2185	4.2290
56 -2-20	11.7215	11.6748	4.2157	4.2185	1.1926	1.1885	4.2195	4.2270
56 -2-27	11.7217	11.6690	4.2159	4.2190	1.1925	1.1885	4.2205	4.2270
56 -3 -5	11.7125	11.6703	4.2160	4.2193	1.1915	1.1885	4.2225	4.2270
56 -3-12	11.7218	11.6700	4.2160	4.2195	1.1912	1.1885	4.2225	4.2255
56 -3-19	11.7268	11.6662	4.2160	4.2195	1.1912	1.1885	4.2217	4.2240
56 -3-26	11.7240	11.6625	4.2160	4.2195	1.1911	1.1885	4.2221	4.2260
56 -4 -2	11.7280	11.6640	4.2161	4.2199	1.1911	1.1885	4.2225	4.2260
56 -4 -9	11.7342	11.6747	4.2154	4.2181	1.1912	1.1885	4.2249	4.2260
56 -4-16	11.7408	11.6775	4.2155	4.2170	1.1916	1.1885	4.2279	4.2263
56 -4-23	11.7375	11.6725	4.2150	4.2167	1.1914	1.1885	4.2395	4.2353
56 -4-30	11.7356	11.6830	4.2148	4.2165	1.1911	1.1885	4.2366	4.2350
56 -5 -7	11.7366	11.6940	4.2139	4.2162	1.1911	1.1885	4.2424	4.2404

DATE	UK L − FFR		UK L − CAN $		US $ − UK L		US $ − CAN $	
YR M DAY	SPOT	3−M FORW	SPOT	3−M FORW	SPOT	3−M FORW	SPOT	3−M FORW
56 −5−14	9.8537	9.8771	2.7851	2.7974	2.8090	2.7942	1.0077	1.0067
56 −5−21	9.8420	9.8620	2.7795	2.7914	2.8075	2.7928	1.0097	1.0089
56 −5−28	9.8333	9.8533	2.7742	2.7837	2.8046	2.7904	1.0108	1.0094
56 −6 −4	9.8199	9.8399	2.7716	2.7815	2.8029	2.7877	1.0149	1.0131
56 −6−11	9.8159	9.8359	2.7642	2.7742	2.8053	2.7899	1.0147	1.0127
56 −6−18	9.8137	9.8337	2.7588	2.7693	2.8044	2.7887	1.0164	1.0143
56 −6−25	9.8034	9.8234	2.7460	2.7543	2.7984	2.7836	1.0188	1.0164
56 −7 −2	9.7974	9.8107	2.7420	2.7507	2.7963	2.7807	1.0198	1.0177
56 −7 −9	9.8044	9.7910	2.7450	2.7537	2.7956	2.7805	1.0189	1.0165
56 −7−16	9.8031	9.7598	2.7455	2.7535	2.7966	2.7814	1.0186	1.0159
56 −7−23	9.8033	9.7333	2.7411	2.7478	2.7916	2.7766	1.0184	1.0156
56 −7−30	9.8026	9.7226	2.7348	2.7425	2.7839	2.7687	1.0165	1.0146
56 −8 −6	9.8174	9.7264	2.7331	2.7417	2.7834	2.7673	1.0176	1.0147
56 −8−13	9.8173	9.7090	2.7272	2.7352	2.7831	2.7681	1.0203	1.0178
56 −8−20	9.8060	9.7144	2.7285	2.7350	2.7839	2.7708	1.0204	1.0179
56 −8−27	9.8042	9.7258	2.73( )	2.7355	2.7834	2.7705	1.0192	1.0166
56 −9 −4	9.8095	9.7561	2.7261	2.7321	2.7832	2.7682	1.0205	1.0178
56 −9−10	9.8115	9.7882	2.7188	2.7250	2.7834	2.7667	1.0235	1.0202
56 −9−17	9.8177	9.8060	2.7180	2.7250	2.7838	2.7668	1.0244	1.0208
56 −9−24	9.8265	9.7948	2.7194	2.7266	2.7836	2.7670	1.0230	1.0208
56−10 −1	9.8303	9.7753	2.7134	2.7188	2.7845	2.7681	1.0260	1.0222
56−10 −8	9.8262	9.7879	2.7143	2.7195	2.7841	2.7684	1.0260	1.0223
56−10−15	9.8305	9.7955	2.7135	2.7188	2.7859	2.7717	1.0266	1.0231
56−10−22	9.8324	9.7891	2.7091	2.7136	2.7856	2.7713	1.0275	1.0243
56−10−29	9.8140	9.7640	2.6974	2.7013	2.7836	2.7675	1.0305	1.0264
56−11 −5	9.8138	9.7588	2.6941	2.6992	2.7832	2.7686	1.0326	1.0288
56−11−13	9.8278	9.7753	2.6840	2.6903	2.7830	2.7669	1.0374	1.0343
56−11−19	9.8224	9.7724	2.6795	2.6877	2.7830	2.7633	1.0383	1.0344
56−11−26	9.8256	9.7823	2.6687	2.6830	2.7832	2.7557	1.0433	1.0396
56−12 −3	9.8304	9.7904	2.6774	2.6936	2.7833	2.7527	1.0390	1.0342
56−12−10	9.8378	9.7978	2.6752	2.6840	2.7855	2.7619	1.0406	1.0352
56−12−17	9.8290	9.7890	2.6724	2.6781	2.7859	2.7584	1.0423	1.0364
56−12−24	9.8320	9.7920	2.6736	2.6764	2.7862	2.7623	1.0429	1.0354
56−12−31	9.8396	9.7996	2.6767	2.677	2.7880	2.7677	1.0409	1.0336
57 −1 −7	9.8549	9.8199	2.6876	2.6879	2.7944	2.7789	1.0385	1.0331
57 −1−14	9.8612	9.8312	2.6880	2.6893	2.7977	2.7837	1.0407	1.0359
57 −1−21	9.8587	9.8287	2.6861	2.6853	2.7994	2.7884	1.0414	1.0370
57 −1−28	9.8608	9.8458	2.6834	2.6830	2.7986	2.7877	1.0429	1.0386
57 −2 −4	9.8515	9.8415	2.6812	2.6800	2.7993	2.7894	1.0436	1.0398
57 −2−11	9.8680	9.8605	2.6824	2.6811	2.7987	2.7894	1.0432	1.0391
57 −2−18	9.8679	9.8642	2.6812	2.6801	2.7984	2.7884	1.0435	1.0393
57 −2−25	9.8685	9.8577	2.6792	2.6759	2.7985	2.7894	1.0440	1.0394
57 −3 −4	9.8706	9.8452	2.6747	2.6697	2.7971	2.7895	1.0453	1.0401
57 −3−11	9.8676	9.8376	2.6722	2.6671	2.7956	2.7871	1.0459	1.0407
57 −3−18	9.8568	9.8043	2.6769	2.6737	2.7906	2.7781	1.0464	1.0415

DATE	DM – UK L		DM – US $		DM – FFR		DM – CAN $	
YR M DAY	SPOT	3-M FORW	SPOT	3-M FORW	SPOT	3-M FORW	SPOT	3-M FORW
56 -5-14	11.7374	11.6938	4.2119	4.2152	1.1911	1.1885	4.2475	4.2420
56 -5-21	11.7216	11.6888	4.2097	4.2138	1.1911	1.1885	4.2509	4.2458
56 -5-28	11.7120	11.6810	4.2059	4.2101	1.1912	1.1885	4.2506	4.2480
56 -6 -4	11.6958	11.6705	4.2012	4.2042	1.1911	1.1878	4.2487	4.2458
56 -6-11	11.6915	11.6590	4.2015	4.2060	1.1911	1.1875	4.2639	4.2552
56 -6-18	11.6883	11.6517	4.2007	4.2048	1.1910	1.1872	4.2694	4.2550
56 -6-25	11.6772	11.6363	4.1967	4.1987	1.1912	1.1861	4.2764	4.2630
56 -7 -2	11.6743	11.6327	4.1944	4.1960	1.1915	1.1860	4.2770	4.2657
56 -7 -9	11.6770	11.6295	4.1939	4.1940	1.1911	1.1837	4.2731	4.2662
56 -7-16	11.6760	11.6105	4.1919	4.1865	1.1911	1.1733	4.2702	4.2573
56 -7-23	11.6752	11.6075	4.1910	4.1810	1.1910	1.1710	4.2675	4.2580
56 -7-30	11.6758	11.6045	4.1910	4.1822	1.1911	1.1680	4.2662	4.2580
56 -8 -6	11.6938	11.6122	4.1910	4.1843	1.1912	1.1690	4.2587	4.2613
56 -8-13	11.6968	11.6118	4.1910	4.1857	1.1915	1.1671	4.2782	4.2637
56 -8-20	11.6812	11.6125	4.1910	4.1870	1.1912	1.1717	4.2752	4.2617
56 -8-27	11.6770	11.6145	4.1911	4.1900	1.1911	1.1745	4.2718	4.2650
56 -9 -4	11.6832	11.6158	4.1913	4.1950	1.1911	1.1770	4.2777	4.2667
56 -9-10	11.6862	11.6110	4.1913	4.1950	1.1911	1.1780	4.2917	4.2770
56 -9-17	11.6980	11.6140	4.1913	4.1950	1.1912	1.1767	4.2929	4.2827
56 -9-24	11.7058	11.6278	4.1921	4.1957	1.1911	1.1795	4.2904	4.2820
56-10 -1	11.7087	11.6415	4.1933	4.1970	1.1911	1.1795	4.3018	4.2902
56-10 -8	11.7025	11.6407	4.1930	4.194	1.1911	1.1795	4.3022	4.2935
56-10-15	11.7088	11.6538	4.1931	4.1940	1.1911	1.1795	4.3040	4.2950
56-10-22	11.7110	11.6667	4.1937	4.1940	1.1910	1.1785	4.3111	4.3002
56-10-29	11.6863	11.6302	4.1938	4.1943	1.1912	1.1782	4.3255	4.3158
56-11 -5	11.6888	11.6252	4.1947	4.1973	1.1911	1.1765	4.3329	4.3217
56-11-13	11.7070	11.6307	4.1950	4.1980	1.1911	1.1765	4.3516	4.3358
56-11-19	11.6996	11.6228	4.1959	4.2004	1.1911	1.1765	4.3592	4.3432
56-11-26	11.7042	11.6173	4.1962	4.2010	1.1912	1.1765	4.3762	4.3565
56-12 -3	11.7107	11.6082	4.1967	4.2027	1.1911	1.1762	4.3632	4.3550
56-12-10	11.7172	11.6317	4.1971	4.2030	1.1911	1.1745	4.3695	4.3575
56-12-17	11.7070	11.6277	4.1976	4.2043	1.1911	1.1745	4.3778	4.3633
56-12-24	11.7117	11.6530	4.1983	4.2060	1.1911	1.1745	4.3767	4.3650
56-12-31	11.7210	11.6332	4.1987	4.2048	1.1912	1.1745	4.3725	4.3638
57 -1 -7	11.7383	11.6565	4.1992	4.2040	1.1912	1.1752	4.3631	4.3530
57 -1-14	11.7497	11.6760	4.1999	4.2048	1.1914	1.1772	4.3718	4.3542
57 -1-21	11.7437	11.6818	4.2003	4.2050	1.1911	1.1772	4.3762	4.3588
57 -1-28	11.7450	11.6918	4.2009	4.2043	1.1911	1.1833	4.3813	4.3710
57 -2 -4	11.7518	11.7115	4.2012	4.2030	1.1911	1.1900	4.3853	4.3737
57 -2-11	11.7548	11.7127	4.2014	4.2030	1.1911	1.1900	4.3837	4.3777
57 -2-18	11.7522	11.7122	4.2016	4.2030	1.1911	1.1900	4.3842	4.3760
57 -2-25	11.7547	11.7182	4.2015	4.2020	1.1911	1.1895	4.3866	4.3767
57 -3 -4	11.7590	11.7218	4.2018	4.2020	1.1911	1.1897	4.3936	4.3813
57 -3-11	11.7538	11.7115	4.2020	4.2035	1.1911	1.1897	4.3955	4.3797
57 -3-18	11.7393	11.6795	4.2020	4.2050	1.1911	1.1842	4.3973	4.3780

DATE YR M DAY	UK L - FFR SPOT	3-M FORW	UK L - CAN $ SPOT	3-M FORW	US $ - UK L SPOT	3-M FORW	US $ - CAN $ SPOT	3-M FORW
57 -3-25	9.8631	9.7956	2.6766	2.6745	2.7910	2.7829	1.0466	1.0428
57 -4 -1	9.8644	9.8060	2.6744	2.6744	2.7878	2.7802	1.0423	1.0398
57 -4-15	9.8711	9.8073	2.6774	2.6787	2.7891	2.7812	1.0417	1.0394
57 -4-22	9.8712	9.7832	2.6771	2.6775	2.7905	2.7831	1.0420	1.0396
57 -4-29	9.8712	9.7512	2.6743	2.6743	2.7923	2.7843	1.0442	1.0417
57 -5 -6	9.8703	9.6961	2.6700	2.6704	2.7924	2.7838	1.0455	1.0427
57 -5-13	9.3571	9.6796	2.6652	2.6665	2.7900	2.7802	1.0467	1.0439
57 -5-20	9.8518	9.5393	2.6645	2.6654	2.7907	2.7808	1.0471	1.0441
57 -5-27	9.8498	9.5590	2.6628	2.6632	2.7914	2.7809	1.0485	1.0450
57 -6 -3	9.8493	9.6159	2.7897	2.7821	2.6592	2.6584	1.0486	1.0451
57 -6-10	9.8438	9.5787	2.6582	2.6571	2.7892	2.7806	1.0494	1.0457
57 -6-17	9.8320	9.5603	2.6607	2.6595	2.7924	2.7842	1.0494	1.0456
57 -6-24	9.8235	9.5119	2.6600	2.6599	2.7916	2.7831	1.0492	1.0468
57 -7 -1	9.8110	9.5760	2.6592	2.6602	2.7920	2.7830	1.0493	1.0470
57 -7 -8	9.8071	9.5071	2.6569	2.6586	2.7907	2.7822	1.0503	1.0465
57 -7-15	9.8044	9.4344	2.6502	2.6515	2.7879	2.7791	1.0517	1.0497
57 -7-22	9.8012	9.3421	2.6442	2.6458	2.7860	2.7762	1.0536	1.0512
57 -7-29	9.8019	9.2235	2.6406	2.6419	2.7846	2.7737	1.0543	1.0511
57 -8 -5	9.8056	9.1706	2.6390	2.6390	2.7837	2.7719	1.0546	1.0506
57 -8-13	11.6833	11.5283	2.6345	2.6398	2.7828	2.7634	1.0559	1.0514
57 -8-20	11.6751	11.6318	2.6292	2.6482	2.7842	2.7482	1.0593	1.0548
57 -8-26	11.6747	11.5897	2.6455	2.6726	2.7832	2.7611	1.0522	1.0479
57 -9 -3	11.6874	11.6649	2.6477	2.6598	2.7831	2.7509	1.0511	1.0467
57 -9-10	11.7469	11.7302	2.6663	2.6813	2.7831	2.7551	1.0489	1.0447
57 -9-16	11.7325	11.7325	2.6758	2.6975	2.7834	2.7453	1.0404	1.0366
57 -9-23	11.7612	11.7537	2.6867	2.7052	2.7902	2.7590	1.0389	1.0348
57 -9-30	11.7796	11.7512	2.7050	2.7229	2.7955	2.7632	1.0342	1.0294
57-10 -7	11.8260	11.8085	2.7134	2.7261	2.8007	2.7734	1.0336	1.0296
57-10-14	11.8285	11.8177	2.7106	2.7229	2.8019	2.7769	1.0361	1.0313
57-10-21	11.8343	11.7760	2.7106	2.7212	2.8011	2.7779	1.0385	1.0338
57-10-28	11.8410	11.6877	2.7038	2.7130	2.7989	2.7766	1.0424	1.0376
57-11 -4	11.8071	11.7087	2.6904	2.7025	2.7998	2.7760	1.0406	1.0371
57-11-12	11.8219	11.6935	2.6919	2.7061	2.8019	2.7791	1.0412	1.0384
57-11-18	11.8337	11.7079	2.6966	2.7111	2.8043	2.7813	1.0401	1.0377
57-11-25	11.8261	11.7095	2.7113	2.7249	2.8069	2.7844	1.0364	1.0336
57-12 -2	11.7919	11.7077	2.7218	2.7329	2.8074	2.7857	1.0313	1.0272
57-12 -9	11.7794	11.6877	2.7318	2.741	2.8056	2.7854	1.0272	1.0232
57-12-16	11.7485	11.6519	2.7532	2.7617	2.8058	2.7861	1.0202	1.0161
57-12-23	11.7384	11.6259	2.7612	2.7691	2.8047	2.7846	1.0164	1.0125
57-12-30	11.7610	11.6410	2.7699	2.7785	2.8094	2.7886	1.0144	1.0102
58 -1 -6	11.7671	11.6896	2.7806	2.7920	2.8114	2.7906	1.0110	1.0079
58 -1-13	11.7650	11.7167	2.7722	2.7862	2.8134	2.7919	1.0148	1.0122
58 -1-21	11.7733	11.7433	2.7642	2.7802	2.8152	2.7928	1.0182	1.0162
58 -1-27	11.7800	11.7633	2.7643	2.7797	2.8158	2.7932	1.0187	1.0163
58 -2 -3	11.8067	11.8008	2.7719	2.787	2.8171	2.7925	1.0160	1.0137

DATE	DM - UK L		DM - US $		DM - FFR		DM - CAN $	
YR M DAY	SPOT	3-M FORW	SPOT	3-M FORW	SPOT	3-M FORW	SPOT	3-M FORW
57 -3-25	11.7483	11.6870	4.2021	4.2050	1.1911	1.1816	4.3968	4.3795
57 -4 -1	11.7485	11.6855	4.2024	4.2054	1.1911	1.1820	4.3811	4.3703
57 -4-15	11.7575	11.6960	4.2024	4.2055	1.1911	1.1810	4.3762	4.3667
57 -4-22	11.7594	11.6952	4.2024	4.2054	1.1911	1.1784	4.3804	4.3724
57 -4-29	11.7596	11.6966	4.2019	4.2050	1.1911	1.1750	4.3884	4.3780
57 -5 -6	11.7570	11.6997	4.2016	4.2042	1.1911	1.1727	4.3940	4.3808
57 -5-13	11.7412	11.6962	4.2011	4.2028	1.1911	1.1703	4.3973	4.3823
57 -5-20	11.7333	11.6902	4.2010	4.2025	1.1910	1.1600	4.3997	4.3878
57 -5-27	11.7322	11.6568	4.2011	4.2025	1.1911	1.1485	4.4043	4.3922
57 -6 -3	11.7304	11.6852	4.2007	4.2025	1.1911	1.1575	4.4050	4.3888
57 -6-10	11.7194	11.6798	4.2006	4.2025	1.1911	1.1575	4.4089	4.3988
57 -6-17	11.7107	11.6725	4.2009	4.2025	1.1911	1.1506	4.4079	4.3987
57 -6-24	11.7018	11.6590	4.2009	4.2018	1.1911	1.1433	4.4088	4.3953
57 -7 -1	11.6862	11.6302	4.2010	4.1979	1.1911	1.1529	4.4091	4.3940
57 -7 -8	11.6793	11.6027	4.2010	4.1918	1.1911	1.1479	4.4119	4.3937
57 -7-15	11.6780	11.6147	4.2010	4.1904	1.1912	1.1450	4.4192	4.3980
57 -7-22	11.6737	11.6040	4.2009	4.1922	1.1910	1.1342	4.4252	4.4047
57 -7-29	11.6742	11.5830	4.2009	4.1864	1.1911	1.1157	4.4286	4.4060
57 -8 -5	11.6790	11.5473	4.2008	4.1768	1.1911	1.1080	4.4293	4.3975
57 -8-13	11.6728	11.4513	4.2007	4.1578	0.9989	0.6325	4.4388	4.3833
57 -8-20	11.6733	11.3483	4.2007	4.1598	1.0000	0.9125	4.4487	4.3850
57 -8-26	11.6722	11.4223	4.2009	4.180	0.9999	0.9529	4.4189	4.3885
57 -9 -3	11.6723	11.3683	4.2011	4.1633	0.9985	0.9550	4.4148	4.3683
57 -9-10	11.6720	11.3757	4.2011	4.1722	0.9937	0.9550	4.3872	4.3538
57 -9-16	11.6733	11.3650	4.2011	4.1783	0.9947	0.9550	4.3698	4.3425
57 -9-23	11.7097	11.4790	4.2011	4.1810	0.9967	0.9570	4.3628	4.3442
57 -9-30	11.7202	11.5158	4.2011	4.1835	0.9950	0.9630	4.3425	4.3298
57-10 -7	11.7540	11.5767	4.2011	4.1915	0.9938	0.9643	4.3360	4.3170
57-10-14	11.7703	11.5950	4.2011	4.1950	0.9953	0.9653	4.3535	4.3242
57-10-21	11.7817	11.5958	4.2011	4.1950	0.9955	0.9665	4.3645	4.3322
57-10-28	11.7727	11.6190	4.2011	4.1950	0.9944	0.9643	4.3797	4.3483
57-11 -4	11.7722	11.6228	4.2011	4.1987	0.9967	0.9640	4.3722	4.3485
57-11-12	11.7767	11.6602	4.2012	4.2030	0.9959	0.9602	4.3733	4.3545
57-11-18	11.7726	11.6552	4.2014	4.2030	0.9947	0.9570	4.3682	4.3514
57-11-25	11.7672	11.6517	4.2015	4.2030	0.9947	0.9570	4.3487	4.3372
57-12 -2	11.7668	11.6522	4.2016	4.2030	0.9975	0.9608	4.3324	4.3240
57-12 -9	11.7692	11.6547	4.2016	4.2030	0.9988	0.9623	4.3154	4.3077
57-12-16	11.7668	11.6700	4.2017	4.2030	1.0013	0.9650	4.2819	4.2757
57-12-23	11.7523	11.6593	4.2017	4.2030	1.0018	0.9650	4.2672	4.2550
57-12-30	11.7600	11.6592	4.2017	4.2030	0.9995	0.9650	4.2603	4.2442
58 -1 -6	11.7738	11.6643	4.2017	4.2030	1.0005	0.9685	4.2470	4.2285
58 -1-13	11.7780	11.6730	4.2018	4.2030	1.0015	0.9717	4.2648	4.2403
58 -1-21	11.7755	11.6768	4.2020	4.2030	1.0003	0.9750	4.2794	4.2665
58 -1-27	11.7743	11.6750	4.2021	4.2030	0.9994	0.9750	4.2803	4.2737
58 -2 -3	11.7742	11.6797	4.2021	4.2017	0.9970	0.9783	4.2699	4.2590

DATE	UK L - FFR		UK L - CAN $		US $ - UK L		US $ - CAN $	
YR M DAY	SPOT	3-M FORW	SPOT	3-M FORW	SPOT	3-M FORW	SPOT	3-M FORW
58 -2-10	11.8042	11.7942	2.7626	2.7797	2.8179	2.7925	1.0196	1.0167
58 -2-17	11.8007	11.7907	2.7602	2.7782	2.8176	2.7929	1.0213	1.0192
58 -2-24	11.8031	11.7931	2.7548	2.7720	2.8133	2.7883	1.0213	1.0187
58 -3 -3	11.8208	11.8108	2.7560	2.7748	2.8152	2.7879	1.0213	1.0187
58 -3-10	11.8272	11.8172	2.7517	2.7707	2.8164	2.7897	1.0234	1.0208
58 -3-17	11.8258	11.8108	2.7491	2.7678	2.8158	2.7907	1.0242	1.0220
58 -3-24	11.8149	11.7832	2.7485	2.7670	2.8162	2.7907	1.0244	1.0222
58 -3-31	11.8212	11.8032	2.7420	2.7636	2.8166	2.7887	1.0276	1.0261
58 -4 -7	11.8222	11.8032	2.7340	2.7569	2.8177	2.7907	1.0307	1.0294
58 -4-14	11.8144	11.7527	2.7342	2.7578	2.8186	2.7911	1.0312	1.0305
58 -4-21	11.7986	11.6570	2.7315	2.7549	2.8168	2.7905	1.0312	1.0303
58 -4-28	11.7817	11.6017	2.7306	2.7538	2.8177	2.7916	1.0317	1.0308
58 -5 -5	11.7906	11.6273	2.7229	2.7425	2.8134	2.7889	1.0335	1.0322
58 -5-12	11.8004	11.5754	2.7241	2.7425	2.8161	2.7919	1.0338	1.0317
58 -5-19	11.8002	11.4494	2.7227	2.7398	2.8169	2.7934	1.0346	1.0327
58 -5-26	11.7925	11.4225	2.7162	2.7337	2.8168	2.7941	1.0361	1.0345
58 -6 -2	11.7903	11.5936	2.7105	2.7274	2.8164	2.7950	1.0388	1.0375
58 -6 -9	11.7767	11.5483	2.7084	2.7249	2.8154	2.7941	1.0393	1.0381
58 -6-16	11.7525	11.5842	2.7060	2.7221	2.8117	2.7913	1.0390	1.0378
58 -6-23	11.7552	11.6069	2.6913	2.7073	2.8055	2.7862	1.0418	1.0404
58 -6-30	11.7408	11.6017	2.6917	2.7068	2.8046	2.7849	1.0426	1.0412
58 -7 -7	11.7373	11.6106	2.6938	2.7070	2.8062	2.7884	1.0422	1.0409
58 -7-14	11.7354	11.6071	2.6879	2.7031	2.8019	2.7823	1.0425	1.0419
58 -7-21	11.7419	11.6135	2.6908	2.7084	2.8045	2.7849	1.0423	1.0422
58 -7-28	11.7444	11.6352	2.6957	2.7122	2.8056	2.7869	1.0410	1.0405
58 -8 -4	11.7437	11.6487	2.6985	2.7136	2.8077	2.7902	1.0403	1.0400
58 -8-11	11.7326	11.6343	2.6981	2.7088	2.8058	2.7929	1.0421	1.0415
58 -8-18	11.7302	11.6302	2.7074	2.7147	2.8064	2.7971	1.0373	1.0369
58 -8-25	11.7218	11.6268	2.7218	2.7286	2.8032	2.7940	1.0304	1.0298
58 -9 -2	11.7321	11.6121	2.7306	2.7374	2.8012	2.7936	1.0256	1.0255
58 -9 -8	11.7457	11.6257	2.7418	2.7490	2.8022	2.7947	1.0210	1.0210
58 -9-15	11.7543	11.6609	2.7371	2.7434	2.8041	2.7988	1.0231	1.0234
58 -9-22	11.7516	11.6541	2.7353	2.7427	2.8064	2.8011	1.0262	1.0270
58 -9-29	11.7592	11.6650	2.7381	2.7447	2.8076	2.8034	1.0251	1.0263
58-10 -6	11.7650	11.6750	2.7290	2.7363	2.8077	2.8036	1.0290	1.0303
58-10-14	11.7646	11.6829	2.7223	2.7305	2.8078	2.8035	1.0313	1.0328
58-10-20	11.7657	11.6757	2.7201	2.7283	2.8075	2.8026	1.0325	1.0336
58-10-27	11.7619	11.6452	2.7203	2.7274	2.8068	2.8005	1.0315	1.0319
58-11 -3	11.7765	11.6448	2.7206	2.7274	2.8073	2.8006	1.0318	1.0318
58-11-10	11.7866	11.6291	2.7212	2.7275	2.8065	2.7998	1.0314	1.0314
58-11-17	11.7885	11.4935	2.7143	2.7191	2.8063	2.8018	1.0334	1.0336
58-11-24	11.7746	11.4304	2.7113	2.7152	2.8052	2.8021	1.0342	1.0348
58-12 -1	11.7777	11.4435	2.7082	2.7107	2.8039	2.8017	1.0352	1.0354
58-12 -8	11.7740	11.3373	2.7036	2.7052	2.8041	2.8029	1.0372	1.0375
58-12-15	11.7698	11.1340	2.7052	2.7034	2.8059	2.8056	1.0372	1.0367

DATE	DM - UK L		DM - US $		DM - FFR		DM - CAN $	
YR M DAY	SPOT	3-M FORW	SPOT	3-M FORW	SPOT	3-M FORW	SPOT	3-M FORW
58 -2-10	11.7762	11.6935	4.2020	4.2030	0.9977	0.9900	4.2857	4.2701
58 -2-17	11.7738	11.6905	4.2020	4.2030	0.9978	0.9900	4.2910	4.2875
58 -2-24	11.7698	11.6845	4.2020	4.2030	0.9973	0.9900	4.2906	4.2825
58 -3 -3	11.7693	11.6852	4.2020	4.2030	0.9958	0.9880	4.2912	4.2800
58 -3-10	11.7683	11.6772	4.2015	4.2030	0.9950	0.9870	4.2992	4.2860
58 -3-17	11.7557	11.6720	4.2018	4.2030	0.9940	0.9867	4.3036	4.2900
58 -3-24	11.7427	11.6662	4.2010	4.2030	0.9939	0.9852	4.3037	4.2907
58 -3-31	11.7472	11.6680	4.2006	4.2030	0.9941	0.9850	4.3120	4.2985
58 -4 -7	11.7438	11.6648	4.2007	4.2030	0.9934	0.9850	4.3285	4.3190
58 -4-14	11.7355	11.6590	4.1999	4.2025	0.9933	0.9833	4.3299	4.3255
58 -4-21	11.7250	11.6503	4.1976	4.2012	0.9937	0.9762	4.3279	4.3247
58 -4-28	11.7198	11.6458	4.1920	4.1982	0.9945	0.9760	4.3256	4.3226
58 -5 -5	11.7082	11.6413	4.1916	4.1990	0.9931	0.9757	4.3308	4.3323
58 -5-12	11.7138	11.6500	4.1890	4.1968	0.9926	0.9680	4.3306	4.3322
58 -5-19	11.7122	11.6514	4.1888	4.1970	0.9926	0.9540	4.3344	4.3360
58 -5-26	11.7050	11.6448	4.1886	4.1970	0.9926	0.9480	4.3420	4.3430
58 -6 -2	11.7060	11.6488	4.1902	4.1966	0.9928	0.9636	4.3510	4.3538
58 -6 -9	11.7052	11.6565	4.1929	4.1992	0.9940	0.9647	4.3565	4.3590
58 -6-16	11.7004	11.6582	4.1911	4.1990	0.9955	0.9686	4.3542	4.3600
58 -6-23	11.6810	11.6515	4.1892	4.1974	0.9937	0.9700	4.3603	4.3664
58 -6-30	11.6795	11.6512	4.1892	4.1983	0.9948	0.9705	4.3664	4.3712
58 -7 -7	11.6808	11.6497	4.1907	4.1992	0.9951	0.9715	4.3652	4.3697
58 -7-14	11.6745	11.6325	4.1910	4.1998	0.9950	0.9720	4.3693	4.3745
58 -7-21	11.6733	11.6413	4.1899	4.1987	0.9942	0.9720	4.3664	4.3715
58 -7-28	11.6763	11.6430	4.1895	4.1962	0.9943	0.9720	4.3602	4.3645
58 -8 -4	11.6847	11.6498	4.1897	4.1967	0.9950	0.9735	4.3596	4.3650
58 -8-11	11.6872	11.6545	4.1897	4.1943	0.9962	0.9815	4.3561	4.3593
58 -8-18	11.6953	11.6652	4.1895	4.1930	0.9970	0.9855	4.3428	4.3455
58 -8-25	11.6978	11.6677	4.1892	4.1925	0.9979	0.9861	4.3148	4.3180
58 -9 -2	11.6983	11.6703	4.1895	4.1930	0.9971	0.9842	4.2978	4.3002
58 -9 -8	11.6902	11.6677	4.1895	4.1930	0.9953	0.9823	4.2815	4.2825
58 -9-15	11.6917	11.6728	4.1894	4.1926	0.9948	0.9845	4.2912	4.2942
58 -9-22	11.6843	11.6730	4.1872	4.1893	0.9944	0.9840	4.2965	4.2987
58 -9-29	11.6873	11.6775	4.1857	4.1870	0.9940	0.9837	4.2923	4.2922
58-10 -6	11.6870	11.6775	4.1841	4.1850	0.9934	0.9837	4.3054	4.3077
58-10-14	11.6863	11.6763	4.1842	4.1860	0.9933	0.9850	4.3147	4.3190
58-10-20	11.6867	11.6738	4.1841	4.1860	0.9933	0.9848	4.3180	4.3227
58-10-27	11.6907	11.6725	4.1842	4.1853	0.9937	0.9827	4.3167	4.3172
58-11 -3	11.6985	11.6758	4.1843	4.1855	0.9933	0.9802	4.3177	4.3183
58-11-10	11.7002	11.6794	4.1843	4.1855	0.9926	0.9762	4.3152	4.3158
58-11-17	11.7006	11.6804	4.1831	4.1830	0.9926	0.9636	4.3248	4.3232
58-11-24	11.6962	11.6787	4.1829	4.1824	0.9933	0.9590	4.3252	4.3248
58-12 -1	11.6964	11.6862	4.1829	4.1825	0.9929	0.9542	4.3276	4.3289
58-12 -8	11.6900	11.6800	4.1827	4.1826	0.9928	0.9577	4.3387	4.3362
58-12-15	11.6913	11.6813	4.1817	4.1810	0.9930	0.9383	4.3374	4.3338

| DATE | UK L − FFR | | UK L − CAN $ | | US $ − UK L | | US $ − CAN $ | |
YR M DAY	SPOT	3−M FORW	SPOT	3−M FORW	SPOT	3−M FORW	SPOT	3−M FORW
58-12-22	11.7808	10.7815	2.7041	2.7022	2.8054	2.8044	1.0372	1.0361
58-12-29	13.7485	13.6994	2.7021	2.7000	2.8028	2.8012	1.0377	1.0364
59 −1 −5	13.7575	13.7008	2.7103	2.7084	2.8056	2.8039	1.0354	1.0343
59 −1-12	13.7585	13.7319	2.7124	2.7105	2.8058	2.8037	1.0344	1.0333
59 −1-19	13.7667	13.7350	2.7150	2.7140	2.8077	2.8057	1.0340	1.0329
59 −1-26	13.7740	13.7490	2.7201	2.7204	2.8097	2.8074	1.0333	1.0326
59 −2 −2	13.7772	13.7522	2.7352	2.7358	2.8107	2.8081	1.0289	1.0285
59 −2-10	13.7710	13.7360	2.7466	2.7448	2.8091	2.8075	1.0238	1.0227
59 −2-16	13.7709	13.7334	2.7422	2.7397	2.8091	2.8071	1.0241	1.0227
59 −2-24	13.7773	13.7473	2.7340	2.7310	2.8102	2.8077	1.0280	1.0261
59 −3 −2	13.7811	13.7511	2.7313	2.7279	2.8112	2.8086	1.0292	1.0271
59 −3 −9	13.7840	13.7565	2.7283	2.7250	2.8116	2.8092	1.0307	1.0288
59 −3-16	13.7913	13.7672	2.7265	2.7222	2.8134	2.8106	1.0318	1.0301
59 −3-23	13.7975	13.7750	2.7241	2.7205	2.8147	2.8114	1.0334	1.0316
59 −3-30	13.8071	13.7866	2.7219	2.7189	2.8163	2.8126	1.0340	1.0320
59 −4 −6	13.8060	13.7860	2.7146	2.7099	2.8161	2.8119	1.0376	1.0345
59 −4-13	13.8106	13.7906	2.7153	2.7103	2.8174	2.8123	1.0378	1.0341
59 −4-20	13.8102	13.7919	2.7116	2.7060	2.8174	2.8124	1.0392	1.0352
59 −4-27	13.8053	13.7886	2.7098	2.7022	2.8163	2.8118	1.0398	1.0352
59 −5 −4	13.8065	13.7915	2.7157	2.7072	2.8119	2.8107	1.0371	1.0322
59 −5-11	13.8040	13.7890	2.7137	2.7050	2.8094	2.8087	1.0377	1.0330
59 −5-18	13.7907	13.7757	2.7062	2.6979	2.8127	2.8123	1.0396	1.0354
59 −5-25	13.7891	13.7728	2.7026	2.6942	2.8127	2.8120	1.0407	1.0369
59 −6 −1	13.7869	13.7785	2.7023	2.6933	2.8113	2.8099	1.0408	1.0369
59 −6 −8	13.7847	13.7797	2.7001	2.6906	2.8115	2.8100	1.0415	1.0377
59 −6-15	13.7874	13.7824	2.6990	2.6904	2.8121	2.8099	1.0424	1.0385
59 −6-22	13.7903	13.7853	2.6899	2.6816	2.8129	2.8108	1.0457	1.0418
59 −6-29	13.7933	13.7883	2.6833	2.6738	2.8109	2.8089	1.0485	1.0443
59 −7 −6	13.8015	13.7965	2.6870	2.6770	2.8108	2.8102	1.0474	1.0426
59 −7-13	13.7975	13.7937	2.6941	2.6820	2.8109	2.8106	1.0438	1.0389
59 −7-20	13.7878	13.7811	2.6959	2.6890	2.8106	2.8099	1.0431	1.0384
59 −7-27	13.7850	13.7771	2.6956	2.6881	2.8107	2.8098	1.0429	1.0381
59 −8 −3	13.7850	13.7762	2.6939	2.6812	2.8112	2.8103	1.0438	1.0387
59 −8-10	13.7826	13.7732	2.6849	2.6684	2.8105	2.8101	1.0466	1.0403
59 −8-17	13.7730	13.7626	2.6751	2.6560	2.8094	2.8097	1.0504	1.0431
59 −8-24	13.7652	13.7540	2.6748	2.6597	2.8050	2.8058	1.0498	1.0452
59 −8-31	13.7442	13.7319	2.6741	2.6573	2.8032	2.8054	1.0483	1.0438
59 −9 −8	13.7381	13.7256	2.6718	2.6541	2.8025	2.8057	1.0492	1.0433
59 −9-14	13.7524	13.7399	2.6674	2.6492	2.8037	2.8081	1.0512	1.0456
59 −9-21	13.7678	13.7524	2.6659	2.6483	2.8066	2.8103	1.0524	1.0468
59 −9-28	13.7628	13.7474	2.6578	2.6410	2.8039	2.8075	1.0554	1.0501
59-10 −5	13.7696	13.7546	2.6615	2.6474	2.8057	2.8095	1.0557	1.0524
59-10-13	13.7815	13.7667	2.6613	2.6456	2.8083	2.8129	1.0556	1.0509
59-10-19	13.7786	13.7622	2.6602	2.6443	2.8079	2.8125	1.0555	1.0507
59-10-26	13.7702	13.7510	2.6566	2.6426	2.8059	2.8104	1.0562	1.0523

DATE	DM – UK L		DM – US $		DM – FFR		DM – CAN $	
YR M DAY	SPOT	3-M FORW	SPOT	3-M FORW	SPOT	3-M FORW	SPOT	3-M FORW
58-12-22	11.7013	11.6847	4.1819	4.1810	0.9927	0.9000	4.3350	4.3300
58-12-29	11.7042	11.6975	4.1776	4.1772	0.8517	0.8405	4.3335	4.3255
59 -1 -5	11.7233	11.7160	4.1793	4.1792	0.8521	0.8440	4.3268	4.3187
59 -1-12	11.7228	11.7124	4.179)	4.1790	0.8522	0.8460	4.3220	4.3124
59 -1-19	11.7280	11.7173	4.1773	4.1778	0.8519	0.8470	4.3193	4.3123
59 -1-26	11.7318	11.7207	4.1759	4.1760	0.8518	0.8470	4.3207	4.3067
59 -2 -2	11.7383	11.7232	4.1771	4.1765	0.8520	0.8470	4.2963	4.2938
59 -2-10	11.7382	11.7274	4.1792	4.1770	0.8524	0.8470	4.2757	4.2738
59 -2-16	11.7414	11.7278	4.1805	4.1784	0.8527	0.8478	4.2815	4.2744
59 -2-24	11.7442	11.7273	4.1794	4.1783	0.8525	0.8490	4.2955	4.2867
59 -3 -2	11.7535	11.7388	4.1813	4.1795	0.8528	0.8490	4.3026	4.2913
59 -3 -9	11.7655	11.7485	4.1847	4.1820	0.8536	0.8495	4.3119	4.3042
59 -3-16	11.7632	11.7438	4.1816	4.1800	0.8531	0.8500	4.3148	4.3046
59 -3-23	11.7600	11.7372	4.1788	4.1775	0.8525	0.8500	4.3192	4.3070
59 -3-30	11.7702	11.7430	4.1794	4.1774	0.8525	0.8500	4.3236	4.3120
59 -4 -6	11.7728	11.7408	4.1807	4.1777	0.8527	0.8500	4.3376	4.3255
59 -4-13	11.7796	11.7464	4.1815	4.178	0.8529	0.8500	4.3389	4.3274
59 -4-20	11.7803	11.7483	4.1821	4.1797	0.8530	0.8500	4.3457	4.3325
59 -4-27	11.7804	11.7498	4.1831	4.1800	0.8533	0.8500	4.3481	4.3300
59 -5 -4	11.7806	11.7532	4.1828	4.1799	0.8533	0.8500	4.3395	4.3156
59 -5-11	11.7762	11.7504	4.1822	4.1795	0.8531	0.8501	4.2810	4.3154
59 -5-18	11.7628	11.7398	4.1813	4.1779	0.8529	0.8505	4.3462	4.3236
59 -5-25	11.7572	11.7372	4.1808	4.1770	0.8529	0.8505	4.3499	4.3276
59 -6 -1	11.7510	11.7367	4.1781	4.1733	0.8523	0.8501	4.3479	4.3287
59 -6 -8	11.7518	11.7340	4.1792	4.1742	0.8526	0.8506	4.3525	4.3292
59 -6-15	11.7525	11.7310	4.1782	4.1737	0.8524	0.8510	4.3551	4.3321
59 -6-22	11.7528	11.7325	4.1775	4.1731	0.8523	0.8510	4.3688	4.3457
59 -6-29	11.7513	11.7323	4.1780	4.1737	0.8520	0.8507	4.3798	4.3543
59 -7 -6	11.7542	11.7325	4.1797	4.1737	0.8516	0.8505	4.3747	4.3420
59 -7-13	11.7548	11.7330	4.1807	4.1732	0.8520	0.8505	4.3645	4.3276
59 -7-20	11.7558	11.7332	4.1815	4.1727	0.8528	0.8505	4.3610	4.3268
59 -7-27	11.7585	11.7347	4.1827	4.1747	0.8531	0.8507	4.3619	4.3253
59 -8 -3	11.7595	11.7343	4.1825	4.1750	0.8531	0.8497	4.3657	4.3303
59 -8-10	11.7608	11.7362	4.1835	4.1754	0.8533	0.8516	4.3784	4.3442
59 -8-17	11.7542	11.7358	4.1840	4.1762	0.8534	0.8516	4.3935	4.3570
59 -8-24	11.7472	11.7300	4.183?	4.1761	0.8534	0.8510	4.3928	4.3557
59 -8-31	11.7317	11.7188	4.1854	4.1763	0.8537	0.8512	4.3877	4.3573
59 -9 -8	11.7255	11.7113	4.1844	4.1753	0.8535	0.8515	4.3883	4.3617
59 -9-14	11.7318	11.7162	4.1844	4.1728	0.8532	0.8513	4.3979	4.3674
59 -9-21	11.7348	11.7215	4.1817	4.1716	0.8523	0.8500	4.4018	4.3713
59 -9-28	11.7253	11.7133	4.1818	4.1723	0.8520	0.8500	4.4128	4.3817
59-10 -5	11.7280	11.7192	4.1798	4.1707	0.8518	0.8496	4.4068	4.3783
59-10-13	11.7404	11.7264	4.1804	4.1698	0.8517	0.8495	4.4116	4.3788
59-10-19	11.7322	11.7203	4.1783	4.1685	0.8514	0.8496	4.4095	4.3777
59-10-26	11.7075	11.7122	4.1726	4.1687	0.8502	0.8487	4.4072	4.3823

DATE YR M DAY	UK L – FFR SPOT	3-M FORW	UK L – CAN $ SPOT	3-M FORW	US $ – UK L SPOT	3-M FORW	US $ – CAN $ SPOT	3-M FORW
59-11 -2	13.7546	13.7371	2.6530	2.6400	2.8034	2.8085	1.0566	1.0535
59-11 -9	13.7541	13.7355	2.6563	2.6484	2.8037	2.8090	1.0560	1.0539
59-11-16	13.7483	13.7250	2.6713	2.6647	2.8030	2.8082	1.0497	1.0476
59-11-23	13.7429	13.7152	2.6713	2.6618	2.8023	2.8074	1.0480	1.0451
59-11-30	13.7256	13.6965	2.6634	2.6533	2.7992	2.8043	1.0507	1.0477
59-12 -7	13.7322	13.7093	2.6631	2.6513	2.7989	2.8037	1.0514	1.0486
59-12-14	13.7396	13.7227	2.6625	2.6506	2.7997	2.8034	1.0517	1.0483
59-12-21	13.7303	13.7066	2.6573	2.6444	2.7979	2.8026	1.0530	1.0497
59-12-28	13.7347	13.7113	2.6642	2.6520	2.7989	2.8035	1.0510	1.0479
60 -1 -4	13.7357	13.7211	2.6701	2.6621	2.7998	2.8039	1.0484	1.0463
60 -1-11	13.7397	13.7205	2.6667	2.6596	2.7985	2.8025	1.0494	1.0481
60 -1-18	13.7408	13.7254	2.6670	2.6630	2.8001	2.8027	1.0499	1.0489
60 -1-25	13.7649	13.7328	2.6684	2.6648	2.8020	2.8021	1.0502	1.0487
60 -2 -1	13.7627	13.7477	2.6686	2.6654	2.8030	2.8023	1.0505	1.0488
60 -2 -8	13.7577	13.7494	2.6695	2.6682	2.8030	2.8007	1.0502	1.0489
60 -2-15	13.7616	13.7566	2.6676	2.6655	2.8044	2.8027	1.0514	1.0502
60 -2-23	13.7610	13.7523	2.6668	2.6651	2.8038	2.8025	1.0513	1.0501
60 -2-29	13.7598	13.7544	2.6647	2.6632	2.8041	2.8031	1.0524	1.0513
60 -3 -7	13.7642	13.7601	2.6658	2.6641	2.8053	2.8034	1.0524	1.0510
60 -3-14	13.7702	13.7674	2.6663	2.6652	2.8065	2.8033	1.0526	1.0510
60 -3-21	13.7725	13.7677	2.6676	2.6682	2.8070	2.8021	1.0525	1.0511
60 -3-28	13.7721	13.7658	2.6795	2.6813	2.8073	2.8024	1.0483	1.0470
60 -4-11	13.7811	13.7824	2.7111	2.7162	2.8097	2.8042	1.0365	1.0364
60 -4-18	13.7837	13.7852	2.7109	2.7167	2.8104	2.8044	1.0370	1.0371
60 -4-25	13.7746	13.7729	2.7085	2.7143	2.8093	2.8030	1.0376	1.0374
60 -5 -2	13.7697	13.7688	2.7174	2.7229	2.8089	2.8029	1.0340	1.0338
60 -5 -9	13.7598	13.7608	2.7318	2.7370	2.8072	2.8022	1.0287	1.0287
60 -5-16	13.7540	13.7540	2.7554	2.7616	2.8057	2.8007	1.0193	1.0196
60 -5-23	13.7437	13.7433	2.7681	2.773	2.8046	2.7995	1.0135	1.0137
60 -5-31	13.7269	13.7273	2.7591	2.7649	2.8013	2.7965	1.0156	1.0158
60 -6 -6	13.7242	13.7245	2.7516	2.7585	2.8013	2.7957	1.0183	1.0187
60 -6-13	13.7293	13.7322	2.7544	2.7637	2.8018	2.7941	1.0167	1.0173
60 -6-20	13.7451	13.7500	2.7543	2.7657	2.8042	2.7950	1.0188	1.0192
60 -6-27	13.7545	13.7836	2.7505	2.7632	2.8065	2.7941	1.0201	1.0203
60 -7 -5	13.7618	13.7947	2.7563	2.7691	2.8090	2.7946	1.0187	1.0185
60 -7-11	13.7597	13.7963	2.7532	2.765	2.8085	2.7948	1.0199	1.0196
60 -7-18	13.7629	13.8067	2.7466	2.7604	2.8091	2.7944	1.0222	1.0218
60 -7-25	13.7595	13.7982	2.7357	2.747	2.8082	2.7933	1.0264	1.0253
60 -8 -1	13.7630	13.8080	2.7331	2.7454	2.8091	2.7956	1.0273	1.0268
60 -8 -8	13.7701	13.8143	2.7245	2.737	2.8104	2.7972	1.0311	1.0310
60 -8-15	13.7735	13.8185	2.7200	2.7329	2.8113	2.7977	1.0337	1.0335
60 -8-22	13.7703	13.8132	2.7224	2.7362	2.8114	2.7900	1.0328	1.0326
60 -9 -6	13.7796	13.8292	2.7288	2.7455	2.8125	2.7970	1.0308	1.0312
60 -9-12	13.7938	13.8463	2.7296	2.7472	2.8152	2.7992	1.0314	1.0321
60 -9-19	13.7905	13.8422	2.7378	2.7571	2.8151	2.7990	1.0244	1.0254

DATE	DM – UK L		DM – US $		DM – FFR		DM – CAN $	
YR M DAY	SPOT	3-M FORW	SPOT	3-M FORW	SPOT	3-M FORW	SPOT	3-M FORW
59-11 -2	11.6935	11.7118	4.1714	4.1704	0.8501	0.8499	4.4073	4.3882
59-11 -9	11.6940	11.7117	4.1714	4.1702	0.8502	0.8500	4.4031	4.3905
59-11-16	11.6920	11.7120	4.1714	4.1700	0.8503	0.8500	4.3781	4.3700
59-11-23	11.6888	11.7090	4.1714	4.1700	0.8505	0.8500	4.3758	4.3650
59-11-30	11.6743	11.6983	4.1714	4.1707	0.8506	0.8502	4.3819	4.3675
59-12 -7	11.6738	11.6957	4.1714	4.1728	0.8503	0.8505	4.3853	4.3720
59-12-14	11.6782	11.6988	4.1713	4.1726	0.8499	0.8504	4.3861	4.3720
59-12-21	11.6682	11.6912	4.1700	4.1710	0.8499	0.8500	4.3899	4.3752
59-12-28	11.6718	11.6840	4.1700	4.1710	0.8496	0.8500	4.3835	4.3710
60 -1 -4	11.6765	11.6927	4.1707	4.1710	0.8501	0.8502	4.3735	4.3653
60 -1-11	11.6700	11.6852	4.1705	4.1706	0.8494	0.8497	4.3756	4.3576
60 -1-18	11.6773	11.6840	4.1704	4.1700	0.8498	0.8495	4.3795	4.3682
60 -1-25	11.6855	11.6840	4.1704	4.1700	0.8487	0.8462	4.3794	4.3710
60 -2 -1	11.6895	11.6858	4.1703	4.1700	0.8495	0.8457	4.3803	4.3733
60 -2 -8	11.6897	11.6818	4.1705	4.1700	0.8497	0.8470	4.3797	4.3740
60 -2-15	11.6936	11.6854	4.1702	4.1700	0.8498	0.8486	4.3832	4.3752
60 -2-23	11.6912	11.6863	4.1700	4.1700	0.8496	0.8488	4.3841	4.3770
60 -2-29	11.6927	11.6860	4.1700	4.1700	0.8498	0.8488	4.3885	4.3808
60 -3 -7	11.6973	11.6917	4.1700	4.1700	0.8498	0.8492	4.3878	4.3820
60 -3-14	11.7022	11.6956	4.1700	4.1700	0.8498	0.8493	4.3891	4.3820
60 -3-21	11.7043	11.6953	4.1700	4.1703	0.8498	0.8493	4.3877	4.3820
60 -3-28	11.7067	11.6905	4.1701	4.1710	0.8500	0.8493	4.3700	4.3678
60 -4-11	11.7150	11.6937	4.1700	4.1710	0.8502	0.8488	4.3206	4.3172
60 -4-18	11.7194	11.6966	4.1700	4.1710	0.8502	0.8488	4.3224	4.3178
60 -4-25	11.7140	11.6907	4.1700	4.1710	0.8503	0.8488	4.3263	4.3262
60 -5 -2	11.7120	11.6893	4.1700	4.1710	0.8506	0.8488	4.3099	4.3082
60 -5 -9	11.7053	11.6855	4.1700	4.1710	0.8507	0.8488	4.2859	4.2843
60 -5-16	11.6994	11.6788	4.1700	4.1710	0.8506	0.8488	4.2495	4.2508
60 -5-23	11.6938	11.6748	4.1700	4.1710	0.8508	0.8488	4.2274	4.2268
60 -5-31	11.6816	11.6674	4.1700	4.1710	0.8510	0.7137	4.2285	4.2306
60 -6 -6	11.6804	11.6634	4.1700	4.1710	0.8509	0.8493	4.2444	4.2440
60 -6-13	11.6810	11.6457	4.1700	4.1687	0.8509	0.8488	4.2428	4.2423
60 -6-20	11.6932	11.6495	4.1700	4.1682	0.8508	0.8487	4.2481	4.2483
60 -6-27	11.7023	11.6483	4.1700	4.1685	0.8507	0.8484	4.2533	4.2510
60 -7 -5	11.7105	11.6487	4.1700	4.166	0.8510	0.8484	4.2489	4.2458
60 -7-11	11.7096	11.7466	4.1700	4.1660	0.8510	0.8484	4.2529	4.2484
60 -7-18	11.7132	11.6467	4.1700	4.1660	0.8510	0.8484	4.2634	4.2603
60 -7-25	11.7097	11.6442	4.1700	4.1660	0.8510	0.8484	4.2795	4.2775
60 -8 -1	11.7123	11.6490	4.1700	4.1660	0.8510	0.8484	4.2838	4.2755
60 -8 -8	11.7197	11.6580	4.1700	4.1660	0.8510	0.8484	4.3020	4.2955
60 -8-15	11.7222	11.6628	4.1700	4.1660	0.8511	0.8484	4.3110	4.3056
60 -8-22	11.7193	11.6635	4.1700	4.1695	0.8510	0.8495	4.3043	4.3040
60 -9 -6	11.7270	11.6618	4.1700	4.1690	0.8510	0.8498	4.2968	4.2985
60 -9-12	11.7380	11.6668	4.1700	4.1686	0.8509	0.8498	4.3005	4.2984
60 -9-19	11.7358	11.6595	4.1700	4.1680	0.8510	0.8490	4.2863	4.2832

DATE	UK L − FFR		UK L − CAN $		US $ − UK L		US $ − CAN $	
YR M DAY	SPOT	3-M FORW	SPOT	3-M FORW	SPOT	3-M FORW	SPOT	3-M FORW
60 −9-26	13.7684	13.8138	2.7461	2.7631	2.8099	2.7958	1.0235	1.0246
50-10 −3	13.7786	13.8278	2.7510	2.7673	2.8104	2.7966	1.0217	1.0226
60-10-10	13.7904	13.8492	2.7511	2.7666	2.8098	2.7965	1.0213	1.0220
60-10-17	13.8106	13.8744	2.7520	2.7658	2.8120	2.7979	1.0217	1.0218
60-10-24	13.8007	13.8561	2.7503	2.7615	2.8134	2.8022	1.0232	1.0231
60-10-31	13.7970	13.8486	2.7442	2.7548	2.8166	2.8047	1.0262	1.0254
60-11 −7	13.8001	13.8409	2.7448	2.7547	2.8160	2.8047	1.0265	1.0259
60-11-14	13.7862	13.8171	2.7528	2.7612	2.8132	2.8028	1.0222	1.0211
60-11-21	13.7826	13.8126	2.7503	2.7558	2.8129	2.8045	1.0224	1.0211
60-11-28	13.7699	13.7999	2.7485	2.7520	2.8086	2.8011	1.0225	1.0209
60-12 −5	13.7697	13.7982	2.7448	2.7466	2.8098	2.8024	1.0238	1.0218
61 −1 −3	13.7576	13.7807	2.7933	2.7973	2.8066	2.7995	1.0050	1.0039
61 −1 −9	13.7542	13.7729	2.7903	2.7954	2.8073	2.8028	1.0059	1.0050
61 −1-16	13.7543	13.7751	2.7883	2.7917	2.8072	2.8006	1.0067	1.0055
61 −1-23	13.7523	13.7673	2.7816	2.7847	2.8068	2.8009	1.0085	1.0075
61 −1-30	13.7397	13.7538	2.7781	2.7813	2.8044	2.7986	1.0097	1.0087
61 −2 −6	13.7294	13.7450	2.7755	2.7792	2.8022	2.7965	1.0096	1.0087
61 −3 −6	13.6975	13.7492	2.7516	2.7600	2.7949	2.7864	1.0166	1.0166
61 −3-13	13.7144	13.7744	2.7634	2.7765	2.7996	2.7869	1.0134	1.0135
61 −3-20	13.7136	13.7736	2.7692	2.7829	2.7986	2.7839	1.0110	1.0104
61 −3-27	13.7102	13.7702	2.7682	2.7822	2.7989	2.7837	1.0110	1.0106
61 −4 −3	13.7135	13.7705	2.7690	2.7825	2.7989	2.7844	1.0112	1.0108
61 −4-10	13.7154	13.7637	2.7692	2.7790	2.7995	2.7883	1.0122	1.0116
61 −4-17	13.7098	13.7598	2.7662	2.7752	2.7985	2.7872	1.0123	1.0112
61 −4-24	13.7155	13.7547	2.7640	2.7735	2.7967	2.7834	1.0127	1.0114
61 −5 −1	13.7032	13.7399	2.7608	2.7693	2.7961	2.7834	1.0132	1.0117
61 −5 −8	13.6967	13.7292	2.7610	2.7696	2.7958	2.7845	1.0125	1.0110
61 −5-15	13.6867	13.7250	2.7594	2.7681	2.7937	2.7816	1.0124	1.0109
61 −5-22	13.6829	13.7204	2.7564	2.7637	2.7928	2.7811	1.0135	1.0118
61 −5-29	13.6749	13.7132	2.7555	2.7645	2.7911	2.7787	1.0132	1.0117
61 −6 −5	13.6710	13.7177	2.7549	2.7655	2.7903	2.7764	1.0131	1.0117
61 −6-12	13.6735	13.7377	2.7738	2.7881	2.7917	2.7750	1.0078	1.0065

| DATE | DM − UK L | | DM − US $ | | DM − FFR | | DM − CAN $ | |
YR M DAY	SPOT	3−M FORW	SPOT	3−M FORW	SPOT	3−M FORW	SPOT	3−M FORW
60 −9−26	11.7178	11.6378	4.1700	4.1598	0.8510	0.8480	4.2661	4.2598
60−10 −3	11.7243	11.6497	4.1719	4.1673	0.8510	0.8481	4.2631	4.2583
60−10−10	11.7230	11.6538	4.1730	4.1690	0.8499	0.8481	4.2605	4.2596
60−10−17	11.7303	11.6597	4.1722	4.1697	0.8495	0.8485	4.2607	4.2558
60−10−24	11.7348	11.6717	4.1712	4.1670	0.8501	0.8487	4.2679	4.2625
60−10−31	11.7447	11.6717	4.1710	4.1662	0.8512	0.8491	4.2800	4.2738
60−11 −7	11.7443	11.6873	4.1710	4.1670	0.8508	0.8491	4.2793	4.2760
60−11−14	11.7312	11.6832	4.1710	4.1670	0.8511	0.8491	4.2645	4.2640
60−11−21	11.7320	11.6890	4.1710	4.1670	0.8511	0.8491	4.2649	4.2580
60−11−28	11.7212	11.6812	4.1710	4.1670	0.8512	0.8491	4.2643	4.2547
60−12 −5	11.7178	11.6810	4.1710	3.4725	0.8509	0.8491	4.2689	4.2598
61 −1 −3	11.7080	11.6610	4.1717	4.1650	0.8510	0.8488	4.1911	4.1807
61 −1 −9	11.7097	11.6605	4.1716	4.1650	0.8513	0.8488	4.1963	4.1857
61 −1−16	11.7084	11.6584	4.1715	4.1650	0.8513	0.8488	4.1985	4.1882
61 −1−23	11.7077	11.6560	4.1716	4.1623	0.8513	0.8481	4.2085	4.1947
61 −1−30	11.7023	11.6610	4.1737	4.1672	0.8517	0.8482	4.2122	4.1998
61 −2 −6	11.6903	11.6565	4.1723	4.1680	0.8515	0.8500	4.2111	4.2000
61 −3 −6	11.1097	10.9958	3.9755	3.9525	0.8114	0.8112	4.0401	3.3408
61 −3−13	11.1128	10.9910	3.9703	3.9420	0.8101	0.8047	4.0216	3.9970
61 −3−20	11.1090	11.0100	3.9702	3.9587	0.8102	0.8064	4.0123	3.9917
61 −3−27	11.1067	10.9997	3.9700	3.9550	0.8101	0.8065	4.0125	3.9850
61 −4 −3	11.1110	11.0062	3.9700	3.9530	0.8102	0.8060	4.0125	3.9900
61 −4−10	11.1134	11.1270	3.9702	3.9550	0.8102	0.8065	4.0131	3.9900
61 −4−17	11.1094	11.1240	3.9701	3.9550	0.8102	0.8061	4.0162	3.9940
61 −4−24	11.1022	10.9996	3.9702	3.9532	0.8098	0.8044	4.0176	3.9982
61 −5 −1	11.1012	11.0037	3.9706	3.9524	0.8101	0.8044	4.0225	4.0040
61 −5 −8	11.0990	11.0095	3.9702	3.9550	0.8102	0.8045	4.0196	4.0100
61 −5−15	11.0906	10.9876	3.9705	3.9550	0.8103	0.8045	4.0189	4.0100
61 −5−22	11.0877	11.0025	3.9701	3.9550	0.8103	0.8052	4.0226	4.0100
61 −5−29	11.0795	10.9812	3.9700	3.9550	0.8102	0.8054	4.0214	4.0100
61 −6 −5	11.0776	10.9720	3.9700	3.9524	0.8102	0.8051	4.0215	4.0090
61 −6−12	11.0834	10.9682	3.9703	3.9526	0.8103	0.8048	4.0017	3.9852

Weekly Interest Rates: July 4, 1955, to June 12, 1961

This appendix lists weekly interest rates on ten types of paper in five markets. New York rates, drawn from the *Federal Reserve Bulletin*, are given for three types of paper: (1) three-month treasury bills, (2) three-month bankers' prime acceptances, and (3) three-month finance paper. London rates, taken from *The Economist*, London, are given for four types of paper: (1) three-month treasury bills, (2) three-month bankers' prime acceptances, (3) three-month prime commercial paper, and (4) day-to-day money. The Frankfurt rates, for three-month treasury bills, were obtained from the *Monthly Reports of the Deutsche Bundesbank*, Frankfurt. The Ottawa rates, also for three-month treasury bills, were drawn from the *Bank of Canada, Statistical Summary, Financial Supplements*, Ottawa. The Paris rates, for day-to-day money, were taken from the internal records of the Bank of France, Paris.

DATE YR M DAY	FRANK- FURT	PARIS	OTTAWA	LONDON (1)	LONDON (2)	LONDON (3)	LONDON (4)	NEW YORK1	NEW YORK2	NEW YORK3
55 -7 -4	2.63	3.55	1.44	3.97	4.50	4.00	2.88	1.54	2.05	1.50
55 -7-11	2.63	3.00	1.42	3.97	4.50	4.00	3.25	1.61	2.06	1.50
55 -7-18	2.68	3.60	1.41	3.97	4.50	4.00	3.63	1.02	2.14	1.50
55 -7-25	2.75	3.13	1.43	3.97	4.50	4.00	3.50	1.72	2.19	1.50
55 -8 -1	2.82	3.20	1.55	4.00	4.75	4.03	3.50	1.85	2.29	1.53
55 -8 -8	3.00	3.00	1.59	4.00	4.75	4.06	3.63	1.89	2.31	1.63
55 -8-15	3.00	2.85	1.57	4.01	4.75	4.06	3.13	1.89	2.31	1.68
55 -8-22	3.00	2.88	1.70	4.00	4.75	4.06	3.38	1.88	2.35	1.75
55 -8-29	3.04	2.90	1.70	4.07	4.75	4.06	3.38	2.09	2.48	1.85
55 -9 -5	3.10	2.88	1.72	4.07	5.18	4.19	3.38	2.13	2.50	2.00
55 -9-12	3.25	2.91	1.78	4.07	5.18	4.19	3.50	2.10	2.55	2.13
55 -9-19	3.25	3.05	1.82	4.07	5.38	4.19	3.50	1.98	2.56	2.13
55 -9-26	3.25	3.10	1.83	4.07	5.38	4.19	3.38	2.12	2.58	2.13
55-10 -3	3.25	3.00	1.85	4.07	5.38	4.19	3.44	2.21	2.63	2.20
55-10-10	3.38	2.94	2.06	4.07	5.38	4.19	3.38	2.26	2.66	2.25
55-10-17	3.38	2.88	2.16	4.07	5.38	4.19	3.50	2.33	2.74	2.25
55-10-24	3.38	2.95	2.20	4.07	5.38	4.19	2.75	2.23	2.75	2.25
55-10-31	3.38	3.00	2.19	4.10	5.38	4.19	3.38	2.18	2.75	2.13
55-11 -7	3.38	3.00	2.23	4.10	5.38	4.19	3.38	2.03	2.75	2.13
55-11-14	3.38	2.94	2.33	4.10	5.38	4.19	3.38	2.25	2.81	2.13
55-11-21	3.38	2.93	2.57	4.10	5.38	4.19	3.38	2.44	2.86	2.25
55-11-28	3.38	3.00	2.58	4.07	5.38	4.19	3.38	2.45	2.88	2.25
55-12 -5	3.38	2.94	2.64	4.07	5.38	4.19	2.50	2.47	3.00	2.35
55-12-12	3.38	2.85	2.60	4.07	5.38	4.19	2.88	2.59	3.00	2.48
55-12-19	3.38	2.98	2.57	4.14	5.38	4.19	3.25	2.62	3.00	2.50
55-12-26	3.38	2.91	2.56	4.07	5.38	4.19	3.25	2.69	3.00	2.50
56 -1 -2	3.38	2.94	2.59	4.07	5.38	4.19	2.75	2.49	3.00	2.50
56 -1 -9	3.38	2.69	2.61	4.07	5.38	4.19	2.63	2.60	3.00	2.50
56 -1-16	3.38	2.83	2.57	4.07	5.38	4.19	2.50	2.49	3.00	2.45
56 -1-23	3.38	2.88	2.53	4.07	5.38	4.19	3.38	2.25	3.00	2.38
56 -1-30	3.38	3.00	2.48	4.13	5.38	4.19	3.38	2.40	3.00	2.38
56 -2 -6	3.38	3.03	2.49	4.14	5.38	4.19	3.38	2.27	3.00	2.38
56 -2-13	3.38	2.98	2.51	5.27	6.25	5.34	4.38	2.39	3.00	2.38
56 -2-20	3.38	2.95	2.52	5.22	6.25	5.34	4.38	2.43	3.00	2.38
56 -2-27	3.38	3.03	2.56	5.20	6.25	5.34	4.38	2.41	3.00	2.38
56 -3 -5	3.75	2.97	2.60	5.21	6.25	5.34	4.38	2.17	3.00	2.38
56 -3-12	4.13	2.94	2.62	5.22	6.25	5.34	4.28	2.37	3.00	2.38
56 -3-19	4.13	2.95	2.62	5.11	6.25	5.34	4.38	2.42	3.00	2.38
56 -3-26	4.00	3.03	2.64	5.17	6.25	5.34	4.38	2.17	3.00	2.38
56 -4 -2	4.00	3.17	2.77	5.17	6.25	5.34	4.38	2.40	3.00	2.38
56 -4 -9	4.00	2.98	2.80	5.12	6.25	5.34	3.75	2.50	3.05	2.38
56 -4-16	4.00	2.93	2.86	5.12	6.25	5.28	3.88	2.77	3.25	2.50
56 -4-23	4.10	3.03	2.89	5.01	6.25	5.28	3.50	2.79	3.25	2.50
56 -4-30	4.25	3.09	2.91	4.95	6.25	5.16	3.88	2.74	3.25	2.50
56 -5 -7	4.25	3.13	2.90	4.95	6.25	5.16	4.00	2.52	3.25	2.50

DATE YR M DAY	FRANK-FURT	PARIS	OTTAWA	LONDON (1)	LONDON (2)	LONDON (3)	LONDON (4)	NEW YORK1	NEW YORK2	NEW YORK3
56 -5-14	4.25	2.88	2.87	4.95	6.25	5.16	4.25	2.71	3.25	2.50
56 -5-21	5.21	2.94	2.78	4.95	6.25	5.16	4.25	2.70	3.25	2.50
56 -5-28	5.25	2.93	2.72	5.01	6.25	5.16	4.25	2.57	3.38	2.50
56 -6 -4	5.31	2.91	2.68	5.02	6.25	5.21	4.13	2.56	3.38	2.50
56 -6-11	5.38	2.53	2.67	5.02	6.25	5.21	4.25	2.58	3.38	2.50
56 -6-18	5.38	2.97	2.63	5.08	6.25	5.21	4.00	2.43	3.38	2.40
56 -6-25	5.38	3.15	2.52	5.14	6.25	5.21	4.25	2.54	3.38	2.38
56 -7 -2	5.38	3.50	2.40	5.06	6.25	5.21	4.25	2.41	3.34	2.38
56 -7 -9	5.38	3.31	2.49	4.99	6.25	5.13	3.88	2.39	3.31	2.38
56 -7-16	5.38	3.08	2.57	5.02	6.25	5.09	4.13	2.24	3.29	2.43
56 -7-23	5.38	3.08	2.65	4.98	6.25	5.09	4.00	2.30	3.19	2.50
56 -7-30	5.38	2.90	2.80	5.02	6.25	5.05	4.25	2.38	3.19	2.50
56 -8 -6	5.38	3.08	2.97	5.02	6.25	5.06	4.63	2.40	3.19	2.50
56 -8-13	5.38	3.08	3.03	5.00	6.25	5.06	3.50	2.60	3.25	2.60
56 -8-20	5.38	3.01	3.00	5.06	6.25	5.06	4.75	2.82	3.35	2.73
56 -8-27	5.38	2.98	2.90	5.03	6.25	5.12	4.38	2.83	3.38	2.85
56 -9 -3	5.13	2.80	2.92	5.07	6.25	5.09	4.25	2.74	3.50	3.13
56 -9-10	4.88	2.81	3.05	5.10	6.25	5.15	4.38	2.77	3.50	3.13
56 -9-17	4.88	2.93	3.09	5.17	6.25	5.18	4.38	2.91	3.50	3.13
56 -9-24	4.88	3.00	3.16	5.09	6.25	5.22	4.25	2.99	3.50	3.15
56-10 -1	4.88	3.53	3.21	5.06	6.25	5.21	4.38	2.90	3.63	2.88
56-10 -8	4.88	3.45	3.26	5.11	6.25	5.16	4.38	3.01	3.63	2.88
56-10-15	4.88	3.81	3.34	5.01	6.25	5.21	4.25	3.02	3.63	2.88
56-10-22	4.88	4.31	3.37	4.99	6.25	5.08	4.13	2.91	3.63	2.88
56-10-29	4.88	4.80	3.34	5.00	6.25	5.08	3.75	2.89	3.63	2.88
56-11 -5	4.88	4.90	3.33	5.00	6.25	5.08	4.00	2.91	3.63	2.88
56-11-12	4.88	3.88	3.32	5.00	6.25	5.08	4.38	2.98	3.63	2.85
56-11-19	4.83	3.58	3.44	5.01	6.25	5.08	4.13	3.04	3.63	3.06
56-11-26	4.69	4.83	3.52	5.02	6.25	5.08	4.25	3.17	3.63	3.13
56-12 -3	4.75	5.70	3.53	5.04	6.25	5.08	4.25	3.10	3.63	3.26
56-12-10	4.75	3.55	3.59	4.96	6.25	5.13	4.25	3.27	3.63	3.38
56-12-17	4.75	4.08	3.64	4.91	6.25	5.13	4.00	3.33	3.63	3.38
56-12-24	4.75	5.66	3.67	4.86	6.25	5.03	4.25	3.22	3.63	3.38
56-12-31	4.75	4.04	3.65	4.79	6.25	4.97	4.13	3.26	3.63	3.38
57 -1 -7	4.70	5.52	3.71	4.77	6.25	4.91	3.75	3.20	3.63	3.38
57 -1-14	4.25	4.60	3.72	4.66	6.25	4.91	4.00	3.22	3.63	3.38
57 -1-21	4.25	3.60	3.72	4.55	6.13	4.77	4.00	3.09	3.63	3.38
57 -1-28	4.25	3.31	3.70	4.54	6.13	4.74	4.00	3.28	3.63	3.38
57 -2 -4	4.25	3.50	3.72	4.23	5.75	4.50	3.75	3.13	3.63	3.38
57 -2-11	4.25	3.50	3.75	4.28	5.75	4.78	3.69	3.06	3.63	3.38
57 -2-18	4.25	3.22	3.81	4.15	5.75	4.78	3.75	3.18	3.63	3.38
57 -2-25	4.25	3.65	3.76	4.00	5.75	4.28	3.63	3.29	3.63	3.38
57 -3 -4	4.43	4.90	3.72	4.02	5.75	4.22	3.63	3.25	3.63	3.38
57 -3-11	4.38	4.33	3.73	4.12	5.75	4.22	3.63	3.24	3.63	3.38
57 -3-18	4.38	3.68	3.69	4.13	5.75	4.28	3.69	3.04	3.63	3.18

DATE YR M DAY	FRANK- FURT	PARIS	OTTAWA	LONDON (1)	LONDON (2)	LONDON (3)	LONDON (4)	NEW YORK1	NEW YORK2	NEW YORK3
57 -3-25	4.38	4.96	3.70	4.10	5.75	4.28	3.50	3.03	3.63	3.13
57 -4 -1	4.38	4.35	3.69	4.15	5.75	4.25	3.75	3.05	3.63	3.13
57 -4-15	4.38	4.19	3.73	3.94	5.75	4.15	3.63	3.19	3.63	3.25
57 -4-22	4.38	6.06	3.75	3.91	5.75	4.09	3.50	3.05	3.63	3.25
57 -4-29	4.38	6.69	3.76	3.74	5.75	4.09	3.13	3.04	3.63	3.25
57 -5 -6	4.38	6.50	3.78	3.81	5.75	3.97	3.56	2.91	3.63	3.25
57 -5-13	4.38	4.88	3.78	3.83	5.75	4.03	3.50	2.89	3.63	3.25
57 -5-20	4.38	4.35	3.76	3.91	5.75	4.03	3.56	3.12	3.63	3.25
57 -5-27	4.38	6.58	3.76	3.92	5.75	4.09	3.56	3.25	3.63	3.25
57 -6 -3	4.38	6.25	3.79	3.91	5.75	4.09	3.38	3.37	3.70	3.30
57 -6-10	4.38	5.03	3.79	3.86	5.75	4.09	3.38	3.26	3.75	3.38
57 -6-17	4.38	6.00	3.80	3.86	5.75	4.06	3.56	3.40	3.85	3.38
57 -6-24	4.38	7.92	3.81	3.85	5.75	4.06	3.56	3.23	3.88	3.38
57 -7 -1	4.34	7.25	3.81	3.85	5.75	4.06	3.13	3.24	3.88	3.38
57 -7 -8	4.25	8.19	3.81	3.85	5.75	4.06	3.50	3.17	3.88	3.38
57 -7-15	4.25	8.50	3.81	3.84	5.75	4.06	3.38	3.09	3.88	3.38
57 -7-22	4.25	0.33	3.80	3.85	5.75	4.06	3.50	3.16	3.88	3.38
57 -7-29	4.25	0.55	3.81	3.82	5.75	4.06	3.63	3.36	3.88	3.38
57 -8 -5	4.25	0.44	3.92	3.88	5.75	4.06	3.56	3.31	3.95	3.53
57 -8-12	4.13	0.25	4.03	3.99	5.75	4.12	3.56	3.50	4.00	3.90
57 -8-19	4.16	6.83	4.08	4.05	5.75	4.18	3.56	3.35	4.00	3.98
57 -8-26	3.82	3.06	4.03	4.12	5.75	4.25	3.63	3.50	4.00	3.88
57 -9 -2	4.04	6.43	4.01	4.22	5.75	4.31	3.63	3.57	4.00	3.88
57 -9 -9	4.08	5.12	4.00	4.23	5.75	4.54	3.69	3.58	4.00	3.88
57 -9-16	4.13	5.50	3.93	6.60	8.00	6.50	5.25	3.63	4.00	3.85
57 -9-23	3.79	7.40	3.80	6.60	8.00	6.81	5.56	3.54	4.00	3.75
57 -9-30	3.79	5.75	3.84	6.61	8.00	6.81	5.81	3.53	4.00	3.75
57-10 -7	3.75	4.73	3.87	6.60	8.00	6.81	5.30	3.53	4.09	3.75
57-10-14	3.71	4.10	3.88	6.60	8.00	6.81	5.50	3.66	4.13	3.75
57-10-21	3.56	4.80	3.83	6.60	8.00	6.81	5.63	3.62	4.13	3.75
57-10-28	3.50	6.17	3.80	6.59	8.00	6.81	5.50	3.62	4.13	3.75
57-11 -4	3.50	5.50	3.79	6.59	8.00	6.81	5.75	3.57	4.13	3.66
57-11-11	3.38	4.88	3.74	6.58	8.00	6.81	5.69	3.47	4.13	3.56
57-11-18	3.38	4.50	3.51	6.47	8.00	6.81	5.75	3.15	4.04	3.38
57-11-25	3.40	5.45	3.58	6.46	8.00	6.69	5.69	3.16	4.00	3.38
57-12 -2	3.58	6.05	3.67	6.46	8.00	6.69	5.50	3.11	3.93	3.38
57-12 -9	3.63	5.80	3.67	6.46	8.00	6.69	5.69	2.99	3.81	3.33
57-12-16	3.63	5.65	3.64	6.44	8.00	6.69	5.69	3.14	3.75	3.33
57-12-23	3.68	7.83	3.62	6.37	8.00	6.69	5.75	3.17	3.75	3.38
57-12-30	3.63	6.63	3.60	6.33	7.63	6.56	5.19	2.75	3.75	3.34
58 -1 -6	3.38	5.73	3.64	6.33	7.63	6.56	5.25	2.86	3.68	3.25
58 -1-13	3.38	4.88	3.65	6.29	7.63	6.56	5.56	2.59	3.55	3.13
58 -1-20	3.29	4.81	3.58	6.28	7.63	6.47	5.25	2.59	3.40	2.98
58 -1-27	3.25	5.42	3.25	6.13	7.63	6.47	5.38	2.20	3.23	2.78
58 -2 -3	3.25	5.25	2.99	6.06	7.63	6.28	5.63	1.58	2.83	2.43

DATE YR M DAY	FRANK-FURT	PARIS	OTTAWA	LONDON (1)	LONDON (2)	LONDON (3)	LONDON (4)	NEW YORK1	NEW YORK2	NEW YORK3
58 -2-10	3.25	5.03	3.06	6.04	7.50	6.16	5.63	1.73	2.63	2.38
58 -2-17	3.25	5.03	3.03	5.97	7.50	6.16	5.57	1.73	2.63	2.35
58 -2-24	3.25	6.75	2.86	6.01	7.50	6.09	5.57	1.20	2.45	2.08
58 -3 -3	3.25	7.00	2.66	6.02	7.50	6.22	5.44	1.35	2.38	1.88
58 -3-10	3.25	3.33	2.42	6.03	7.13	6.15	5.63	1.53	2.38	1.88
58 -3-17	3.25	5.60	2.39	5.56	6.13	5.15	4.75	1.34	2.38	1.88
58 -3-24	3.25	6.25	2.27	5.52	6.63	5.65	4.50	1.19	2.23	1.63
58 -3-31	3.25	5.00	1.83	5.43	6.63	5.59	4.77	1.15	2.13	1.63
58 -4 -7	3.25	5.44	1.89	5.33	6.63	5.49	4.75	1.07	2.00	1.63
58 -4-14	3.25	5.56	1.58	5.20	6.63	5.47	4.56	1.23	1.88	1.58
58 -4-21	3.25	6.60	1.37	5.18	6.63	5.40	4.69	1.06	1.75	1.38
58 -4-28	3.25	1.19	1.58	5.06	6.63	5.40	4.75	1.37	1.75	1.38
58 -5 -5	3.25	2.90	1.63	5.20	6.63	5.28	4.69	1.19	1.75	1.38
58 -5-12	3.25	0.	1.54	5.20	6.63	5.40	4.50	1.11	1.75	1.38
58 -5-19	3.25	9.19	1.53	4.82	6.63	5.40	4.19	0.93	1.70	1.28
58 -5-26	3.25	3.31	1.54	4.82	6.25	4.97	4.19	0.64	1.63	1.13
58 -6 -2	3.25	9.35	1.72	4.72	6.25	4.97	4.19	0.72	1.63	1.13
58 -6 -9	3.25	6.95	1.76	4.51	6.25	4.84	4.19	0.84	1.55	1.13
58 -6-16	3.25	5.50	1.78	4.29	5.88	4.59	3.69	0.95	1.50	1.13
58 -6-23	3.04	8.15	1.72	4.29	5.38	4.40	3.50	1.01	1.50	1.13
58 -6-30	2.75	9.00	1.61	4.17	5.38	4.40	3.50	0.77	1.50	1.13
58 -7 -7	2.66	5.95	1.66	4.02	5.38	4.28	3.69	0.93	1.50	1.13
58 -7-14	2.63	5.62	1.45	4.25	5.38	4.15	3.44	1.14	1.50	1.13
58 -7-21	2.63	7.35	0.97	4.16	5.38	4.40	3.69	0.99	1.50	1.13
58 -7-28	2.63	7.29	0.87	4.01	5.38	4.34	3.69	0.98	1.50	1.13
58 -8 -4	2.63	9.83	1.23	3.87	5.38	4.15	3.75	1.17	1.50	1.15
58 -8-11	2.50	5.00	1.16	3.72	5.38	4.15	3.19	1.52	1.68	1.58
58 -8-18	2.50	4.95	1.26	3.73	4.88	3.90	3.19	1.90	2.14	1.88
58 -8-25	2.50	5.70	1.49	3.75	4.88	3.90	3.19	2.16	2.63	2.13
58 -9 -1	2.50	5.62	1.71	3.70	4.88	3.90	3.19	2.46	2.88	2.25
58 -9 -8	2.50	5.56	1.94	3.68	4.88	3.84	3.19	2.36	2.88	2.25
58 -9-15	2.50	5.04	2.17	3.59	4.88	3.84	3.19	2.61	2.90	2.45
58 -9-22	2.50	7.33	2.27	3.63	4.88	3.73	3.19	2.51	3.00	2.50
58 -9-29	2.50	7.16	2.37	3.71	4.88	3.78	3.19	2.92	3.20	2.70
58-10 -6	2.50	5.57	2.39	3.65	4.88	3.84	3.25	2.67	3.25	2.75
58-10-13	2.50	5.30	2.35	3.61	4.88	3.78	3.19	2.93	3.25	2.75
58-10-20	2.50	4.53	2.48	3.68	4.88	3.72	3.19	2.80	3.25	2.75
58-10-27	2.38	5.20	2.63	3.58	4.88	3.84	3.19	2.65	3.15	2.75
58-11 -3	2.38	6.75	2.95	3.58	4.88	3.72	3.19	2.65	3.13	2.75
58-11-10	2.38	4.40	3.16	3.55	4.88	3.72	3.19	2.77	3.00	2.75
58-11-17	2.38	4.25	3.00	3.42	4.88	3.72	2.38	2.88	3.08	2.75
58-11-24	2.38	6.20	2.88	3.31	4.63	3.84	2.38	2.72	3.13	2.75
58-12 -1	2.38	5.10	3.07	3.22	4.63	3.47	2.25	2.81	3.20	2.75
58-12 -8	2.38	4.91	3.52	3.12	4.63	3.40	2.63	2.81	3.38	2.75
58-12-15	2.38	4.50	3.56	3.15	4.63	3.28	2.50	2.90	3.38	2.75

DATE YR M DAY	FRANK- FURT	PARIS	OTTAWA	LONDON (1)	LONDON (2)	LONDON (3)	LONDON (4)	NEW YORK1	NEW YORK2	NEW YORK3
58-12-22	2.38	7.25	3.64	3.15	4.63	3.28	2.62	2.74	3.38	2.75
58-12-29	2.38	4.50	3.49	3.15	4.63	3.28	2.56	2.69	3.31	2.75
59 -1 -5	2.38	4.16	3.25	3.14	4.63	3.28	2.62	2.68	3.25	2.75
59 -1-12	2.25	3.25	2.36	3.11	4.63	3.28	2.62	2.81	3.25	2.75
59 -1-19	2.25	3.58	3.46	3.11	4.63	3.28	2.62	3.04	3.33	2.75
59 -1-26	2.25	4.68	3.28	3.11	4.63	3.28	2.62	2.98	3.38	2.75
59 -2 -2	2.25	4.63	3.37	3.00	4.63	3.24	2.77	2.72	3.30	2.75
59 -2 -9	2.25	3.88	3.57	3.00	4.63	3.16	2.76	2.81	3.25	2.75
59 -2-16	2.25	3.80	3.78	3.09	4.63	3.20	2.67	2.73	3.25	2.75
59 -2-23	2.25	4.65	4.07	3.28	4.63	3.32	2.74	2.59	3.25	2.75
59 -3 -2	2.25	5.10	4.06	3.30	4.63	3.41	2.69	2.82	3.25	2.83
59 -3 -9	2.25	4.09	4.05	3.30	4.63	3.41	2.65	3.06	3.38	2.98
59 -3-16	2.25	3.97	4.22	3.29	4.63	3.41	2.50	2.76	3.38	2.88
59 -3-23	2.25	4.16	4.30	3.30	4.63	3.41	2.74	2.77	3.38	2.58
59 -3-30	2.25	4.56	4.33	3.30	4.63	3.41	2.73	2.84	3.38	2.88
59 -4 -6	2.19	4.13	4.42	3.20	4.63	3.41	2.76	2.95	3.38	3.00
59 -4-13	2.06	3.80	4.61	3.23	4.63	3.36	2.63	3.08	3.38	3.00
59 -4-20	2.00	4.18	4.72	3.28	4.63	3.41	2.70	3.11	3.48	3.10
59 -4-27	2.00	4.22	4.76	3.31	4.63	3.42	2.74	2.83	3.50	3.13
59 -5 -4	2.00	4.25	4.91	3.31	4.63	3.42	2.78	2.94	3.50	3.13
59 -5-11	2.00	3.66	5.05	3.31	4.63	3.42	2.71	2.72	3.50	3.13
59 -5-18	2.00	3.75	5.05	3.34	4.63	3.42	2.50	2.87	3.63	3.20
59 -5-25	2.00	3.98	4.90	3.38	4.63	3.47	2.64	2.88	3.63	3.25
59 -6 -1	2.00	3.70	5.08	3.43	4.63	3.50	2.69	3.15	3.73	3.25
59 -6 -8	2.00	3.28	5.17	3.45	4.63	3.54	2.79	3.28	3.85	3.25
59 -6-15	2.00	3.35	5.22	3.47	4.63	3.56	2.78	3.28	3.88	3.35
59 -6-22	2.00	3.94	5.11	3.45	4.63	3.56	2.72	3.28	3.88	3.38
59 -6-29	2.00	4.44	5.01	3.45	4.63	3.56	2.75	3.16	3.88	3.38
59 -7 -6	2.00	4.35	5.06	3.45	4.63	3.56	2.84	3.27	3.88	3.38
59 -7-13	2.00	4.38	5.19	3.45	4.63	3.56	2.80	3.40	3.88	3.48
59 -7-20	2.00	3.68	5.41	3.45	4.63	3.56	2.79	3.34	3.88	3.50
59 -7-27	2.00	4.70	5.47	3.48	4.63	3.59	3.58	3.05	3.88	3.50
59 -8 -3	2.00	4.13	5.73	3.48	4.63	3.63	2.69	3.04	3.88	3.50
59 -8-10	2.00	3.97	6.16	3.48	4.63	3.59	2.76	3.15	4.00	3.50
59 -8-17	2.00	3.57	6.04	3.48	4.63	3.59	2.82	3.42	3.90	3.50
59 -8-24	2.00	4.03	5.33	3.49	4.63	3.59	2.73	3.82	4.10	3.63
59 -8-31	2.13	3.98	5.64	3.49	4.63	3.59	2.84	3.89	4.40	3.83
59 -9 -7	2.50	3.95	5.80	3.49	4.63	3.59	2.82	3.98	4.50	3.93
59 -9-14	2.50	3.97	5.88	3.48	4.63	3.59	2.85	4.17	4.70	4.10
59 -9-21	2.57	4.13	5.60	3.47	4.63	3.59	2.73	3.96	4.75	4.18
59 -9-28	2.70	4.05	5.50	3.49	4.63	3.60	2.73	4.19	4.75	4.25
59-10 -5	2.75	3.95	5.25	3.44	4.63	3.60	2.84	4.01	4.75	4.25
59-10-12	2.70	3.55	5.01	3.42	4.63	3.56	2.81	4.26	4.75	4.25
59-10-19	2.63	3.47	4.93	3.43	4.63	3.56	2.81	4.10	4.75	4.25
59-10-26	3.13	4.05	5.02	3.39	4.63	3.55	2.85	4.02	4.68	4.25

DATE YR M DAY	FRANK-FURT	PARIS	OTTAWA	LONDON (1)	LONDON (2)	LONDON (3)	LONDON (4)	NEW YORK1	NEW YORK2	NEW YORK3
59-11 -2	3.13	4.25	4.83	3.37	4.63	3.53	2.68	4.14	4.63	4.25
59-11 -9	3.13	4.13	4.88	3.39	4.63	3.54	2.84	4.09	4.63	4.25
59-11-16	3.13	3.64	4.91	3.40	4.63	3.56	2.82	4.33	4.63	4.25
59-11-23	3.13	4.08	4.86	3.40	4.63	3.56	2.73	4.28	4.75	4.25
59-11-30	3.13	4.05	4.93	3.53	4.63	3.59	2.81	4.50	4.85	4.35
59-12 -7	3.13	4.03	5.02	3.58	4.63	3.68	2.76	4.64	4.88	4.50
59-12-14	3.13	4.00	4.98	3.64	4.63	3.74	2.93	4.54	4.88	4.50
59-12-21	3.75	4.08	5.03	3.69	4.63	3.79	2.92	4.67	4.88	4.50
59-12-28	3.75	4.33	5.12	3.73	4.63	3.83	2.83	4.52	4.88	4.50
60 -1 -4	3.75	4.05	5.14	3.75	4.63	3.88	2.68	4.60	4.88	4.62
60 -1-11	3.75	3.93	4.82	3.78	4.63	3.89	2.84	4.59	5.00	4.83
60 -1-18	3.75	3.73	4.66	4.55	4.81	4.22	3.19	4.44	4.99	4.83
60 -1-25	3.75	3.93	4.60	4.54	5.63	4.69	3.81	4.12	4.85	4.83
60 -2 -1	3.75	4.25	4.76	4.55	5.63	4.69	3.88	4.04	4.75	4.63
60 -2 -8	3.75	4.05	4.75	4.55	5.63	4.69	3.94	3.56	4.53	4.38
60 -2-15	3.75	3.85	4.62	4.54	5.63	4.69	3.66	4.05	4.53	4.38
60 -2-22	3.75	4.20	4.61	4.55	5.63	4.69	3.65	4.17	4.73	4.38
60 -2-29	3.93	4.43	4.57	4.54	5.63	4.69	3.88	4.28	4.83	4.38
60 -3 -7	4.00	4.23	4.34	4.58	5.63	4.71	3.91	3.64	4.73	4.13
60 -3-14	4.00	3.98	4.02	4.61	5.63	4.76	3.94	3.45	4.55	3.88
60 -3-21	4.00	3.98	3.41	4.62	5.63	4.78	3.94	3.03	4.30	3.73
60 -3-28	4.00	4.40	3.01	4.62	5.63	4.78	3.90	2.79	4.13	3.63
60 -4-11	4.00	4.19	3.58	4.65	5.63	4.81	3.83	3.62	4.09	3.94
60 -4-18	4.00	3.91	3.50	4.65	5.63	4.81	3.59	3.31	4.25	4.00
60 -4-25	4.00	4.53	3.26	4.65	5.63	4.81	3.55	3.32	4.25	4.00
60 -5 -2	4.00	4.93	2.82	4.67	5.63	4.82	3.90	3.00	4.25	3.88
60 -5 -9	4.00	4.08	2.67	4.56	5.63	4.80	3.74	3.27	4.25	3.75
60 -5-16	4.00	3.83	2.99	4.56	5.63	4.72	3.87	3.79	4.25	3.75
60 -5-23	4.00	4.13	3.01	4.56	5.63	4.72	3.95	3.50	4.25	3.75
60 -5-30	4.33	4.15	2.92	4.56	5.63	4.72	3.65	3.18	4.16	3.63
60 -6 -6	4.88	4.25	2.65	4.61	5.63	4.74	3.69	2.72	4.10	3.48
60 -6-13	4.88	3.95	2.71	4.68	5.63	4.80	3.74	2.29	3.70	3.18
60 -6-20	4.88	3.95	2.98	5.68	5.63	5.18	4.23	2.61	3.63	3.13
60 -6-27	4.88	4.88	3.07	5.68	5.63	5.84	4.42	2.40	3.63	3.13
60 -7 -4	4.88	4.68	3.17	5.66	6.75	5.84	4.90	2.31	3.44	3.13
60 -7-11	4.88	4.46	3.24	5.51	6.75	5.79	4.68	2.57	3.38	3.13
60 -7-18	4.88	4.10	3.19	5.49	6.75	5.69	4.75	2.31	3.38	3.13
60 -7-25	4.88	4.58	2.92	5.55	6.75	5.71	4.69	2.40	3.38	3.13
60 -8 -1	4.88	4.15	2.83	5.58	6.75	5.75	4.73	2.13	3.38	3.13
60 -8 -8	4.88	4.10	2.91	5.57	6.75	5.75	4.76	2.22	3.38	3.08
60 -8-15	4.88	3.88	2.66	5.59	6.75	5.75	4.81	2.28	3.38	2.93
60 -8-22	4.88	3.90	2.25	5.59	6.75	5.75	4.81	2.52	3.33	3.05
60 -9 -5	4.88	4.05	2.09	5.51	6.75	5.73	4.82	2.52	3.25	3.00
60 -9-12	4.88	4.08	2.07	5.51	6.75	5.69	4.88	2.65	3.38	3.00
60 -9-19	4.88	4.10	1.68	5.49	6.75	5.69	4.82	2.43	3.50	3.00

DATE YR M DAY	FRANK- FURT	PARIS	OTTAWA	LONDON (1)	LONDON (2)	LONDON (3)	LONDON (4)	NEW YORK1	NEW YORK2	NEW YORK3
60 -9-26	4.88	4.45	1.70	5.57	6.75	5.71	4.82	2.29	3.50	3.00
60-10 -3	4.88	4.60	2.20	5.56	6.75	5.75	4.88	2.47	3.38	3.00
60-10-10	4.88	3.80	2.48	5.48	6.75	5.71	4.88	2.70	3.38	3.00
60-10-17	4.88	3.63	2.87	5.33	6.75	5.59	4.87	2.41	3.30	3.00
60-10-24	4.88	3.95	3.03	5.09	6.75	5.45	4.57	2.13	3.40	3.00
60-10-31	4.77	3.96	3.22	4.89	6.25	5.21	4.36	2.13	3.12	3.00
60-11 -7	4.38	4.22	3.21	4.77	6.06	5.03	4.34	2.39	3.17	3.00
60-11-14	4.00	3.60	3.48	4.67	6.06	4.94	4.32	2.62	3.15	3.00
60-11-21	4.00	3.58	3.77	4.64	5.94	4.86	4.22	2.40	3.38	3.00
60-11-28	4.00	3.60	3.95	4.62	5.94	4.83	4.23	2.33	3.38	3.00
60-12 -5	4.00	3.58	3.70	4.48	5.94	4.75	4.09	2.33	3.30	3.00
61 -1 -2	3.75	4.00	3.34	4.34	5.70	4.53	3.69	2.23	3.13	2.88
61 -1 -9	3.75	3.83	3.18	4.31	5.70	4.53	3.73	2.39	3.00	2.88
61 -1-16	3.63	3.33	3.22	4.18	5.70	4.43	3.81	2.36	3.00	2.90
61 -1-23	3.25	3.50	3.04	4.17	5.70	4.34	3.83	2.23	2.90	2.88
61 -1-30	3.25	3.75	3.13	4.17	5.70	4.34	3.83	2.30	2.93	2.75
61 -2 -6	3.19	3.58	3.10	4.30	5.70	4.41	3.77	2.37	3.00	2.75
61 -3 -6	2.91	3.88	3.21	4.49	5.70	4.61	3.86	2.49	3.13	2.98
61 -3-13	2.79	3.58	3.16	4.49	5.70	4.63	3.65	2.35	3.05	3.00
61 -3-20	2.56	3.55	3.28	4.49	5.70	4.63	3.75	2.28	2.93	2.93
61 -3-27	2.50	3.75	3.21	4.49	5.70	4.63	3.53	2.39	2.97	2.88
61 -4 -3	2.50	3.81	3.25	4.44	5.70	4.61	3.73	2.47	3.00	2.88
61 -4-10	2.50	3.63	3.34	4.48	5.70	4.61	3.39	2.36	2.98	2.88
61 -4-17	2.50	3.55	3.32	4.49	5.70	4.66	3.82	2.29	2.88	2.80
61 -4-24	2.44	3.78	3.28	4.40	5.70	4.64	3.84	2.19	2.78	2.75
61 -5 -1	2.33	4.22	3.22	4.37	5.70	4.55	3.88	2.30	2.75	2.75
61 -5 -8	2.25	3.96	3.20	4.32	5.70	4.52	3.73	2.23	2.75	2.63
61 -5-15	2.25	3.68	3.16	4.41	5.70	4.51	3.83	2.26	2.75	4.51
61 -5-22	2.25	3.75	3.17	4.43	5.70	4.59	3.66	2.35	2.75	4.59
61 -5-29	2.25	3.95	3.14	4.44	5.70	4.59	3.74	2.44	2.88	4.59
61 -6 -5	2.25	3.83	3.05	4.46	5.70	4.60	3.74	2.52	3.00	4.60
61 -6-12	2.25	3.65	3.00	4.50	5.70	4.64	3.70	2.30	3.00	4.64

Selected Bibliography

A more complete bibliography, including foreign-language publications, has been assembled by Paul Einzig, in *A Dynamic Theory of Forward Exchange*, London: Macmillan, 1961.

Aliber, Robert Z., "Counter-Speculation and the Forward Exchange Market: A Comment," *Journal of Political Economy*, December 1962.
——, "More About Counter-Speculation in the Forward Exchange Market," *Journal of Political Economy*, December 1963.
Altman, Oscar, "Foreign Markets for Dollars, Sterling, and Other Currencies," *International Monetary Fund Staff Paper*, December 1961.
Auten, John H., "Counter-Speculation and the Forward Exchange Market," *Journal of Political Economy*, February 1961.
——, "Monetary Policy and the Forward Exchange Market," *Journal of Finance*, December 1961.
Bloomfield, Arthur I., "Official Intervention in the Forward Exchange Market: Some Recent Experiences," *Banca Nazionale Del Lavoro Quarterly Review*, March 1964.
Einzig, Paul, *A Dynamic Theory of Forward Exchange*, London: Macmillan, 1961.
——, "Some Recent Changes in Forward Exchange Practices," *Economic Journal*, September 1960.
——, "Some Recent Developments in Official Forward Exchange Operations," *Economic Journal*, June 1963.
——, "Some Theoretical Aspects of Forward Exchanges," *Economic Journal*, September 1936.
——, "Some Theoretico-Technical Aspects of Official Forward Exchange Operation," *Economic Journal*, June 1938.
——, "The Relation Between the Practice and Theory of Forward Exchange," *Banca Nazionale Del Lavoro Quarterly Review*, September 1962.
——, *The Theory of Forward Exchange*, London: Macmillan, 1937.
Fleming, Marcus J., and Robert A. Mundell, "Official Intervention in the Forward Exchange Market: A Simplified Analysis," *International Monetary Fund Staff Paper*, March 1964.
Goldstein, Henry N., "Counter Speculation in the Forward Exchange Market: Some Further Comments," *Journal of Political Economy*, October 1963.

Grubel, Herbert G., "A Multicountry Model of Forward Exchange: Theory, Policy, and Empirical Evidence," *Yale Economic Essays*, Spring 1963.

———, "A Neglected Aspect of Forward Exchange Theory and Policy," *Journal of Finance*, September 1963.

———, "Reply," *Journal of Finance*, September 1964.

———, "Profits from Forward Exchange Speculation," *Quarterly Journal of Economics*, May 1965.

Hansen, Bent, "Interest Policy and Foreign Exchange Policy," *Skandinaviska Banken Quarterly Review*, October 1958.

Jasay, Anthony Egan, "Bank Rate or Forward Exchange Policy," *Banca Nazionale Del Lavoro Quarterly Review*, March 1958.

———, "Case for Official Support," *The Banker*, April 1958.

———, "Forward Exchange: The Case for Intervention," *Lloyds Bank Review*, October 1958.

———, "Making Currency Reserves Go Round," *Journal of Political Economy*, August 1958.

———, "Speculation, Arbitrage and Sterling: A Comment," *Economic Journal*, September 1959.

Keynes, John Maynard, "The Forward Market in Foreign Exchanges," *Manchester Guardian Reconstruction Supplement*, April 20, 1922.

———, "The Future of the Foreign Exchanges," *Lloyds Bank Monthly Review*, December 1935.

———, *A Tract on Monetary Reform*, London: Macmillan, 1923.

Kindleberger, Charles P., *International Short Term Capital Movements*, New York: Columbia University Press, 1937.

———, "Speculation and Forward Exchange," *Journal of Political Economy*, April 1939.

Morgenstern, Oscar, *International Financial Transactions*, Princeton: Princeton University Press, 1960.

Reading, B., "The Forward Pound 1951–59," *Economic Journal*, June 1960.

Report of the Committee on the Working of the Monetary System, Command 827, London: H.M. Stationery Office, 1959; and *Principal Memoranda of Evidence*, London: H.M. Stationery Office, 1960.

Sohmen, Egon, *Flexible Exchange Rates*, Chicago: University of Chicago Press, 1961.

Spraos, John, "Exchange Policy in the Forward Market: Case for an Official Peg," *The Banker*, April 1958.

———, "Speculation, Arbitrage and Pound Sterling," *Economic Journal*, March 1959.

———, "The Theory of Forward Exchange and Recent Practice," *Manchester School of Economic and Social Studies*, May 1953.

Stein, Jerome L., *The Nature and Efficiency of the Foreign Exchange Market*, Essays in International Finance, No. 40, Princeton: Princeton University Press, 1962.

———, "The Rationality of Official Intervention in the Forward Exchange Market," *Quarterly Journal of Economics*, May 1963.

Trued, Merlyn N., "Interest Arbitrage, Exchange Rates, and Dollar Reserves," *Journal of Political Economy*, October 1957.

Tsiang, S. C., "A Theory of Foreign Exchange Speculation under a Floating Exchange System," *Journal of Political Economy*, October 1958.

———, "The Theory of the Forward Exchange Market," *International Monetary Fund Staff Papers*, April 1959.

White, William H., "Interest Rate Differences, Forward Exchange Mechanism, and Scope for Short-Term Capital Movements," *International Monetary Fund Staff Papers*, November 1963.